SPECTRUM®

Math

Grade 8

Spectrum®

An imprint of Carson-Dellosa Publishing LLC
Greensboro, North Carolina

Spectrum®
An imprint of Carson-Dellosa Publishing LLC
P.O. Box 35665
Greensboro, NC 27425 USA

ISBN 978-0-7696-3698-6

09-090137811

Table of Contents Grade 8

Chapter 1   Whole Numbers, Decimals, and Fractions

Chapter 1 Pretest 1
Lessons 1–12 3–14
Chapter 1 Posttest 15

Chapter 2   Ratio and Proportion

Chapter 2 Pretest 17
Lessons 1–4 19–22
Chapter 2 Posttest 23

Chapter 3   Percents and Interest

Chapter 3 Pretest 25
Lessons 1–8 27–38
Chapter 3 Posttest 39

Chapter 4   Customary Measurement

Chapter 4 Pretest 41
Lessons 1–6 43–48
Chapter 4 Posttest 49

Chapter 5   Metric Measurement

Chapter 5 Pretest 51
Lessons 1–4 53–56
Chapter 5 Posttest 57

Chapters 1–5 Mid-Test 59

Chapter 6   Probability and Statistics

Chapter 6 Pretest 63
Lessons 1–12 65–78
Chapter 6 Posttest 79

Chapter 7   Geometry

Chapter 7 Pretest 81
Lessons 1–12 83–100
Chapter 7 Posttest 101

Chapter 8   Perimeter, Area, and Volume

Chapter 8 Pretest 103
Lessons 1–18 105–122
Chapter 8 Posttest 123

Table of Contents, continued

Chapter 9 Preparing for Algebra

Chapter 9 Pretest 125
Lessons 1–14 127–144
Chapter 9 Posttest 145

Chapters 1–9 Final Test 147

Scoring Record for Posttests, Mid-Test, and Final Test 153
Grade 8 Answers 155

Check What You Know

Whole Numbers, Decimals, and Fractions

Add or subtract. Write your answer in simplest form.

	a	b	c	d	e
1.	$\begin{array}{r} 473052 \\ 946721 \\ 423106 \\ +157646 \\ \hline \end{array}$	$\begin{array}{r} 4\frac{1}{2} \\ 1\frac{1}{3} \\ +5\frac{1}{4} \\ \hline \end{array}$	$\begin{array}{r} 716.24 \\ -513.757 \\ \hline \end{array}$	$\begin{array}{r} \frac{2}{3} \\ \frac{2}{7} \\ +\frac{5}{6} \\ \hline \end{array}$	$\begin{array}{r} 476392 \\ -103477 \\ \hline \end{array}$
2.	$\begin{array}{r} 710263 \\ -\ \ 94317 \\ \hline \end{array}$	$\begin{array}{r} 1.072 \\ -0.76 \\ \hline \end{array}$	$\begin{array}{r} 3\frac{3}{4} \\ -1\frac{1}{8} \\ \hline \end{array}$	$\begin{array}{r} 42.761 \\ -33.014 \\ \hline \end{array}$	$\begin{array}{r} 46.102 \\ -39.4679 \\ \hline \end{array}$
3.	$\begin{array}{r} 14.07 \\ 4.267 \\ +\ \ 9.105 \\ \hline \end{array}$	$\begin{array}{r} 12\frac{1}{3} \\ -9\frac{7}{8} \\ \hline \end{array}$	$\begin{array}{r} 10397 \\ 52797 \\ +43798 \\ \hline \end{array}$	$\begin{array}{r} 3\frac{1}{4} \\ +7\frac{3}{5} \\ \hline \end{array}$	$\begin{array}{r} 4.218 \\ 1.07 \\ +19.2376 \\ \hline \end{array}$

Multiply or divide. Write your answer in simplest form.

	a	b	c	d
4.	$4\frac{1}{3} \div \frac{3}{5} =$	$\frac{3}{7} \times 9\frac{1}{3} \times \frac{4}{5} =$	$3\frac{3}{7} \div 1\frac{1}{8} =$	$\begin{array}{r} 7.016 \\ \times\ \ \ \ 0.5 \\ \hline \end{array}$
5.	$4.6 \overline{)35.88}$	$\begin{array}{r} 25.063 \\ \times\ \ \ 0.477 \\ \hline \end{array}$	$\begin{array}{r} 14376 \\ \times\ \ \ \ \ \ 92 \\ \hline \end{array}$	$512 \overline{)462717}$
6.	$\begin{array}{r} 3147 \\ \times\ \ \ 518 \\ \hline \end{array}$	$0.58 \overline{)2.4766}$	$\frac{5}{6} \times 2\frac{7}{8} =$	$25 \overline{)47102}$

NAME _____

🔍 Check What You Know

Whole Numbers, Decimals, and Fractions

SHOW YOUR WORK

Solve each problem.

7. Yumi has $14.50, Jess has $12.75, Tamara has $16.35, and Alex has $15.55. How much do they have altogether?

   They have _____.

8. Isaac had to write a long paper. He wrote $3\frac{1}{4}$ pages Monday, $2\frac{1}{3}$ pages Tuesday, and $\frac{4}{5}$ page on Wednesday. How many pages did he write?

   Isaac wrote _____ pages.

9. Keisha also had to write a paper. She decided to write exactly $2\frac{1}{4}$ pages each day. How many pages did she write after 5 days?

   Keisha wrote _____ pages.

10. The Johnsons had $72,498.33 in a savings account. They spent $64,934.50 on a down payment for a home. How much was left in their savings?

    The Johnsons had _____ left in their savings.

11. Jake makes $116.25 each week, before taxes, at the bookstore. How much money will he make in a year if he works the same number of hours each week?

    Jake will make _____.

12. Jake works 15 hours per week. If he makes $116.25 each week, how much does he make per hour?

    Jake makes _____ per hour.

13. Students collected 6,549 cans in a food drive. They want to give an equal number of cans to 11 homeless shelters. How many cans will each shelter receive? How many will be left over?

    Each shelter will receive _____ cans. There will be _____ left over.

7.	8.
9.	**10.**
11.	**12.**
13.	

Lesson 1.1 Addition

Add ones. Add tens.	Add hundreds.	Continue adding from right to left.

Addends

$$\begin{array}{r} 3\,0\,4\,\overset{2}{7}\,\overset{1}{9}\,7 \\ 1\,2\,7\,5\,6\,4 \\ +\,4\,9\,3\,0\,8\,6 \\ \hline 4\,7 \end{array} \longrightarrow \begin{array}{r} 3\,0\,\overset{1}{4}\,\overset{2}{7}\,\overset{1}{9}\,7 \\ 1\,2\,7\,5\,6\,4 \\ +\,4\,9\,3\,0\,8\,6 \\ \hline 4\,4\,7 \end{array} \longrightarrow \begin{array}{r} \overset{1}{3}\,\overset{1}{0}\,\overset{1}{4}\,\overset{2}{7}\,\overset{1}{9}\,7 \\ 1\,2\,7\,5\,6\,4 \\ +\,4\,9\,3\,0\,8\,6 \\ \hline 9\,2\,5\,4\,4\,7 \end{array} \longleftarrow \text{sum}$$

Add.

	a	b	c	d	e
1.	27 +19	430 +109	6037 +7262	10263 +47918	406334 +921180
2.	62 13 +75	434 106 +757	1463 1802 +4769	40729 49333 +21201	540624 915002 +479293
3.	47 69 67 +19	129 306 472 +545	3904 1676 2490 +4601	27503 42656 10276 +47901	247093 403430 192371 +690467
4.	17 43 15 28 +33	462 103 906 575 +123	5062 1504 3344 6293 +7240	92118 14174 11201 24267 +37642	476052 915450 321737 423705 +640818
5.	26 43 10 29 72 +15	137 406 271 424 929 +533	4263 9015 6260 4176 1472 +3550	42973 17090 28473 91555 32174 +84727	192763 427074 371508 572916 319470 +540976

Lesson 1.2 Subtraction

To subtract, start with ones.
Rename 1 ten as 10 ones.

Continue subtracting from right to left.
Rename as necessary.

minuend ⟶ $\overset{\scriptscriptstyle 8\ 11\ 13}{407\cancel{923}}$
subtrahend ⟶ -146797
                         6

$\overset{\scriptscriptstyle 3\ 10\quad 8\ 11\ 13}{\cancel{40}7\cancel{923}}$
-146797
261126 ⟵ difference

Subtract.

	a	b	c	d	e
1.	42 −39	617 − 79	4762 −2379	24971 −10792	426707 − 92109
2.	76 − 9	462 −107	5455 −4909	82793 − 4074	847910 −703247
3.	87 −49	921 − 88	3712 − 909	61735 −54269	543072 − 81794
4.	54 − 6	654 − 91	7932 −1049	46246 − 7292	401263 −329104
5.	77 −67	327 −144	7213 − 846	92719 −81041	612910 −104763
6.	46 − 7	801 −629	1497 − 546	51927 − 4307	729040 − 81065

Lesson 1.3 Multiplication

Multiply the top number by the bottom number. Use 4 steps.

$$
\begin{array}{r}
\text{factors} \left\{ \begin{array}{r} 4376 \\ \times \quad 642 \end{array} \right. \\
\hline
8752 \quad (1.\ 4376 \times 2) \\
175040 \quad (2.\ 4376 \times 40) \\
+2625600 \quad (3.\ 4376 \times 600) \\
\hline
\text{product} \longrightarrow \quad 2809392 \quad (4.\ \text{Add})
\end{array}
$$

Multiply.

	a	b	c	d	e
1.	29 × 6	57 × 8	371 × 5	476 × 7	1432 × 9
2.	18 ×77	84 ×92	747 × 36	107 × 18	4704 × 4
3.	57 ×27	5072 × 65	339 × 81	4216 × 52	6790 × 25
4.	371 ×403	463 ×369	4276 × 483	5312 × 811	2897 × 632

Lesson 1.4 Division

$$424\overline{)91472}$$

The divisor is 3 digits. The first digit in the quotient will be in the hundreds place.

424 fits into 914 about 2 times.

$$424\overline{)91472}$$
$$-848$$
$$\overline{667}$$

424 fits into 667 only once.

$$\begin{array}{r} 21 \\ 424\overline{)91472} \\ -848 \\ \hline 667 \\ -424 \\ \hline 2432 \end{array}$$

424 fits into 2432 about 5 times.

$$\begin{array}{r} 215 \\ 424\overline{)91472} \\ -848 \\ \hline 667 \\ -424 \\ \hline 2432 \\ -2120 \\ \hline \end{array}$$

Remainder ⟶ 312

Divide. Include the remainder in your answer.

	a	b	c	d
1.	$6\overline{)479}$	$27\overline{)481}$	$119\overline{)865}$	$8\overline{)1699}$
2.	$8\overline{)915}$	$45\overline{)848}$	$201\overline{)976}$	$9\overline{)4793}$
3.	$4\overline{)54672}$	$6\overline{)14757}$	$27\overline{)11973}$	$81\overline{)41262}$
4.	$42\overline{)1247}$	$81\overline{)9076}$	$106\overline{)53727}$	$9\overline{)4279}$

Lesson 1.5 Adding and Subtracting Decimals

Add 0s if they help you. Add.

```
  1 9.4 7 5          ² ¹
    7.3 4 0 3        1 9.4 7 5 0
+ 2 5.0 5              7.3 4 0 3
                   + 2 5.0 5 0 0
                   ─────────────
                     5 1.8 6 5 3
```

Add 0s if they help you. Subtract.

```
                        ⁶ ¹¹ ¹⁰ ⁹ ¹² ⁹ ¹⁰
  7 2 1.0 3            7 2 1.0 3 0 0
−   6 4.9 7 2 5      −   6 4.9 7 2 5
                     ───────────────
                      6 5 6.0 5 7 5
```

Line up the decimal point in the answer with the decimal points in the problem.

Add or subtract.

	a	b	c	d	e
1.	4 5.3 + 9.7	1.2 1 3 − 0.9 0 6	1 3 7.5 6 + 5 4.0 9	1 5.0 7 4 − 7.8 3 5	6 7 2.9 1 − 5 0 1.5 0 4
2.	1.0 2 + 0.7 3	4.2 6 2 + 4.1 0 5	4 7.0 5 2 − 8.7 6	9.0 5 6 − 4.7 1 7 5	5 9.0 7 4 5 + 7.5 5 4
3.	4.3 3 − 1.7 9	1 5.6 5 − 9.4	5 0 1.3 7 − 1 0 7.5	4.2 3 7 4 + 0.8 1 0 4	7 7 5.0 3 5 − 6 9.6 7
4.	1 2.7 − 6.9	3 7.7 6 + 1 2.5 5	9.2 1 6 4 + 5.1 0 5	1 2 7.0 8 − 1 0 4.2	1 2.0 7 − 9.4 3 6 5
5.	1 2.3 9.4 + 4 5	1.0 4 5 0.1 2 + 3.6 7 5	4 4.0 4 5 9.1 5 + 1 7.3 8 1	6 2.7 5 1 9.0 6 3 + 4 4.6	4 2 1.0 6 3 1 9.8 4 + 1 0 7.4 4

Lesson 1.6 Multiplying Decimals

```
  1 4.3 6      2
×     9.5    + 1
  7 1 8 0      3
+1 2 9 2 4 0
1 3 6.4 2 0
      3 2 1
```

Where does the decimal go in the product? Count how many numbers are decimals in *both* factors of the problem. Add them together and count that number of places from the right.

```
  1.0 8 5       3
×   2.2 5     + 2
  5 4 2 5       5
2 1 7 0 0
+2 1 7 0 0 0
2.4 4 1 2 5
    5 4 3 2 1
```

Multiply.

	a	b	c	d	e
1.	2 7.2 5 × 1.4	4.3 6 × 2 9	1 2.2 ×0.7 6	4 6.3 3 × 1.5	0.9 2 ×0.7 4
2.	3 6.1 2 × 0.7	1 6.3 × 7	7 2.0 6 × 0.8	4 5.5 ×0.0 9	1 2.0 7 × 0.6
3.	1.8 2 × 1.7	1 4.7 6 × 9.3	7.0 9 5 × 0.7 3	0.1 9 6 × 4.6	7 6 7.5 × 0.2 7
4.	1 7 3 ×1.2 9	4 2.9 5 × 4.4 6	1.4 6 ×0.7 9 5	9 2.7 5 × 7 6.4	0.3 6 7 × 5.6 4
5.	1 2.0 7 × 0.0 9	4 6.7 × 5	0.1 9 7 × 0.6	1 2.0 7 × 0.7	8 9.7 7 ×0.0 0 8

Lesson 1.5 Adding and Subtracting Decimals

Add 0s if they help you. Add.

```
  19.475        2 1
   7.3403      19.4750
 +25.05         7.3403
             +25.0500
             _____
              51.8653
```

Add 0s if they help you. Subtract.

```
  721.03      6 11 10 9 12 9 10
 - 64.9725    7 2 1 . 0 3 0 0
             - 64.9725
             _____
             656.0575
```

Line up the decimal point in the answer with the decimal points in the problem.

Add or subtract.

	a	b	c	d	e
1.	45.3 +9.7	1.213 -0.906	137.56 +54.09	15.074 -7.835	672.91 -501.504
2.	1.02 +0.73	4.262 +4.105	47.052 -8.76	9.056 -4.7175	59.0745 +7.554
3.	4.33 -1.79	15.65 -9.4	501.37 -107.5	4.2374 +0.8104	775.035 -69.67
4.	12.7 -6.9	37.76 +12.55	9.2164 +5.105	127.08 -104.2	12.07 -9.4365
5.	12.3 9.4 +45	1.045 0.12 +3.675	44.045 9.15 +17.381	62.75 19.063 +44.6	421.063 19.84 +107.44

Lesson 1.6 Multiplying Decimals

```
    1 4.3 6      | 2 |     Where does the decimal go in the        1.0 8 5      | 3 |
  ×     9.5      |+ 1|     product? Count how many numbers are    ×   2.2 5      |+ 2|
  ───────────    |───|     decimals in both factors of the problem. ───────────    |───|
    7 1 8 0      | 3 |     Add them together and count that          5 4 2 5      | 5 |
+ 1 2 9 2 4 0             number of places from the right.         2 1 7 0 0
  ───────────                                                    + 2 1 7 0 0 0
  1 3 6.4 2 0                                                      ───────────
      ‿‿‿                                                          2.4 4 1 2 5
      3 2 1                                                            ‿‿‿‿‿
                                                                      5 4 3 2 1
```

Multiply.

	a	b	c	d	e
1.	$\begin{array}{r} 2\,7.2\,5 \\ \times\quad 1.4 \\ \hline \end{array}$	$\begin{array}{r} 4.3\,6 \\ \times\quad 2\,9 \\ \hline \end{array}$	$\begin{array}{r} 1\,2.2 \\ \times\,0.7\,6 \\ \hline \end{array}$	$\begin{array}{r} 4\,6.3\,3 \\ \times\quad 1.5 \\ \hline \end{array}$	$\begin{array}{r} 0.9\,2 \\ \times\,0.7\,4 \\ \hline \end{array}$
2.	$\begin{array}{r} 3\,6.1\,2 \\ \times\quad 0.7 \\ \hline \end{array}$	$\begin{array}{r} 1\,6.3 \\ \times\quad 7 \\ \hline \end{array}$	$\begin{array}{r} 7\,2.0\,6 \\ \times\quad 0.8 \\ \hline \end{array}$	$\begin{array}{r} 4\,5.5 \\ \times\,0.0\,9 \\ \hline \end{array}$	$\begin{array}{r} 1\,2.0\,7 \\ \times\quad 0.6 \\ \hline \end{array}$
3.	$\begin{array}{r} 1.8\,2 \\ \times\quad 1.7 \\ \hline \end{array}$	$\begin{array}{r} 1\,4.7\,6 \\ \times\quad 9.3 \\ \hline \end{array}$	$\begin{array}{r} 7.0\,9\,5 \\ \times\quad 0.7\,3 \\ \hline \end{array}$	$\begin{array}{r} 0.1\,9\,6 \\ \times\quad 4.6 \\ \hline \end{array}$	$\begin{array}{r} 7\,6\,7.5 \\ \times\quad 0.2\,7 \\ \hline \end{array}$
4.	$\begin{array}{r} 1\,7\,3 \\ \times\,1.2\,9 \\ \hline \end{array}$	$\begin{array}{r} 4\,2.9\,5 \\ \times\quad 4.4\,6 \\ \hline \end{array}$	$\begin{array}{r} 1.4\,6 \\ \times\,0.7\,9\,5 \\ \hline \end{array}$	$\begin{array}{r} 9\,2.7\,5 \\ \times\quad 7\,6.4 \\ \hline \end{array}$	$\begin{array}{r} 0.3\,6\,7 \\ \times\quad 5.6\,4 \\ \hline \end{array}$
5.	$\begin{array}{r} 1\,2.0\,7 \\ \times\quad 0.0\,9 \\ \hline \end{array}$	$\begin{array}{r} 4\,6.7 \\ \times\quad 5 \\ \hline \end{array}$	$\begin{array}{r} 0.1\,9\,7 \\ \times\quad 0.6 \\ \hline \end{array}$	$\begin{array}{r} 1\,2.0\,7 \\ \times\quad 0.7 \\ \hline \end{array}$	$\begin{array}{r} 8\,9.7\,7 \\ \times\,0.0\,0\,8 \\ \hline \end{array}$

Lesson 1.7 Dividing Decimals

$0.25)\overline{1\,3\,2.5}$

is the same as

$25)\overline{1\,3\,2\,5\,0}$

Make the divisor a whole number by moving the decimal point to the right. Move the decimal point in the dividend the same number of places. Then, divide.

$$
\begin{array}{r}
5\,3\,0 \\
25)\overline{1\,3\,2\,5\,0} \\
-\,1\,2\,5 \\
\hline
7\,5 \\
-\,7\,5 \\
\hline
0\,0
\end{array}
$$

Divide.

	a	b	c	d

1. $0.1\,7)\overline{5.9\,5}$ $0.6)\overline{8\,8.8}$ $5.8)\overline{8.1\,2}$ $0.8)\overline{2\,8.8}$

2. $2.3)\overline{2\,2.4\,2\,5}$ $0.8\,9)\overline{0.9\,9\,6\,8}$ $1.5\,6)\overline{1\,3.7\,2\,8}$ $0.9)\overline{4\,6\,0.8}$

3. $0.5\,5)\overline{2\,5\,0.8}$ $1.8)\overline{4\,6\,2.6}$ $.7\,5)\overline{0.9\,4\,5\,0}$ $4\,2.5)\overline{2\,7\,6\,2.5}$

4. $5.2)\overline{5.5\,1\,2}$ $.2\,3)\overline{0.2\,0\,4\,7}$ $2.6\,4)\overline{1\,1.5\,1\,0\,4}$ $0.7)\overline{3.7\,5\,2}$

Lesson 1.8 Reducing to Simplest Form

Reduce a fraction to simplest form by dividing both the numerator and denominator by their **greatest common factor (GCF)**.

$\frac{18}{30}$ Factors of 18: 1, 2, 3, 6, 9, 18
Factors of 30: 1, 2, 3, 5, 6, 10, 15, 30
The GCF is 6.

$$\frac{18}{30} \div \frac{6}{6} = \frac{3}{5}$$

Reduce mixed numerals to simplest form by reducing the fractional part using the greatest common factor.

$4\frac{12}{15}$ Factors of 12: 1, 2, 3, 4, 6, 12
Factors of 15: 1, 3, 5, 15
The GCF is 3.

$$4\frac{12}{15} = 4 + \frac{12}{15} \div \frac{3}{3} = 4 + \frac{4}{5} = 4\frac{4}{5}$$

Write the fraction or mixed numeral in simplest form.

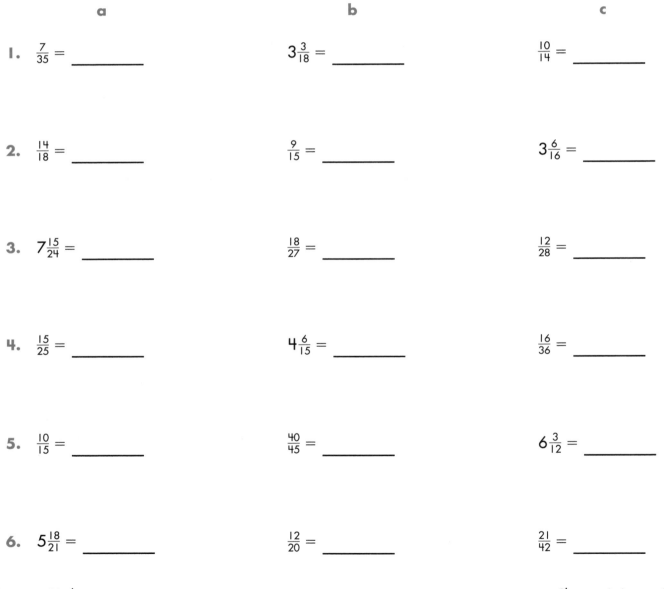

	a	b	c
1.	$\frac{7}{35} =$ _____	$3\frac{3}{18} =$ _____	$\frac{10}{14} =$ _____
2.	$\frac{14}{18} =$ _____	$\frac{9}{15} =$ _____	$3\frac{6}{16} =$ _____
3.	$7\frac{15}{24} =$ _____	$\frac{18}{27} =$ _____	$\frac{12}{28} =$ _____
4.	$\frac{15}{25} =$ _____	$4\frac{6}{15} =$ _____	$\frac{16}{36} =$ _____
5.	$\frac{10}{15} =$ _____	$\frac{40}{45} =$ _____	$6\frac{3}{12} =$ _____
6.	$5\frac{18}{21} =$ _____	$\frac{12}{20} =$ _____	$\frac{21}{42} =$ _____

Lesson 1.9 Renaming Fractions and Mixed Numerals

You can change an **improper fraction** into a **mixed numeral.**

$\frac{18}{7}$ means $18 \div 7$. Solve.

$$\begin{array}{r} 2 \\ 7\overline{)\,18} \\ -14 \\ \hline 4 \end{array}$$ $4 \div 7 = \frac{4}{7}$ $\frac{18}{7} = 2\frac{4}{7}$

You can change a **mixed numeral** into an **improper fraction.**

Multiply the whole number by the denominator and add the numerator.

Place this number over the denominator.

$$4\frac{3}{5} = \frac{(4 \times 5) + 3}{5} = \frac{23}{5}$$

Rewrite these two fractions so they have a common denominator.

$\frac{3}{4}, \frac{2}{5}$ What is their least common denominator? 4: 4, 8, 12, 16, 20

5: 5, 10, 15, 20

$\frac{3}{4} = \frac{?}{20}$ Multiply 4×5 to get 20.
Then, multiply 3×5 to get 15.

$\frac{2}{5} = \frac{?}{20}$ Multiply 5×4 to get 20.
Then, multiply 2×4 to get 8.

$\frac{3}{4} = \frac{15}{20}$

$\frac{2}{5} = \frac{8}{20}$

Change improper fractions to mixed numerals and mixed numerals to improper fractions.

	a	b	c	d
1.	$5\frac{3}{7} = $ _____	$\frac{19}{2} = $ _____	$\frac{21}{5} = $ _____	$2\frac{8}{9} = $ _____
2.	$4\frac{7}{9} = $ _____	$\frac{12}{5} = $ _____	$3\frac{2}{3} = $ _____	$\frac{23}{12} = $ _____

Rewrite each pair of fractions so they have a common denominator.

	a	b	c
3.	$\frac{3}{5}, \frac{4}{9}$ _____	$\frac{7}{12}, \frac{10}{18}$ _____	$\frac{9}{10}, \frac{18}{25}$ _____
4.	$\frac{4}{7}, \frac{1}{2}$ _____	$\frac{2}{9}, \frac{5}{12}$ _____	$\frac{3}{8}, \frac{7}{10}$ _____

Lesson 1.10 Adding and Subtracting Fractions and Mixed Numerals

To add or subtract fractions or mixed numerals with different denominators, give all of the fractions the same denominator.

$$4\frac{7}{12} \rightarrow 4\frac{21}{36}$$
$$+ \frac{7}{12} \rightarrow + \frac{20}{36}$$
$$\overline{\quad 4\frac{41}{36}} \quad \text{Rename the improper fraction.}$$

$$7\frac{1}{6} \rightarrow 7\frac{5}{30} \rightarrow 6+1+\frac{5}{30} \rightarrow 6+\frac{30}{30}+\frac{5}{30} = 6\frac{35}{30}$$
$$-1\frac{2}{5} \rightarrow 1\frac{12}{30} \xrightarrow{\hspace{5cm}} -1\frac{12}{30}$$
$$\text{Subtract numerators.} \quad \overline{5\frac{23}{30}}$$
$$\text{Subtract whole numbers.}$$

$$4\frac{41}{36} = 4 + \frac{41}{36} = 4 + 1 + \frac{5}{36} = 5\frac{5}{36}$$

Add or subtract. Write each sum or difference in simplest form.

	a	b	c	d
1.	$4\frac{3}{8}$ $+5\frac{2}{3}$	$\frac{7}{9}$ $+ \frac{1}{2}$	$2\frac{3}{5}$ $- \frac{3}{4}$	$\frac{15}{16}$ $+ \frac{3}{4}$
2.	$4\frac{3}{5}$ $+2\frac{1}{8}$	$\frac{13}{16}$ $+ \frac{7}{12}$	$4\frac{9}{10}$ $-3\frac{2}{3}$	$\frac{17}{18}$ $- \frac{5}{12}$
3.	$4\frac{1}{3}$ $+ \frac{3}{4}$	$6\frac{1}{4}$ $+1\frac{5}{8}$	$\frac{4}{5}$ $- \frac{3}{8}$	$\frac{11}{12}$ $+ \frac{9}{10}$
4.	$1\frac{3}{5}$ $2\frac{1}{4}$ $+4\frac{3}{8}$	$\frac{7}{10}$ $\frac{3}{4}$ $+ \frac{3}{5}$	$2\frac{1}{3}$ $\frac{4}{9}$ $+5\frac{1}{6}$	$\frac{4}{5}$ $\frac{7}{8}$ $+2\frac{1}{4}$

Lesson 1.11 Multiplying Fractions and Mixed Numerals

To multiply fractions, multiply numerators, then multiply denominators.

$\frac{3}{5} \times \frac{1}{6} = \frac{3 \times 1}{5 \times 6} = \frac{3}{30}$ Simplify. $\frac{3}{30} \div \frac{3}{3} = \frac{1}{10}$

You can also reduce fractions by dividing a numerator and a denominator by a common factor.

$\frac{\overset{1}{\cancel{3}}}{5} \times \frac{1}{\underset{2}{\cancel{6}}} = \frac{1 \times 1}{5 \times 2} = \frac{1}{10}$

To multiply mixed numerals or whole numbers, make them into fractions.

$2\frac{1}{5} \times \frac{3}{4} \times \frac{1}{6} = \frac{11}{5} \times \frac{3}{4} \times \frac{1}{\underset{2}{\cancel{6}}} = \frac{11 \times 1 \times 1}{5 \times 4 \times 2} = \frac{11}{40}$

$4\frac{1}{2} \times 3\frac{2}{5} \times 1\frac{2}{9} = \frac{\overset{9}{\cancel{9}}}{2} \times \frac{17}{5} \times \frac{11}{\underset{1}{\cancel{9}}} = \frac{1 \times 17 \times 11}{2 \times 5 \times 1} = \frac{187}{10} = 18\frac{7}{10}$

Multiply. Write each product in simplest form.

	a	b	c
1.	$1\frac{3}{7} \times \frac{2}{3} = $ _____	$\frac{4}{7} \times \frac{6}{11} = $ _____	$2\frac{1}{6} \times 3\frac{1}{5} \times 4 = $ _____
2.	$4\frac{2}{3} \times 5\frac{1}{5} = $ _____	$\frac{7}{10} \times \frac{2}{7} = $ _____	$\frac{1}{8} \times \frac{2}{9} \times \frac{3}{7} = $ _____
3.	$\frac{3}{4} \times \frac{8}{9} = $ _____	$1\frac{1}{2} \times 3\frac{3}{7} = $ _____	$\frac{11}{12} \times 4\frac{1}{3} \times 1\frac{1}{5} = $ _____
4.	$1\frac{1}{7} \times 3\frac{3}{7} = $ _____	$\frac{7}{18} \times \frac{1}{3} = $ _____	$4 \times \frac{1}{5} \times 1\frac{3}{8}$ _____
5.	$\frac{6}{7} \times 1\frac{3}{4} = $ _____	$\frac{11}{12} \times \frac{10}{13} = $ _____	$\frac{8}{9} \times 1\frac{3}{4} \times 2 = $ _____
6.	$4\frac{1}{6} \times \frac{2}{3} = $ _____	$\frac{1}{10} \times 2\frac{1}{8} = $ _____	$\frac{4}{9} \times \frac{3}{5} \times \frac{4}{7} = $ _____

Lesson 1.12 Dividing Fractions and Mixed Numerals

To divide a number, multiply by its **reciprocal.**
To make a reciprocal, reverse the numerator and denominator.

$\frac{2}{5}$ Reciprocal is $\frac{5}{2}$. $6 = \frac{6}{1}$ Reciprocal is $\frac{1}{6}$. $3\frac{1}{4} = \frac{13}{4}$ Reciprocal is $\frac{4}{13}$.

Any number multiplied by its reciprocal is 1.

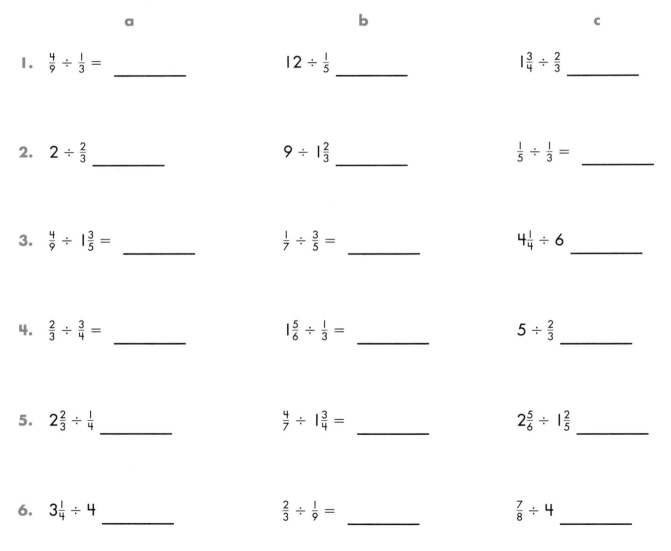

Divide. Write each quotient in simplest form.

	a	b	c
1.	$\frac{4}{9} \div \frac{1}{3} =$ _____	$12 \div \frac{1}{5}$ _____	$1\frac{3}{4} \div \frac{2}{3}$ _____
2.	$2 \div \frac{2}{3}$ _____	$9 \div 1\frac{2}{3}$ _____	$\frac{1}{5} \div \frac{1}{3} =$ _____
3.	$\frac{4}{9} \div 1\frac{3}{5} =$ _____	$\frac{1}{7} \div \frac{3}{5} =$ _____	$4\frac{1}{4} \div 6$ _____
4.	$\frac{2}{3} \div \frac{3}{4} =$ _____	$1\frac{5}{6} \div \frac{1}{3} =$ _____	$5 \div \frac{2}{3}$ _____
5.	$2\frac{2}{3} \div \frac{1}{4}$ _____	$\frac{4}{7} \div 1\frac{3}{4} =$ _____	$2\frac{5}{6} \div 1\frac{2}{5}$ _____
6.	$3\frac{1}{4} \div 4$ _____	$\frac{2}{3} \div \frac{1}{9} =$ _____	$\frac{7}{8} \div 4$ _____

NAME ____________________

Check What You Learned

Whole Numbers, Decimals, and Fractions

Add or subtract. Write your answer in simplest form.

	a	b	c	d	e
1.	$\begin{array}{r} 426173 \\ 109246 \\ 471926 \\ +\,102203 \\ \hline \end{array}$	$\begin{array}{r} 26.371 \\ 42.03 \\ 12.44 \\ +\,91.22 \\ \hline \end{array}$	$\begin{array}{r} 46125 \\ 91383 \\ +\,24797 \\ \hline \end{array}$	$\begin{array}{r} 42.076 \\ 10.36 \\ 92.257 \\ +\,89.1 \\ \hline \end{array}$	$\begin{array}{r} 5\frac{1}{3} \\ -\,1\frac{3}{8} \\ \hline \end{array}$
2.	$\begin{array}{r} 143.95 \\ -\,99.763 \\ \hline \end{array}$	$\begin{array}{r} 927693 \\ -\,814727 \\ \hline \end{array}$	$\begin{array}{r} 342.06 \\ -\,299.075 \\ \hline \end{array}$	$\begin{array}{r} 52.075 \\ +\,49.36 \\ \hline \end{array}$	$\begin{array}{r} 146848 \\ -\,97359 \\ \hline \end{array}$
3.	$\begin{array}{r} 2\frac{1}{3} \\ 4\frac{1}{4} \\ +\,6\frac{2}{3} \\ \hline \end{array}$	$\begin{array}{r} 5\frac{3}{4} \\ +\,4\frac{1}{6} \\ \hline \end{array}$	$\begin{array}{r} 2\frac{1}{4} \\ 3\frac{5}{8} \\ +\,\frac{3}{4} \\ \hline \end{array}$	$\begin{array}{r} 10\frac{2}{3} \\ -\,8\frac{4}{5} \\ \hline \end{array}$	$\begin{array}{r} 3\frac{1}{3} \\ -\,1\frac{1}{5} \\ \hline \end{array}$

Multiply or divide. Write your answer in simplest form.

	a	b	c	d
4.	$4\frac{3}{7} \div \frac{2}{3}$ ______	$6\frac{1}{3} \times 1\frac{3}{4} \times 1\frac{1}{5}$ ______	$\frac{4}{7} \times 1\frac{2}{7}$ ______	$8\frac{1}{4} \div 2\frac{1}{5}$ ______
5.	$96\overline{)834926}$	$\begin{array}{r} 23719 \\ \times\,546 \\ \hline \end{array}$	$0.36\overline{)255.456}$	$\begin{array}{r} 406.075 \\ \times\,9.3 \\ \hline \end{array}$

Check What You Learned

Whole Numbers, Decimals, and Fractions

Solve each problem.

6. Fred works 3.5 hours per day, 5 days per week. He makes $6.70 per hour. How much does Fred earn in a week?

   Fred earns _____ in a week.

7. Last year, Fred earned $156 every week that he worked. He made a total of $4,680. How many weeks did he work?

   Fred worked _____ weeks.

8. There are 3 gallons of milk in the refrigerator. One is $\frac{1}{3}$ full, one is $\frac{1}{5}$ full, and one is $\frac{1}{2}$ full. How much milk is in the refrigerator?

   There are _____ gallons of milk in the refrigerator.

9. Luis had $263.45 in savings. He spent $207.48 on computer equipment. How much does he have left in savings?

   Luis has _____ left in savings.

10. In a charity fund drive, grade 5 raised $1,298.15, grade 6 raised $1,378.25, grade 7 raised $1,545.35, and grade 8 raised $2,056.15. How much did the four grades raise in all?

    They raised _____ in all.

11. The park covers $8\frac{1}{3}$ acres. Fifteen volunteers are going to clean it up. If they each work on the same amount of space, what part of an acre will each volunteer clean?

    Each volunteer will clean _____ acre.

12. Kareem worked 2,016 hours last year. He worked the same number of hours per week for 48 weeks. How many hours did he work per week?

    He worked _____ hours per week.

6.	7.
8.	9.
10.	11.
12.	

Check What You Know

Ratio and Proportion

Cross-multiply to check each proportion. Circle the ratios that are true.

	a	b	c

1. $\frac{4}{7} = \frac{12}{21}$ _____ $\frac{15}{9} = \frac{10}{6}$ _____ $\frac{4}{3} = \frac{8}{7}$ _____

2. $\frac{5}{7} = \frac{15}{28}$ _____ $\frac{8}{5} = \frac{24}{18}$ _____ $\frac{9}{7} = \frac{27}{21}$ _____

3. $\frac{8}{6} = \frac{12}{9}$ _____ $\frac{9}{6} = \frac{15}{10}$ _____ $\frac{14}{12} = \frac{21}{18}$ _____

4. $\frac{11}{14} = \frac{22}{30}$ _____ $\frac{15}{14} = \frac{8}{7}$ _____ $\frac{9}{12} = \frac{15}{20}$ _____

Solve for n in each proportion.

5. $\frac{7}{5} = \frac{28}{n}$ _____ $\frac{4}{6} = \frac{n}{21}$ _____ $\frac{6}{n} = \frac{15}{20}$ _____

6. $\frac{n}{9} = \frac{14}{18}$ _____ $\frac{15}{18} = \frac{10}{n}$ _____ $\frac{n}{30} = \frac{13}{10}$ _____

7. $\frac{10}{8} = \frac{n}{24}$ _____ $\frac{11}{12} = \frac{44}{n}$ _____ $\frac{n}{2} = \frac{9}{6}$ _____

8. $\frac{12}{n} = \frac{4}{5}$ _____ $\frac{10}{14} = \frac{n}{35}$ _____ $\frac{10}{n} = \frac{25}{15}$ _____

Check What You Know

SHOW YOUR WORK

Ratio and Proportion

| Apples 12 for $4 | Peaches 8 for $2 | Corn 6 for $2 | Tomatoes 5 for $2 |

Use a proportion to solve each problem.
Refer to the picture at the top of this page.

9. Carmen bought 24 ears of corn. How much did she spend?

   Carmen spent _____.

10. Keith spent $8 on tomatoes. How many did he get?

    Keith got _____ tomatoes.

11. Jill bought 12 peaches. How much did she spend?

    Jill spent _____.

12. Isabel spent $3 on corn. How many ears did she get?

    Isabel got _____ ears.

13. Itsu spent $6 on apples. How many did he get?

    Itsu got _____ apples.

14. Maria bought 9 apples. How much did she spend?

    Maria spent _____.

15. Roberto spent $7 on peaches. How many did he get?

    Roberto got _____ peaches.

16. Ruth bought 15 tomatoes. How much did she spend?

    Ruth spent _____.

9.	10.
11.	**12.**
13.	14.
15.	16.

Lesson 2.1 Ratio and Proportion

A **ratio** compares the numbers in 2 sets.

□ □ □ □   ○ ○

The ratio of □ to ○ is 4 to 2 or $\frac{4}{2}$.

The ratio of ○ to □ is 2 to 4 or $\frac{2}{4}$.

A **proportion** expresses the equality of 2 ratios. To check if a proportion is true, cross-multiply.

$\frac{4}{2} \bowtie \frac{2}{1}$ $4 \times 1 = 2 \times 2$, so it is true.

$\frac{3}{4} = \frac{2}{3}$ $3 \times 3 \neq 4 \times 2$, so it is **not** true.

Cross-multiply to check each proportion. Circle the ratios that are true.

	a	b	c
1.	$\frac{4}{3} = \frac{6}{4}$ _____	$\frac{1}{4} = \frac{3}{12}$ _____	$\frac{4}{5} = \frac{16}{20}$ _____
2.	$\frac{8}{12} = \frac{2}{3}$ _____	$\frac{30}{25} = \frac{6}{5}$ _____	$\frac{7}{3} = \frac{5}{2}$ _____
3.	$\frac{9}{1} = \frac{18}{3}$ _____	$\frac{15}{4} = \frac{45}{12}$ _____	$\frac{2}{5} = \frac{4}{12}$ _____
4.	$\frac{7}{4} = \frac{21}{12}$ _____	$\frac{9}{2} = \frac{18}{6}$ _____	$\frac{5}{6} = \frac{15}{18}$ _____
5.	$\frac{5}{9} = \frac{10}{19}$ _____	$\frac{4}{3} = \frac{16}{12}$ _____	$\frac{7}{4} = \frac{14}{10}$ _____
6.	$\frac{12}{8} = \frac{18}{12}$ _____	$\frac{14}{7} = \frac{6}{3}$ _____	$\frac{1}{5} = \frac{3}{16}$ _____
7.	$\frac{2}{1} = \frac{6}{2}$ _____	$\frac{8}{6} = \frac{12}{8}$ _____	$\frac{5}{4} = \frac{10}{8}$ _____
8.	$\frac{2}{5} = \frac{6}{15}$ _____	$\frac{14}{6} = \frac{21}{8}$ _____	$\frac{4}{5} = \frac{10}{16}$ _____
9.	$\frac{3}{5} = \frac{9}{20}$ _____	$\frac{1}{3} = \frac{4}{12}$ _____	$\frac{9}{6} = \frac{12}{8}$ _____
10.	$\frac{7}{5} = \frac{28}{20}$ _____	$\frac{5}{4} = \frac{25}{16}$ _____	$\frac{10}{13} = \frac{30}{26}$ _____

Lesson 2.2 Solving Proportion Equations

Find the unknown number in each proportion. Follow these steps.

	1. Cross-multiply to make an equation.	**2.** Divide both sides by the number with n.	**3.** What is n?
$\frac{4}{5} = \frac{n}{15}$	$4 \times 15 = 5 \times n$ $60 = 5n$	$60 \div 5 = 5n \div 5$ $12 = n$	12
$\frac{14}{7} = \frac{4}{n}$	$14 \times n = 4 \times 7$ $14n = 28$	$14n \div 14 = 28 \div 14$ $n = 2$	2
$\frac{n}{5} = \frac{4}{20}$	$n \times 20 = 4 \times 5$ $20n = 20$	$20n \div 20 = 20 \div 20$ $n = 1$	1
$\frac{6}{n} = \frac{9}{3}$	$6 \times 3 = 9 \times n$ $18 = 9n$	$18 \div 9 = 9n \div 9$ $2 = n$	2

Solve for n in each proportion.

	a	b	c
1.	$\frac{3}{4} = \frac{n}{16}$ _____	$\frac{9}{n} = \frac{3}{5}$ _____	$\frac{n}{7} = \frac{16}{28}$ _____
2.	$\frac{4}{6} = \frac{12}{n}$ _____	$\frac{15}{12} = \frac{n}{8}$ _____	$\frac{20}{12} = \frac{5}{n}$ _____
3.	$\frac{n}{9} = \frac{8}{6}$ _____	$\frac{8}{n} = \frac{6}{3}$ _____	$\frac{5}{8} = \frac{n}{24}$ _____
4.	$\frac{7}{n} = \frac{21}{18}$ _____	$\frac{n}{15} = \frac{4}{3}$ _____	$\frac{3}{5} = \frac{30}{n}$ _____
5.	$\frac{5}{4} = \frac{n}{12}$ _____	$\frac{24}{n} = \frac{8}{3}$ _____	$\frac{11}{7} = \frac{n}{49}$ _____
6.	$\frac{14}{n} = \frac{21}{18}$ _____	$\frac{7}{5} = \frac{n}{25}$ _____	$\frac{45}{30} = \frac{6}{n}$ _____

Lesson 2.3 Problem Solving

Problem: The Longs drove 680 miles in 2 days. At that rate, how far will they drive in 5 days?

You can solve the problem using a proportion.
Let *n* equal the unknown number; that is, how far the Longs will drive in 5 days. You can make the proportion in different ways. Then, cross-multiply to solve.

Compare the number of days to the number of miles. Either number of days can be on top, but the matching number of miles must also be on top.

$$\frac{2}{5} = \frac{680}{n} \quad \text{or} \quad \frac{5}{2} = \frac{n}{680}$$

Compare the number of days to the number of miles, or compare the number of miles to the number of days. Whichever you choose, do the same for both proportions.

$$\frac{2}{680} = \frac{5}{n} \quad \text{or} \quad \frac{680}{2} = \frac{n}{5}$$

Solve for *n*. In each case, $n = 1700$.

SHOW YOUR WORK

Use a proportion to solve each problem.

1. Lisa ran 3 miles in 21 minutes. At that rate, how long would it take her to run 5 miles?

   It would take Lisa _____ minutes to run 5 miles.

   1.

2. Manuel biked 12 miles in 45 minutes. At that rate, how far could he go in 1 hour?

   Manuel could bike _____ miles in 1 hour.

   2.

3. Alicia walked 5 miles in 65 minutes. At that rate, how long would it take her to walk 7 miles?

   It would take Alicia _____ minutes to walk 7 miles.

   3.

4. Marcus skated 5 miles in 40 minutes. At that rate, how far could he go in 2 hours?

   Marcus could skate _____ miles in 2 hours.

   4.

5. Karen swam 2 miles in 28 minutes. At that rate, how long would it take her to swim 3 miles?

   It would take Karen _____ minutes to swim 3 miles.

   5.

Lesson 2.4 Problem Solving

This compact hybrid car uses 1 gallon of gas every 45 miles.

This sedan uses 1 gallon of gas every 27 miles.

This SUV uses 1 gallon of gas every 15 miles.

This truck uses 1 gallon of gas every 9 miles.

SHOW YOUR WORK

Use the information above. Make a proportion to solve each problem.

1. The sedan and truck drove the same distance at the same speed. When the sedan used 2 gallons of gas, how many gallons did the truck use?

   The truck used _____ gallons of gas.

2. The truck used 5 gallons of gas on a trip. How many gallons did the SUV use on the same trip?

   The SUV used _____ gallons of gas.

3. The hybrid car drove 450 miles. The sedan used the same amount of gas as the hybrid. How far did the sedan drive?

   The sedan drove _____ miles.

4. The SUV drove 90 miles. The truck used the same amount of gas as the SUV. How far did the truck drive?

   The truck drove _____ miles.

5. The sedan used 12 gallons of gas on a trip. How many gallons of gas did the truck use on the same trip?

   The truck used _____ gallons of gas.

6. The hybrid car used 5 gallons of gas. The SUV drove the same distance. How many gallons of gas did the SUV use?

   The SUV used _____ gallons.

1.	2.
3.	4.
5.	
6.	

Check What You Learned

Ratio and Proportion

Cross-multiply to check each proportion. Circle the ones that are true.

	a	b	c

1. $\frac{5}{8} = \frac{15}{20}$ _____ $\frac{16}{10} = \frac{24}{15}$ _____ $\frac{4}{6} = \frac{6}{9}$ _____

2. $\frac{3}{15} = \frac{1}{6}$ _____ $\frac{5}{4} = \frac{15}{13}$ _____ $\frac{8}{6} = \frac{12}{9}$ _____

3. $\frac{7}{9} = \frac{21}{27}$ _____ $\frac{4}{8} = \frac{5}{10}$ _____ $\frac{1}{7} = \frac{4}{27}$ _____

4. $\frac{8}{5} = \frac{32}{25}$ _____ $\frac{11}{13} = \frac{22}{33}$ _____ $\frac{24}{18} = \frac{20}{15}$ _____

Solve for n in each proportion.

5. $\frac{n}{12} = \frac{5}{4}$ _____ $\frac{18}{16} = \frac{n}{24}$ _____ $\frac{2}{n} = \frac{10}{15}$ _____

6. $\frac{15}{21} = \frac{n}{7}$ _____ $\frac{n}{8} = \frac{18}{24}$ _____ $\frac{10}{14} = \frac{15}{n}$ _____

7. $\frac{5}{n} = \frac{20}{24}$ _____ $\frac{4}{7} = \frac{n}{28}$ _____ $\frac{8}{6} = \frac{20}{n}$ _____

8. $\frac{n}{10} = \frac{21}{15}$ _____ $\frac{15}{n} = \frac{20}{12}$ _____ $\frac{3}{12} = \frac{n}{16}$ _____

Check What You Learned

Ratio and Proportion

GOING OUT OF BUSINESS SALE!

| T-shirts 3 for $18 | Sweaters 3 for $50 | Jeans 2 for $20 | Skirts 4 for $30 |

Solve each problem. Use the information in the picture.

9. Kerry spent $40 on jeans. How many pairs did she buy?

   Kerry bought _____ pairs of jeans.

10. Marta and her sisters bought 6 skirts. How much did they pay?

    They paid _____.

11. Leslie and her mother spent $100 on sweaters. How many did they buy?

    They bought _____ sweaters.

12. Tia bought 4 T-shirts. How much did she spend?

    Tia spent _____.

13. The store has 18 pairs of jeans left. If it can sell them all at the current price, how much money will it make?

    The store will make _____.

14. The store has $250 worth of sweaters still in stock. How many sweaters do they still have?

    They have _____ sweaters still in stock.

15. The store still has 22 T-shirts to sell. If they all sell at the current price, how much money will the store make?

    The store will make _____.

16. Diana bought 5 pairs of jeans. How much did she spend?

    Diana spent _____.

9.	10.
11.	12.
13.	14.
15.	16.

Check What You Know

Percents and Interest

Fill in the missing information about each loan.

	Principal	Rate	Time	Compounded	Interest	Total Amount
1.	$700	$7\frac{1}{2}\%$	3 years	no	_____	_____
2.	$800	_____	$1\frac{1}{2}$ years	no	$72	$872
3.	_____	5%	2 years	no	$90	_____
4.	$1,000	6%	$1\frac{1}{2}$ years	semi-annually	_____	_____
5.	$750	4%	_____	no	$75	$825
6.	$800	8%	1 year	quarterly	_____	_____

Write the equivalent decimal and fraction.

		a	b		c	d
	Percent	Decimal	Fraction	Percent	Decimal	Fraction
7.	15%	_____	_____	22%	_____	_____
8.	120%	_____	_____	54%	_____	_____
9.	36%	_____	_____	205%	_____	_____

For each fraction or decimal, write the equivalent percent.

a	b	c
10. $\frac{3}{25} =$ _____	$0.01 =$ _____	$\frac{2}{5} =$ _____
11. $4.06 =$ _____	$\frac{1}{8} =$ _____	$0.6 =$ _____

Complete each sentence.

12. 90% of 120 is _____.   18 is 40% of _____.

13. 3.6 is 5% of _____.   27 is _____% of 108.

14. $37\frac{1}{2}\%$ of 64 is _____.   35 is 25% of _____.

15. 39 is _____% of 52.   32% of 65 is _____.

16. 110% of 55 is _____.   28 is _____% of 20.

NAME _____

Check What You Know

Percents and Interest

Solve each problem.

17. Brendan took out a loan for 3 years. The interest rate was 6%, not compounded. The amount of interest he paid was $135. How much did he borrow?

Brendan borrowed _____.

18. Of the 275 students at David's school, 72% own pets. How many students own pets?

_____ students own pets.

19. Patrick borrowed $1,200 at 7% simple interest for 2 years. How much money will he have to pay back, including both principal and interest?

He will have to pay _____.

20. Lily is 56 inches tall. This is 80% of her brother's height. How tall is her brother?

Her brother is _____ inches tall.

21. Lupe put $500 in an account that pays 5% interest compounded semi-annually. How much did she have in the account after $1\frac{1}{2}$ years, including principal?

She had _____ in the account.

22. Kevin's book is 288 pages long. He has read 252 pages. What percent of the book has he read?

Kevin has read _____ of the book.

23. Two accounts contain $1,000 and pay 4% interest. One of them compounds the interest quarterly. The other pays simple interest. How much more will the account that compounds quarterly contain after 1 year?

The account that compounds quarterly will contain

_____ more.

17.	18.
19.	**20.**
21.	**22.**
23.	

Lesson 3.1 Understanding Percents

Percent (%) means *out of 100.* I percent (1%) = 0.01 or $\frac{1}{100}$

$125\% = 1.25$ or $1\frac{25}{100}$ You can reduce the fraction. $125\% = 1.25 = 1\frac{1}{4}$

Write each percent as a decimal and as a fraction. Write the fractions in simplest form.

	Percent	a Decimal	b Fraction	Percent	c Decimal	d Fraction
1.	19%	_____	_____	44%	_____	_____
2.	36%	_____	_____	345%	_____	_____
3.	55%	_____	_____	110%	_____	_____
4.	20%	_____	_____	56%	_____	_____
5.	38%	_____	_____	40%	_____	_____
6.	86%	_____	_____	275%	_____	_____
7.	15%	_____	_____	205%	_____	_____
8.	27%	_____	_____	95%	_____	_____
9.	230%	_____	_____	80%	_____	_____
10.	150%	_____	_____	154%	_____	_____
11.	18%	_____	_____	30%	_____	_____
12.	16%	_____	_____	108%	_____	_____

Lesson 3.2 Percent to Fraction and Fraction to Percent

Use this method to change a percent into a fraction:

$$12\% = \frac{12}{100} \div \frac{4}{4} = \frac{3}{25}$$

$$4\tfrac{1}{2}\% = \frac{4\tfrac{1}{2}}{100} = 4\tfrac{1}{2} \times \frac{1}{100} = \frac{9}{2} \times \frac{1}{100} = \frac{9}{200}$$

Use this method to change a fraction or mixed numeral into a percent:

$$\frac{5}{8} = \frac{n}{100} \quad 500 = 8n \quad 62\tfrac{1}{2} = n \quad \frac{5}{8} = 62\tfrac{1}{2}\%$$

$$1\tfrac{3}{10} = \frac{13}{10} = \frac{n}{100} \quad \begin{array}{c} 1300 = 10n \\ 130 = n \end{array} \quad 1\tfrac{3}{10} = 130\%$$

For each fraction or mixed numeral, write the equivalent percent. For each percent, write the equivalent fraction or mixed numeral.

	a	b	c
1.	$10\% =$ _____	_____$\% = 1\tfrac{1}{4}$	$34\% =$ _____
2.	_____$\% = \tfrac{4}{5}$	$95\% =$ _____	$130\% =$ _____
3.	$37\tfrac{1}{2}\% =$ _____	_____$\% = 2\tfrac{3}{5}$	$65\% =$ _____
4.	_____$\% = \tfrac{2}{5}$	$175\% =$ _____	_____$\% = \tfrac{3}{20}$
5.	$225\% =$ _____	_____$\% = \tfrac{17}{100}$	_____$\% = \tfrac{1}{5}$
6.	_____$\% = \tfrac{3}{25}$	$12\tfrac{1}{2}\% =$ _____	_____$\% = 1\tfrac{1}{10}$
7.	$45\% =$ _____	_____$\% = \tfrac{3}{5}$	$48\% =$ _____
8.	$105\% =$ _____	_____$\% = 2\tfrac{9}{100}$	_____$\% = 1\tfrac{2}{25}$
9.	_____$\% = \tfrac{7}{8}$	$450\% =$ _____	$16\% =$ _____
10.	$114\% =$ _____	_____$\% = \tfrac{3}{4}$	_____$\% = 2\tfrac{9}{10}$

Lesson 3.3 Percent to Decimal and Decimal to Percent

Use this method to change a decimal
to a percent:

$$0.165 = \frac{16.5}{100} = 16.5\%$$

$$1.4 = 1.40 = \frac{140}{100} = 140\%$$

Use this method to change a percent
to a decimal:

$$49.5\% = \frac{49.5}{100} = 0.495$$

$$180\% = \frac{180}{100} = 1.8$$

For each decimal, write the equivalent percent. For each percent, write the equivalent decimal.

	a	b	c
1.	19.5% = _____	_____% = 0.07	120% = _____
2.	_____% = 0.45	11.5% = _____	_____% = 0.225
3.	24.75% = _____	_____% = 1.4	8% = _____
4.	_____% = 0.625	_____% = 0.011	11% = _____
5.	365% = _____	4% = _____	2.5% = _____
6.	_____% = 1.9	_____% = 0.046	36% = _____
7.	8.75% = _____	_____% = 1.8	2.3% = _____
8.	_____% = 1.25	50% = _____	67.5% = _____
9.	_____% = 0.0436	_____% = 0.0115	_____% = 0.036
10.	_____% = 0.5	18.75% = _____	_____% = 1.02

Lesson 3.4 Finding Percent

What number is 20% of 15?	What number is $17\frac{1}{2}\%$ of 80?	What number is 125% of 42?
$n = 20\% \times 15 = 0.2 \times 15 = 3$	$n = 17\frac{1}{2}\% \times 80 =$	$n = 125\% \times 42$
20% of 15 is 3.	$0.175 \times 80 = 14$	$1.25 \times 42 = 52.5$
	$17\frac{1}{2}\%$ of 80 is 14.	125% of 42 is 52.5.

Complete each sentence.

a   **b**

1. 40% of 50 is _____.   18% of 55 is _____.

2. 32% of 32 is _____.   22% of 56 is _____.

3. 19% of 60 is _____.   16.5% of 40 is _____.

4. 1.05% of 200 is _____.   45% of 7 is _____.

5. 6% of 105 is _____.   11.5% of 37 is _____.

6. 72% of 96 is _____.   60% of 60 is _____.

7. 4% of 200 is _____.   140% of 20 is _____.

8. 85% of 63 is _____.   75% of 112 is _____.

9. 69% of 45 is _____. $37\frac{1}{2}\%$ of 80 is _____.

10. 33% of 63 is _____.   4.5% of 12 is _____.

Lesson 3.4 Finding Percent

Use these methods to find the percent one number is of another number:

50 is what percent of 80?

$$50 = n\% \times 80$$

$$50 = \frac{n}{100} \times 80 \quad 50 = \frac{80n}{100}$$

$$5000 = 80n$$

$$5000 \div 80 = 80n \div 80$$

$$62.5 = n$$

50 is 62.5% of 80.

$\frac{1}{4}$ is what percent of $\frac{5}{8}$?

$$\frac{1}{4} = n\% \times \frac{5}{8}$$

$$\frac{1}{4} = \frac{n}{100} \times \frac{5}{8} \quad \frac{1}{4} = \frac{5n}{800}$$

$$800 = 20n$$

$$800 \div 20 = 20n \div 20$$

$$40 = n$$

$\frac{1}{4}$ is 40% of $\frac{5}{8}$.

Complete.

	a	b
1.	12 is _____ % of 20.	0.9 is _____ % of 4.5.
2.	15 is _____ % of 100.	16 is _____ % of 25.
3.	0.9 is _____ % of 6.	$\frac{1}{3}$ is _____ % of $\frac{5}{6}$.
4.	1.8 is _____ % of 18.	45 is _____ % of 50.
5.	48 is _____ % of 64.	16 is _____ % of 40.
6.	19 is _____ % of 95.	39 is _____ % of 26.
7.	1.8 is _____ % of 6.	5.6 is _____ % of 2.8.
8.	12 is _____ % of 32.	64 is _____ % of 51.2.
9.	$\frac{3}{8}$ is _____ % of $\frac{3}{4}$.	1.4 is _____ % of 5.6.
10.	0.6 is _____ % of 0.5.	$\frac{7}{10}$ is _____ % of $\frac{7}{8}$.

Lesson 3.4 Finding Percent

15 is 30% of what number?	1.2 is 4.8% of what number?

15 is 30% of what number?

$15 = 30\% \times n$

$15 = \frac{30}{100} \times n \quad 15 = \frac{3n}{10}$

$150 = 3n \quad 50 = n$

15 is 30% of 50.

1.2 is 4.8% of what number?

$1.2 = 4.8\% \times n$

$1.2 = \frac{4.8}{100} \times n \quad 1.2 = \frac{4.8n}{100}$

$120 = 4.8n \quad 25 = n$

1.2 is 4.8% of 25.

Complete.

a

b

1. 3.6 is 30% of _____.

9 is 15% of _____.

2. 12 is 25% of _____.

150 is 150% of _____.

3. 125 is 40% of _____.

21 is 14% of _____.

4. 16 is 32% of _____.

12 is 12.5% of _____.

5. 36 is 75% of _____.

7 is 5% of _____.

6. 75 is 75% of _____.

7.2 is 12% of _____.

7. 5.4 is 3% of _____.

0.7 is 7% of _____.

8. 35 is 62.5% of _____.

4 is 8% of _____.

9. 36 is 1.8% of _____.

7.2 is 120% of _____.

10. 19 is 38% of _____.

10 is 2.5% of _____.

Lesson 3.5   Problem Solving

Solve each problem.

1. The Jacksons' dinner cost $125. They left $21.25 for a tip. What percent did they tip?

   The Jacksons tipped _____.

2. A sweater was originally $55. It is now marked down to 65% of its original price. How much is the sweater now?

   The sweater now costs _____.

3. Ms. Martino's new home cost $260,000. She paid $39,000 in a down payment. What percent of the home cost did she pay in the down payment?

   Ms. Martino paid _____.

4. Workers have painted 920 square feet of an office. They have completed 80% of their job. How many square feet do they need to paint in all?

   They need to paint _____ square feet.

5. The Franklins are taking a cross-country trip. They will drive 3,150 miles in all. On the first day, they drove 567 miles. What percent of their trip did they drive?

   The Franklins drove _____ of their trip.

6. Jen is reading a 276-page book. She is 25% finished. How many pages has she read?

   Jen has read _____ pages.

7. Pete's dog weighed 30 pounds. It then lost 16% of its weight. How much did Pete's dog lose?

   The dog lost _____ pounds.

8. Karla has read 85% of her book which amounts to 238 pages. How long is the book?

   The book is _____ pages long.

1. _____

2. _____

3. _____

4. _____

5. _____

6. _____

7. _____

8. _____

Lesson 3.6 Figuring Simple Interest

interest = principal × rate × time (in years)

Carla took out a $3,000 car loan, to be paid in 2 years. The interest rate is 6%. What will the interest be at the end of the 2 years?

$$i = 3000 \times 0.06 \times 2$$

$$i = 360 \qquad \text{The interest will be } \$360.$$

Find the interest for each of the loans below.

	Principal	Rate	Time	Interest
1.	$2,500	7%	$1\frac{1}{2}$ years	_____
2.	$1,000	$5\frac{1}{2}$%	3 years	_____
3.	$750	8%	$\frac{1}{2}$ year	_____
4.	$3,500	$5\frac{1}{2}$%	$2\frac{1}{2}$ years	_____
5.	$2,700	$6\frac{1}{4}$%	2 years	_____
6.	$3,200	7%	$3\frac{1}{2}$ years	_____
7.	$850	8%	1 year	_____
8.	$1,650	$7\frac{1}{2}$%	2 years	_____
9.	$2,200	$5\frac{3}{4}$%	2 years	_____
10.	$1,800	$6\frac{1}{2}$%	$3\frac{3}{4}$ years	_____

Lesson 3.6 Figuring Simple Interest

Mike got a $500 loan for $1\frac{1}{2}$ years. He paid $60 in interest. What was the interest rate?

$$i = prt$$
$$60 = 500 \times r \times 1\frac{1}{2}$$
$$60 = 750r$$
$$\frac{2}{25} = r \left(\frac{2}{25} \times \frac{4}{4} = \frac{8}{100} \right)$$

The interest rate was 8%.

Terri got a loan for 2 years. The interest rate was 6%. She paid $120 in interest. How much was the principal?

$$i = prt$$
$$120 = p \times \frac{6}{100} \times 2$$
$$120 = \frac{12p}{100} \quad 12000 = 12p$$

The principal was $1,000.

Ken got a loan for $1,700. The interest rate was 5%. He paid $212.50 in interest. What was the length of the loan?

$$i = prt$$
$$212.5 = 1700 \times \frac{5}{100} \times t$$
$$212.5 = 85t$$
$$2.5 = t$$

The loan was for $2\frac{1}{2}$ years.

Fill in the missing information about each loan.

	Principal	Rate	Time	Interest
1.	$1,600	_____	$1\frac{1}{2}$ years	$168
2.	$750	$6\frac{1}{2}$%	_____	$97.50
3.	_____	5%	$2\frac{1}{2}$ years	$181.25
4.	$1,1000	$5\frac{1}{2}$%	$3\frac{1}{2}$ years	_____
5.	$2,500	6%	_____	$225
6.	_____	$4\frac{1}{2}$%	3 years	$1215
7.	$3,500	_____	$1\frac{1}{2}$ years	$393.75
8.	$6,650	5%	$2\frac{1}{2}$ years	_____
9.	_____	$8\frac{1}{4}$%	$1\frac{1}{4}$ years	$123.75
10.	$900	_____	$\frac{1}{2}$ year	$29.25

Lesson 3.7 Figuring Compound Interest

Compound interest is interest paid on principal and interest already earned.

A savings account earns 3% interest, compounded annually.
If the amount in the account is $500 at the start of the loan, how much will be in the account after 4 years?

Year 1:
$i = 500 \times 0.03 \times 1 = 15$ New principal $= 500 + 15 = 515$

Year 2:
$i = 515 \times 0.03 \times 1 = 15.45$ New principal $= 515 + 15.45 = 530.45$

Year 3:
$i = 530.45 \times 0.03 \times 1 = 15.9135\,(15.91)$ New principal $= 530.45 + 15.91 = 546.36$

Year 4:
$i = 546.36 \times 0.03 \times 1 = 16.3908\,(16.39)$ New principal $= 546.36 + 16.39 = 562.75$

$500 in an account that earns 3% compounded annually will contain $562.75 after 4 years.

Assume interest is compounded annually. Find the total amount that will be in each account after the given time. Round to cents.

	Principal	Rate	Time	Total Amount
1.	$1,200	4%	3 years	_____
2.	$750	6%	2 years	_____
3.	$2,000	$7\frac{1}{2}$%	2 years	_____
4.	$1,500	5%	4 years	_____
5.	$600	3%	3 years	_____
6.	$700	$3\frac{1}{2}$%	2 years	_____
7.	$1,000	$4\frac{1}{2}$%	4 years	_____
8.	$400	4%	3 years	_____

Lesson 3.7 Figuring Compound Interest

Sometimes interest is paid more often than once a year (annually).

It can be paid semi-annually (twice a year), quarterly (four times a year), monthly (12 times a year, or once a month), or daily (once a day).

If it is compounded more than once annually, the amount compounded each time must be divided by the number of times it is compounded annually.

If it is compounded semi-annually, divide by 2 (multiply by $\frac{1}{2}$).

If it is compounded quarterly, divide by 4 (multiply by $\frac{1}{4}$).

If it is compounded monthly, divide by 12 (multiply by $\frac{1}{12}$).

An account of $500 pays 5% interest compounded monthly. How much will be in the account in 4 months?

Month 1: $500 \times 0.05 \times \frac{1}{12} = 2.08$ Month 2: $502.08 \times 0.05 \times \frac{1}{12} = 2.09$

Month 3: $504.17 \times 0.05 \times \frac{1}{12} = 2.10$ Month 4: $506.27 \times 0.05 \times \frac{1}{12} = 2.11$

After 4 months, $500 put into an account paying 5% interest compounded monthly will have earned $8.38 in interest. The total amount in the account will be $508.38.

Find the total amount in each account after the given amount of time. Round to cents.

	Principal	Rate	Time	Compounded	Total Amount
1.	$1,000	6%	2 years	semi-annually	_____
2.	$500	7%	$\frac{3}{4}$ year	quarterly	_____
3.	$750	8%	$\frac{1}{4}$ year	monthly	_____
4.	$2,000	$7\frac{1}{2}$%	1 year	quarterly	_____
5.	$1,500	5%	$\frac{1}{4}$ year	monthly	_____
6.	$800	$7\frac{1}{2}$%	$1\frac{1}{2}$ years	semi-annually	_____
7.	$1,200	6%	$\frac{1}{2}$ year	quarterly	_____
8.	$600	3%	2 years	semi-annually	_____

Lesson 3.8 Problem Solving

SHOW YOUR WORK

Solve each problem.

1. Kelly borrowed $1,600 for 2 years. The interest she must pay annually is 8%, not compounded. How much will she pay in interest? How much will she pay back in all, including principal?

   Kelly will pay _____ in interest.

   Kelly will pay _____ in all.

2. The interest on a 2-year $2,500 loan is $416 compounded annually. What is the interest rate of the loan?

   The interest rate is _____.

3. Gary put some money in a savings account that paid 3% interest. At the end of the year, the account had earned $19.50. How much did he put in the account?

   He put _____ in the account.

4. An account that pays simple interest pays interest on the original principal only. Lola wants to earn the most money with her $400 savings. She can put it in an account that earns 6% compounded annually or in an account that earns 7% simple interest. After 3 years, how much will each account contain, including the principal?

   The 6% account will contain _____.

   The 7% account will contain _____.

   She should choose the _____ account.

5. Paul put $200 in an account that earned 3% interest, compounded semi-annually. After 2 years, how much money was in the account?

   There was _____ in the account.

6. An account contains $400 and pays 5% interest. How much more would it contain after 2 years if it were compounded annually instead of paying simple interest?

   It would contain _____ more.

1.	
2.	**3.**
4.	
5.	**6.**

Check What You Learned

Percents and Interest

Write the equivalent decimal and fraction.

		a	b		c	d
	Percent	Decimal	Fraction	Percent	Decimal	Fraction
1.	24%	_____	_____	110%	_____	_____
2.	37%	_____	_____	55%	_____	_____
3.	6%	_____	_____	235%	_____	_____

For each fraction or decimal, write the equivalent percent.

a	b	c
4. $\frac{4}{25}$ = _____	0.05 = _____	$\frac{3}{5}$ = _____
5. 0.8 = _____	$\frac{7}{8}$ = _____	1.3 = _____

Complete each sentence.

6. 24 is 30% of _____.   42 is _____% of 50.

7. 20% of 75 is _____.   112 is 70% of _____.

8. 6.2 is _____% of 124.   32% of 85 is _____.

9. 9 is 12.5% of _____.   7 is _____% of 56.

10. 125% of 48 is _____.   5.5 is 125% of _____.

11. 10 is _____% of 62.5.   15% of 630 is _____.

Fill in the missing information about each loan.

	Principal	Rate	Time	Compounded	Interest	Total Amount
12.	$1200	$7\frac{1}{2}$%	3 years	no	_____	_____
13.	_____	8%	$2\frac{1}{2}$ years	no	$100	_____
14.	$850	5%	_____	no	$85	$935
15.	$1000	7%	1 year	quarterly	_____	_____
16.	$750	_____	$1\frac{1}{2}$ years	no	$90	$840

Check What You Learned

Percents and Interest

Solve each problem.

17. There were 32 items on the test. Bill got 28 correct. What percent of the items did Bill answer correctly?

   He answered _____ correctly.

18. Marla put $600 in an account that earns 4% interest compounded annually. How much will be in the account after 4 years, including the principal?

   There will be _____ in the account.

19. At Fairview High School, 62 students have dogs. This represents 40% of all the students polled. How many students were polled?

   _____ students were polled.

20. Alicia borrowed $780 at 5% simple interest for 2 years. How much did she pay back, including the principal?

   She paid back _____, including principal.

21. Tim took out a loan of $850 for 2 years. He had to pay $119 in interest, not compounded. What was the interest rate of the loan?

   The interest rate of the loan was _____.

22. Fifty-six percent of Sara's classmates voted for her for class president. She has 125 classmates. How many voted for her?

   _____ classmates voted for her.

23. Two accounts are opened with $2,000. Both earn 3% interest. One is compounded annually, and the other is compounded semi-annually. How much more will the account that is compounded semi-annually earn over 2 years?

   The account compounded semi-annually will earn

   _____ more.

17.	18.
19.	20.
21.	22.
23.	

CHAPTER 3 POSTTEST

Check What You Know

Customary Measurement

Complete each equation.

	a	b	c
1.	7 lb. 3 oz. = _____ oz.	2 yd. 1 ft. = _____ in.	3 qt. = _____ c.
2.	2 hr. 15 min. = _____ min.	6 pt. = _____ qt.	72 oz. = _____ lb.
3.	117 in. = _____ ft.	210 min. = _____ hr.	5 ft. 2 in. = _____ in.
4.	8 c. = _____ qt.	9 lb. 4 oz. = _____ oz.	1 hr. 24 min. = _____ min.
5.	$\frac{3}{4}$ T. = _____ lb.	100 min. = _____ hr.	2 qt. 1 pt. = _____ c.
6.	$9\frac{1}{3}$ yd. = _____ ft.	80 oz. = _____ lb.	9 min. 5 sec. = _____ sec.
7.	9 pt. = _____ qt.	$3\frac{1}{3}$ yd. = _____ in.	3 lb. 10 oz. = _____ oz.
8.	630 sec. = _____ min.	1 gal. 1 qt. = _____ c.	12 ft. 8 in. = _____ in.

Add or subtract.

	a	b	c	d
9.	1 lb. 5 oz. − 15 oz.	8 hr. 23 min. − 7 hr. 44 min.	2 yd. 2 ft. + 3 yd. 1 ft.	2 qt. 1 pt. + 3 qt.
10.	5 ft. 5 in. − 2 ft. 9 in.	3 qt. 1 pt. + 4 qt. 1 pt.	9 min. 20 sec. + 2 min. 45 sec.	3 lb. 6 oz. + 4 lb. 10 oz.
11.	9 ft .10 in. + 2 ft . 4 in.	13 oz. + 12 oz.	3 qt. − 1 pt.	2 hr. 45 min. − 1 hr. 40 min.
12.	10 min. 23 sec. + 5 min. 37 sec.	5 pt. 1 c. − 3 pt. 1 c.	12 lb. 2 oz. − 3 lb. 11 oz.	4 ft. 5 in. − 9 in.

Check What You Know

Customary Measurement

SHOW YOUR WORK

Solve each problem.

13. Anita brought 3 quarts of ice cream to the school fair. Pedro brought 1 gallon 2 quarts. How much ice cream did they bring together?

    Anita and Pedro brought _____ gallons _____ quart of ice cream to the fair.

14. Paula was hired to babysit for $4\frac{1}{2}$ hours. She was hired for how many minutes?

    Paula was hired for _____ minutes.

15. The McNeils bought a turkey weighing 6 pounds 8 ounces. They stuffed it with 12 ounces of stuffing. How much did it weigh when it was stuffed?

    The turkey weighed _____ pounds _____ ounces.

16. A fence is 16 feet long. How many yards long is it?

    The fence is _____ yards long.

17. Pedro ran for 40 minutes on Monday. He ran for 45 minutes on Tuesday. How long did he run in all?

    Pedro ran for _____ hour _____ minutes.

18. Kara bought a quart of juice. She drank 1 cup. How much juice does she have left?

    Kara has _____ pint _____ cup or _____ cups left.

19. Phil was 4 feet 11 inches tall in sixth grade. By the time he finished growing, he had grown another 11 inches. How tall is he now?

    Phil is _____ feet _____ inches tall.

13.	14.
15.	16.
17.	18.
19.	

Lesson 4.1 Units of Length
(inches, feet, yards, and miles)

12 inches (in.) = 1 foot (ft.)	How many inches is 2 yd. 1 ft.?
3 feet = 1 yard (yd.)	1 yd. = 36 in. 1 ft. = 12 in.
36 inches = 1 yard	2 yd. 1 ft. = $(2 \times 36) + 12 = 84$ in.
5,280 feet = 1 mile (mi.)	
1,760 yards = 1 mile	How many feet is 108 inches?
	1 ft. = 12 in. 108 in. = $108 \div 12 = 9$ ft.

Complete each equation.

	a	**b**	**c**
1.	72 in. = _____ yd.	10 ft. = _____ yd.	2 ft. 9 in. = _____ in.
2.	$\frac{1}{2}$ mi. = _____ yd.	$6\frac{1}{2}$ yd. = _____ ft.	2,640 yd. = _____ mi.
3.	3 yd. = _____ in.	99 in. = _____ ft.	528 ft. = _____ mi.
4.	54 in. = _____ ft.	6 ft. 4 in. = _____ in.	$\frac{3}{4}$ mi. = _____ ft.
5.	3,520 yd. = _____ mi.	33 ft. = _____ yd.	$3\frac{1}{3}$ yd. = _____ in.

SHOW YOUR WORK

Solve each problem.

6. A floor is 126 inches long. How many 1-foot tiles will be needed to cover the length?

_____ 1-foot tiles will be needed.

7. A patio is 144 inches wide. How many yards wide is it?

The patio is _____ yards wide.

8. Trina walks 1,760 feet to school each day. What fraction of a mile does she walk?

Trina walks _____ of a mile to school.

9. Brandon walks $\frac{2}{3}$ of a mile to school. How many yards does he walk?

Brandon walks _____ yards.

6.	7.
8.	9.

Lesson 4.2 Liquid Volume
(cups, pints, quarts, and gallons)

2 cups (c.) = 1 pint (pt.)	How many cups are in 1 gallon?	How many pints are in 3 quarts?
2 pints = 1 quart (qt.)	1 gal. = 4 qt. × 2 pt. × 2 c.	1 qt. = 2 pt.
4 quarts = 1 gallon (gal.)	1 gal. = 4 × 2 × 2 = 16 c.	3 qt. = 3 × 2 = 6 pt.

Complete each equation.

	a	b	c
1.	32 c. = _____ qt.	3 pt. = _____ qt.	1 gal. = _____ pt.
2.	1 gal. 2 pt. = _____ c.	5 qt. = _____ gal.	8 c. = _____ qt.
3.	3 pt. 1 c. = _____ c.	3 qt. = _____ c.	1 gal. 1 qt. = _____ pt.
4.	9 c. = _____ pt.	6 pt. = _____ gal.	6 qt. = _____ gal.
5.	3 qt. 1 pt. = _____ c.	11 c. = _____ pt.	2 gal. = _____ qt.

SHOW YOUR WORK

Solve each problem.

6. A punch recipe calls for $1\frac{1}{2}$ pints of cranberry juice. How many cups is that?

   The recipe calls for _____ cups.

7. Three gallons of lemonade were served at a picnic. How many quarts of lemonade were served?

   _____ quarts of lemonade were served.

8. Mike has $\frac{3}{4}$ gallon of milk in his refrigerator. How many cups of milk does he have?

   Mike has _____ cups.

9. Students served 24 cups of iced tea at parent-teacher night. How many quarts of iced tea did they serve?

   Students served _____ quarts.

6.	7.
8.	9.

Lesson 4.3 Weight and Time (ounces, pounds, and tons)

16 ounces (oz.) = 1 pound (lb.)
2,000 pounds = 1 ton (T.)

How many ounces are in $3\frac{1}{2}$ pounds?

1 lb. = 16 oz.

$3\frac{1}{2}$ lb. = $3\frac{1}{2} \times 16$ = 56 oz.

60 seconds (sec.) = 1 minute (min.)
60 minutes = 1 hour (hr.)
24 hours = 1 day

How many minutes are 420 seconds?

1 min. = 60 sec.

420 sec. = (420 ÷ 60) min. = 7 min.

Complete each equation.

	a	b	c
1.	80 oz. = _____ lb.	$3\frac{1}{2}$ hr. = _____ min.	1000 lb. = _____ T.
2.	72 hr. = _____ days	6 lb. 5 oz. = _____ oz.	200 min. = _____ hr.
3.	$3\frac{1}{2}$ T. = _____ lb.	$9\frac{1}{2}$ min. = _____ sec.	2500 lb. = _____ T.
4.	17 lb. = _____ oz.	108 hr. = _____ days	14 min. = _____ sec.
5.	$1\frac{1}{2}$ T. = _____ lb.	1 day = _____ min.	100 oz. = _____ lb.

SHOW YOUR WORK

Solve each problem.

6. Kim's cat weighs 136 ounces. How much does the cat weigh in pounds?

The cat weighs _____ pounds.

7. Larry's road trip took 2 full days. How many hours did he drive?

Larry drove _____ hours.

8. Mr. Chang's truck can carry 5,000 pounds of cargo. How many tons can it carry?

The truck can carry _____ tons.

9. Mia ran a half mile in 3 minutes 45 seconds. In how many seconds did she run the half mile?

She ran the half mile in _____ seconds.

6.

7.

8.

9.

Lesson 4.4 Adding Measures
(length, liquid volume, weight, and time)

You can add measures.

4 ft. 7 in. + 1 ft. 6 in. ———————— 13 in. = (1 ft.) 1 in. ———————— 6 ft. 1 in.	1 hr. 45 min. + 2 hr. 23 min. ———————— 68 min. = (1 hr.) 8 min. ———————— 4 hr. 8 min.	2 qt. 1 pt. + 1 qt. 1 pt. ———————— 2 pt. = (1 qt.) ———————— 4 qt. or 1 gal.

Add measures.

	a	b	c	d
1.	7 lb. 8 oz. + 2 lb. 10 oz.	3 min. 30 sec. + 5 min. 15 sec.	3 pt. 1 c. + 1 c.	3 yd. 2 ft. + 1 yd. 2 ft.
2.	2 pt. 1 c. + 1 pt. 1 c.	2 ft. 8 in. + 2 ft. 8 in.	1 hr. 45 min. + 1 hr. 25 min.	1 lb. 7 oz. + 4 lb. 12 oz.
3.	9 min. 20 sec. + 10 min. 40 sec.	31 lb. 9 oz. + 15 oz.	1 yd. 1 ft. + 2 yd. 2 ft.	2 qt. 1 pt. + 2 qt. 1 pt.
4.	9 ft. 6 in. + 2 ft. 8 in.	1 gal. 3 qt. + 2 gal. 3 qt.	14 oz. + 12 oz.	8 hr. 50 min. + 7 hr. 40 min.
5.	5 lb. 10 oz. + 6 lb. 10 oz.	2 min. 30 sec. + 55 sec.	3 qt. 1 pt. + 1 qt. 1 pt.	2 yd. 2 ft. + 4 yd. 1 ft.
6.	1 pt. + 3 qt. 1 pt.	1 ft. 10 in. + 10 in.	2 pt. 1 c. + 3 pt. 1 c.	3 hr. 15 min. + 2 hr. 25 min.
7.	5 min. 50 sec. + 2 min. 30 sec.	12 lb. 10 oz. + 3 lb. 7 oz.	2 yd. 2 ft. + 3 yd. 2 ft.	1 gal. 2 qt. + 2 gal. 3 qt.

Lesson 4.5 Subtracting Measures
(length, liquid volume, weight, and time)

You can subtract measures.

$\overset{0}{\cancel{1}}$ lb. $\overset{5+16=21}{\cancel{5}}$ oz.
$-$ 12 oz.
      9 oz.

$\overset{2}{\cancel{3}}$ gal. $\overset{4+1=5}{\cancel{1}}$ qt.
$-$ 1 gal. 2 qt.
   1 gal. 3 qt.

$\overset{1}{\cancel{2}}$ hr. $\overset{30+60=90}{\cancel{30}}$ min.
$-$ 45 min.
   1 hr. 45 min.

$\overset{3}{\cancel{4}}$ ft. $\overset{5+12=17}{\cancel{5}}$ in.
$-$ 1 ft. 10 in.
   2 ft. 7 in.

Subtract measures.

	a	b	c	d
1.	2 qt. 1 pt. − 1 qt. 1 pt.	3 yd. 1 ft. − 2 ft.	4 lb. 10 oz. − 12 oz.	2 min. 20 sec. − 40 sec.
2.	3 lb. 2 oz. − 8 oz.	4 hr. 8 min. − 1 hr. 30 min.	2 gal. − 3 qt.	4 ft. 6 in. − 3 ft. 9 in.
3.	3 yd. − 2 ft.	3 pt. 1 c. − 2 pt.	4 min. 45 sec. − 1 min. 55 sec.	9 lb. 2 oz. − 3 lb. 12 oz.
4.	4 hr. 15 min. − 2 hr. 45 min.	4 lb. 10 oz. − 3 lb. 2 oz.	10 ft. 6 in. − 5 ft. 10 in.	3 qt. − 1 pt.
5.	1 gal. 1 qt. − 3 qt.	4 ft. 5 in. − 7 in.	15 lb. 1 oz. − 4 lb. 7 oz.	6 min. 10 sec. − 3 min. 24 sec.
6.	9 lb. 5 oz. − 5 lb. 3 oz.	16 hr. 15 min. − 8 hr. 19 min.	3 qt. 1 pt. − 2 qt. 1 pt.	4 yd. − 2 ft.
7.	9 ft. 4 in. − 3 ft. 7 in.	4 pt. − 1 pt. 1 c.	7 min. 12 sec. − 2 min. 5 sec.	8 lb. 1 oz. − 15 oz.

Lesson 4.6 Problem Solving

SHOW YOUR WORK

Solve each problem.

1. Josh has a 4-foot-long board. How much of it does he need to cut off to get a length of 20 inches?

   Josh needs to cut off _____ feet _____ inches or

   _____ feet.

2. The community center had 3 gallons 1 quart of milk. 1 gallon 2 quarts were served. How much milk was left?

   _____ gallon _____ quarts of milk were left.

3. Craig studied for his math test 1 hour and 40 minutes at night and another 35 minutes in the morning. How long did he study for the test in all?

   Craig studied for _____ hours _____ minutes.

4. Baby Trista weighed 7 pounds 4 ounces at birth. She now weighs 9 pounds 2 ounces. How much weight has she gained?

   Baby Trista has gained _____ pound _____ ounces.

5. Mr. Franco put up 12 feet 6 inches of fencing yesterday. He put up another 7 feet 6 inches today. How much fencing did he put up in all?

   He put up _____ feet of fencing.

6. Mei's swim practice is 2 hours 15 minutes. 1 hour 40 minutes have gone by. How much practice time is left?

   _____ minutes of practice time are left.

7. A fish stew recipe calls for 1 pound of one type of fish and 8 ounces each of two other types of fish. How much fish does the recipe call for in all?

   The recipe calls for _____ pounds of fish.

1.	2.
3.	4.
5.	6.
7.	

Check What You Learned

Customary Measurement

Complete each equation.

	a	b	c
1.	40 oz. = _____ lb.	3 hr. 12 min. = _____ min.	1 yd. 2 ft. = _____ in.
2.	4 c. = _____ qt.	13 ft. = _____ yd.	8 lb. 5 oz. = _____ oz.
3.	200 sec. = _____ min.	1 gal. 1 qt. = _____ pt.	4 ft. 8 in. = _____ in.
4.	72 oz. = _____ lb.	4 hr. 13 min. = _____ min.	3 qt. 1 pt. = _____ pt.
5.	3 yd. 2 ft. = _____ ft.	2 pt. 1 c. = _____ c.	6 lb. 2 oz. = _____ oz.
6.	450 sec. = _____ min.	9 ft. 2 in. = _____ in.	3 qt. 2 pt. = _____ gal.
7.	3 qt. = _____ pt.	2 hr. 42 min. = _____ min.	200 oz. = _____ lb.
8.	17 ft. = _____ yd.	5 lb. 5 oz. = _____ oz.	9 min. 24 sec. = _____ sec.

Add or subtract.

	a	b	c	d
9.	2 lb. 6 oz. + 4 lb. 8 oz.	9 min. 30 sec. − 5 min. 42 sec.	3 yd. − 1 yd. 2 ft.	3 qt. 1 pt. − 2 qt.
10.	4 hr. 15 min. + 2 hr. 50 min.	2 gal. 3 qt. + 3 gal. 2 qt.	5 lb. 9 oz. − 4 lb. 12 oz.	3 ft. 6 in. + 4 ft. 10 in.
11.	2 yd. 2 ft. + 4 yd. 2 ft.	12 lb. − 9 lb. 5 oz.	3 pt. − 1 pt. 1 c.	2 min. 45 sec. + 3 min. 48 sec.
12.	1 qt. 1 pt. + 2 qt. 1 pt.	8 hr. 12 min. − 5 hr. 35 min.	13 oz. + 3 lb. 7 oz.	12 ft. 8 in. − 4 ft. 10 in.

Check What You Learned

Customary Measurement

Solve each problem.

13. Wanda's dog weighed 15 pounds 5 ounces. She put it on a diet and it lost 1 pound 8 ounces. How much does the dog weigh now?

    The dog weighs _____ pounds _____ ounces.

14. Mrs. Alvarez drew a border along one wall. It was 150 inches long. How many feet long was it?

    The border was _____ feet long.

15. Kyle brought 3 quarts of juice to a picnic. 1 quart and 1 pint were served. How much juice does he have left?

    Kyle has _____ quart _____ pint of juice left.

16. Pramy got 7 hours 30 minutes of sleep on Monday night and 6 hours 50 minutes of sleep on Tuesday night. What is the difference in the amount of sleep she got on the two nights?

    She got _____ minutes less sleep on Tuesday night.

17. Jon was 5 feet 8 inches tall in eighth grade. When he graduated from high school, he was 6 feet 3 inches tall. How much did he grow during that time?

    Jon grew _____ inches.

18. A punch recipe calls for 1 pint 1 cup of cranberry juice, 1 pint of pineapple juice, and 1 cup of raspberry soda. How much punch does the recipe make?

    It makes _____ pints or _____ quart _____ pint of punch.

19. Jim's truck can haul $2\frac{1}{4}$ tons. How many pounds can it haul?

    It can haul _____ pounds.

13.	14.
15.	16.
17.	18.
19.	

NAME _____

Check What You Know

Metric Measurement

Incorrect

Complete each equation.

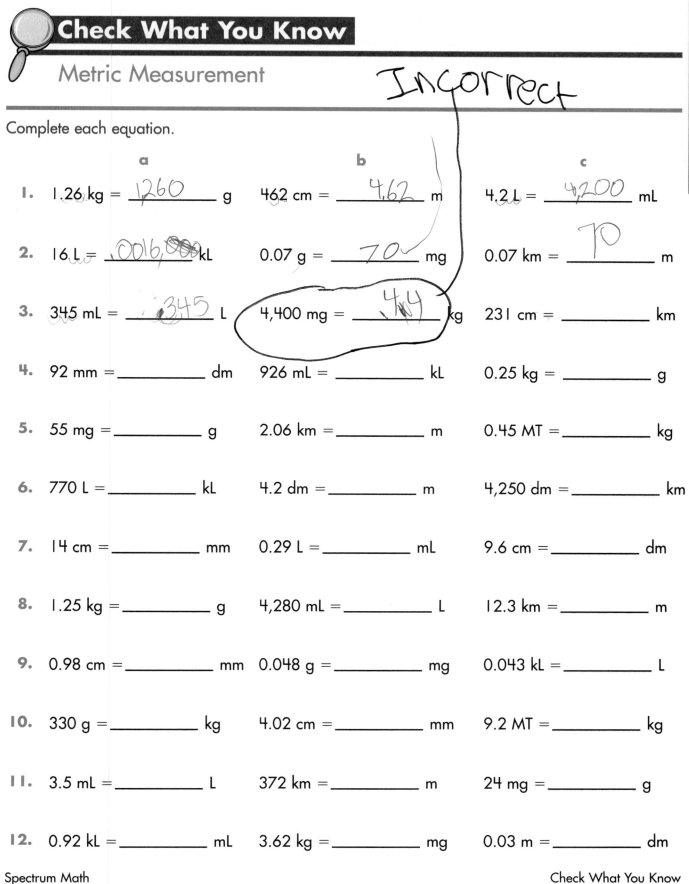

	a	b	c
1.	1.26 kg = __1260__ g	462 cm = __4.62__ m	4.2 L = __4,200__ mL
2.	16 L = __0016,000__ kL	0.07 g = __70__ mg	0.07 km = __70__ m
3.	345 mL = __0.345__ L	4,400 mg = __4.4__ kg	231 cm = _____ km
4.	92 mm = _____ dm	926 mL = _____ kL	0.25 kg = _____ g
5.	55 mg = _____ g	2.06 km = _____ m	0.45 MT = _____ kg
6.	770 L = _____ kL	4.2 dm = _____ m	4,250 dm = _____ km
7.	14 cm = _____ mm	0.29 L = _____ mL	9.6 cm = _____ dm
8.	1.25 kg = _____ g	4,280 mL = _____ L	12.3 km = _____ m
9.	0.98 cm = _____ mm	0.048 g = _____ mg	0.043 kL = _____ L
10.	330 g = _____ kg	4.02 cm = _____ mm	9.2 MT = _____ kg
11.	3.5 mL = _____ L	372 km = _____ m	24 mg = _____ g
12.	0.92 kL = _____ mL	3.62 kg = _____ mg	0.03 m = _____ dm

Check What You Know

SHOW YOUR WORK

Metric Measurement

Solve each problem.

13. Penny was 1.54 meters tall last year. Now she is 1.57 meters tall. How much did she grow in the past year?

    She grew _____ meter or _____ cm.

14. Mrs. Park had a 2.5 liter bottle of juice. She served 1,500 mL of it. How much does she have left?

    She has _____ L or _____ mL left.

15. A candy shop sells chocolate at $3.25 for 200 grams. How much does 1 kilogram of chocolate cost?

    1 kilogram of chocolate costs _____ .

16. Rita jogged 0.6 kilometer, walked 450 meters, then jogged 0.75 kilometer more. How far did she go in all?

    She went _____ kilometers or _____ meters in all.

17. A box of cereal contains 3.6 grams of sodium. There are 10 servings of cereal in the box. How much sodium does each serving contain?

    Each serving contains _____ grams or

    _____ milligrams of sodium.

18. A test tube contained 0.054 liter of iodine. Nineteen milliliters were removed. How much iodine does the test tube contain now?

    It contains _____ L or _____ mL.

19. Frank is driving 4,254 kilometers on a cross-country road trip. He plans to divide his trip into 8 stages. If he drives exactly the same distance each day, how far would he drive?

    He would drive _____ kilometers each day.

13.	14.
15.	16.
17.	18.
19.	

Lesson 5.1 Units of Length (millimeters, centimeters, decimeters, meters, and kilometers)

Metric units of length are organized by 10s.
1 meter = 10 decimeters = 100 centimeters = 1,000 millimeters
1 kilometer = 1,000 meters

To change from	to millimeters, multiply by	to centimeters, multiply by	to decimeters, multiply by	to meters, multiply by	to kilometers, multiply by
millimeters (mm)		0.1	0.01	0.001	0.000001
centimeters (cm)	10		0.1	0.01	0.00001
decimeters (dm)	100	10		0.1	0.0001
meters (m)	1,000	100	10		0.001
kilometers (km)	1,000,000	100,000	10,000	1,000	

12 m = _____ km 　　　　6.9 dm = _____ mm
1 m = 0.001 km 　　　　　 1 dm = 100 mm
12 m = (12 × 0.001) km 　 6.9 dm = (100 × 6.9) mm
12 m = 0.012 km 　　　　　6.9 dm = 690 mm

Complete each equation.

　　　　　　　a 　　　　　　　　　　　b 　　　　　　　　　　　c

1. 200 m = _____ cm 　13 dm = _____ m 　0.6 m = _____ cm

2. 0.89 km = _____ m 　45 mm = _____ dm 　1.04 m = _____ mm

3. 13.2 m = _____ km 　88 dm = _____ m 　0.075 km = _____ dm

4. 972 cm = _____ m 　23 m = _____ km 　672 mm = _____ dm

5. 0.35 km = _____ cm 　908 dm = _____ km 　1.05 m = _____ mm

SHOW YOUR WORK

Solve each problem.

6. A deck is 360 decimeters long. How many meters long is it?

It is _____ meters long.

7. A hummingbird is 45 millimeters long. How many centimeters long is it?

It is _____ centimeters long.

8. Darla ran 2,430 meters. How far did she run in kilometers?

She ran _____ kilometers.

6.

7. 　　　　　8.

Lesson 5.2 Liquid Volume (milliliters, liters, and kiloliters)

Metric units of liquid volume, or capacity, are organized by multiples of 10.

1,000 mL = 1 L
1,000 L = 1 kL

To change from	to milliliters, multiply by	to liters, multiply by	to kiloliters, multiply by
milliliters (mL)		0.001	0.000001
liters (L)	1,000		0.001
kiloliters (kL)	1,000,000	1,000	

45 mL = _____ L
1 mL = 0.001 L
45 mL = (45 × 0.001) L
45 mL = 0.045 L

9.05 kL = _____ L
1 kL = 1,000 L
9.05 kL = (1,000 × 9.05) L
9.05 kL = 9,050 L

Complete each equation.

	a	b	c
1.	873 mL = _____ L	12.3 L = _____ mL	0.02 kL = _____ mL
2.	56 L = _____ kL	7,290 mL = _____ L	36,550 mL = _____ kL
3.	391 L = _____ mL	6.04 kL = _____ L	205 L= _____ kL
4.	5,073 mL = _____ L	0.009 L = _____ mL	4,600 mL = _____ kL
5.	0.015 kL = _____ mL	78 mL = _____ L	3.03 L = _____ kL

SHOW YOUR WORK

Solve each problem.

6. A recipe calls for 1,500 milliliters of cream. How many liters of cream is this?

   The recipe calls for _____ liters of cream.

7. The restaurant made 5.6 kiloliters of soup. How many 1-liter containers of the soup can they sell?

   They can sell _____ 1-liter containers.

8. A science experiment calls for 0.02 liter of iodine. How many milliliters of iodine is this?

   It is _____ milliliters of iodine.

6.

7.

8.

Lesson 5.3 Weight (milligrams, grams, kilograms, and metric tons)

Metric units of weight are organized by 10s.
1 gram = 1,000 milligrams   1 kilogram = 1,000 grams   1 metric ton = 1,000 kilograms

To change from	to milligrams, multiply by	to grams, multiply by	to kilograms, multiply by	to metric tons, multiply by
milligrams (mg)		0.001	0.000001	0.000000001
grams (g)	1,000		0.001	0.000001
kilograms (kg)	1,000,000	1,000		0.001
metric tons (MT)	1,000,000,000	1,000,000	1,000	

90 kg = _____ MT   569 g = _____ mg
1 kg = 0.001 MT   1 g = 1,000 mg
90 kg = (0.001 × 90) MT   569 g = (1,000 × 569) mg
90 kg = 0.09 MT   569 g = 569,000 mg

Complete each equation.

         a   **b**   **c**

1. 67 mg = _____ g   0.04 MT = _____ g   856 g = _____ kg

2. 3.65 kg = _____ MT   6.7 g = _____ mg   45,000 mg = _____ kg

3. 0.86 kg = _____ mg   520 kg = _____ MT   24 kg = _____ g

4. 1.2 MT = _____ kg   0.04 kg = _____ mg   782 g = _____ MT

5. 0.09 kg = _____ g   24.8 kg = _____ MT   3.3 g = _____ mg

SHOW YOUR WORK

Solve each problem.

6. A granola bar contains 0.85 gram of protein. How many milligrams of protein does it contain?

   The granola bar contains _____ milligrams of protein.

6.

7. Bill's cat weighs 4,825 grams. What is the cat's weight in kilograms?

   The cat's weight is _____ kilograms.

7.

Lesson 5.4 Problem Solving

SHOW YOUR WORK

Solve each problem.

1. Peter bought 0.5 kilogram of fish. He divided it into four equal pieces. How much does each piece weigh?

   Each piece weighs _____ kilogram or _____ grams.

2. A soup recipe calls for 0.35 liter of tomato juice, 0.25 liter of clam juice, and 0.5 liter of water. How much liquid is in the soup in all?

   There are _____ liters of liquid in the soup.

3. Crystal is 1.76 meters tall. Sam is 181 centimeters tall. Who is taller? How much taller?

   _____ is _____ centimeters taller.

4. Mrs. Jamison's truck can carry a maximum of 1.2 metric tons of cargo. It is carrying furniture weighing 270 kilograms. How much more weight could the truck carry?

   The truck could carry _____ metric ton or _____ kilograms more.

5. Manny was 1.66 meters tall a year ago. Since then he has grown 4 centimeters. How tall is he now?

   Manny is _____ meters or _____ centimeters tall.

6. Bill built a pond that holds 2.3 kiloliters of water. He put 450 liters in it already. How much more water can he put in the pond?

   He can put _____ liters or _____ kiloliters more in the pond.

7. Gavin ran 2.01 kilometers Monday, 1.89 kilometers Tuesday, and 2,032 meters Wednesday. How far did he run over the three days?

   He ran _____ kilometers or _____ meters.

8. Erica put 32 milliliters of water into each of 25 test tubes. How much water did she use in all?

   She used _____ milliliters or _____ liter in all.

1.	2.
3.	4.
5.	6.
7.	8.

Check What You Learned

Metric Measurement

Complete each equation.

	a	b	c
1.	1.06 m = _____ cm	42 kg = _____ g	0.03 kL = _____ L
2.	290 mL = _____ L	429 mm = _____ m	196 g = _____ kg
3.	240 m = _____ km	4,460 mg = _____ g	8.3 dm = _____ cm
4.	925 mm = _____ cm	7,600 L = _____ kL	0.05 g = _____ mg
5.	25,000 mg = _____ kg	1,020 m = _____ km	1.2 L = _____ mL
6.	4.75 kL = _____ L	14.2 g = _____ mg	0.05 km = _____ dm
7.	0.02 L = _____ mL	3.1 cm = _____ mm	71 mg = _____ g
8.	2.03 m = _____ cm	50 g = _____ kg	38,000 mL = _____ kL
9.	0.003 kg = _____ mg	0.005 kL = _____ L	18,000 cm = _____ km
10.	750 mm = _____ dm	4.6 m = _____ cm	0.163 kg = _____ g
11.	4,690 L = _____ kL	75 g = _____ kg	0.012 m = _____ mm
12.	19 dm = _____ m	0.72 L = _____ mL	2.04 g = _____ mg

Check What You Learned

Metric Measurement

Solve each problem.

13. During a game, the softball team drank 12 bottles of water and 7 bottles of juice. Each bottle contained 0.75 liter. How much liquid did they drink in all?

    The team drank _____ liters in all.

14. Jenna plans to run 12 kilometers each week. On Monday, she ran 1,800 meters. On Tuesday, she ran 2.1 kilometers. How much farther does she plan to run this week?

    She plans to run _____ kilometers or _____ meters farther.

15. Cherries were on sale for $2.18 per kilogram. Mr. Ortiz bought 2,500 grams. How much did he pay?

    Mr. Ortiz paid _____.

16. A goldfinch is 108 millimeters long. A robin is 21 centimeters long. How much longer is the robin than the goldfinch?

    The robin is _____ centimeters or _____ millimeters longer.

17. Derek takes a 500-milligram vitamin every day. How much does he consume in a week?

    He consumes _____ grams or _____ milligrams of vitamins in a week.

18. Alison brought three 2-liter bottles of lemonade to the picnic. At the end of the picnic, only 750 milliliters of lemonade were left. How much lemonade was consumed?

    _____ liters of lemonade were consumed.

19. A puppy weighs 3.6 kilograms. The vet says he will weigh 13 kilograms when full grown. How much weight is the puppy expected to gain?

    He is expected to gain _____ kilograms.

13.	
14.	**15.**
16.	**17.**
18.	**19.**

Mid-Test   Chapters 1–5

Cross-multiply to check each proportion. Circle the ones that are true.

	a	b	c	d
1.	$\frac{8}{9} = \frac{24}{30}$ _____	$\frac{6}{9} = \frac{10}{15}$ _____	$\frac{14}{18} = \frac{35}{45}$ _____	$\frac{4}{12} = \frac{6}{18}$ _____
2.	$\frac{2}{5} = \frac{6}{18}$ _____	$\frac{15}{18} = \frac{20}{25}$ _____	$\frac{10}{30} = \frac{15}{50}$ _____	$\frac{12}{16} = \frac{21}{28}$ _____

Solve for *n* in each proportion.

	a	b	c
3.	$\frac{3}{5} = \frac{n}{20}$ _____	$\frac{n}{15} = \frac{7}{21}$ _____	$\frac{12}{n} = \frac{20}{15}$ _____
4.	$\frac{8}{5} = \frac{40}{n}$ _____	$\frac{10}{24} = \frac{n}{60}$ _____	$\frac{3}{n} = \frac{21}{49}$ _____

Write the missing equivalent fraction, decimal, or percent.

	Percent	Fraction	Decimal	Percent	Fraction	Decimal
5.	35%	_____	_____	_____	$\frac{3}{25}$	_____
6.	_____	$\frac{3}{5}$	0.6	154%	_____	_____
7.	18%	_____	_____	_____	$\frac{7}{10}$	0.7
8.	_____	$\frac{1}{8}$	_____	4%	_____	_____
9.	225%	_____	_____	_____	$\frac{3}{20}$	_____
10.	_____	_____	4.2	36%	_____	_____

Fill in the missing information about each loan.

	Principal	Rate	Time	Compounded	Interest	Total Amount
11.	$800	5%	2 years	no	_____	_____
12.	_____	6%	3 years	no	$216	_____
13.	$750	_____	1 year	no	$48.75	$798.75
14.	$1,500	3%	2 years	semi-annually	_____	_____

Mid-Test Chapters 1–5

Solve.

	a	b	c
15.	$4\frac{1}{2} \times \frac{3}{4} =$ _____	$\frac{7}{12} \div 1\frac{2}{3} =$ _____	$9\frac{1}{2} + 2\frac{7}{12} + 1\frac{1}{3} =$ _____

	a	b	c	d
16.	$\begin{array}{r} 1\,1\,4\,7\,6\,3 \\ 2\,1\,9\,0\,7\,5 \\ +\,8\,2\,3\,0\,4\,7 \\ \hline \end{array}$	$0.1\,9\,\overline{)\,3\,0\,4.7\,6}$	$\begin{array}{r} 2\,5.0\,8 \\ \times\quad .7\,6 \\ \hline \end{array}$	$1\,2\,7\,\overline{)\,4\,5\,3\,6}$
17.	$\begin{array}{r} 3\,9\,2.0\,8\,1 \\ -\,1\,0\,7.6\,3\,5 \\ \hline \end{array}$	$\begin{array}{r} 9\,5.1\,2\,7 \\ \times\quad 0.0\,9 \\ \hline \end{array}$	$\begin{array}{r} 4\,1\,7\,0\,4\,2 \\ -\quad 8\,1\,9\,7\,6 \\ \hline \end{array}$	$\begin{array}{r} 3\,1.1\,7\,2 \\ \times\quad\quad 8 \\ \hline \end{array}$
18.	$\begin{array}{r} 5\frac{1}{2} \\ -\,2\frac{1}{3} \\ \hline \end{array}$	$\begin{array}{r} 4\,7\,8.3\,2 \\ 9\,1\,4.1\,5\,7 \\ 2\,1\,6.0\,6 \\ +\quad 4\,9.9\,1\,2 \\ \hline \end{array}$	$4.8\,\overline{)\,2\,6\,2.0\,8}$	$\begin{array}{r} 5\,2\,1\,7\,4 \\ \times\quad 2\,0\,6 \\ \hline \end{array}$

Complete each equation.

	a	b	c
19.	3 qt. 1 pt. = _____ c.	1.06 m = _____ km	3 yd. 2 ft. = _____ ft.
20.	95 cm = _____ dm	3 min. 2 sec. = _____ sec.	4.26 kg = _____ g
21.	9 lb. 2 oz. = _____ oz.	1,190 mL= _____ L	116 in. = _____ ft.
22.	15 qt. = _____ gal.	1,056 mg = _____ g	420 mm = _____ m
23.	2.3 kg = _____ g	136 oz. = _____ lb.	20,500 mL = _____ L
24.	4 yd. 2 ft. = _____ in.	0.029 kL = _____ L	5 c. = _____ pt.
25.	44.2 dm = _____ m	4 min. 39 sec. = _____ sec.	29 mg = _____ g
26.	$2\frac{1}{4}$ lb. = _____ oz.	4.6 L = _____ mL	111 in. = _____ ft.

Mid-Test Chapters 1–5

Solve each problem.

27. Ivy put $500 in a savings account that pays 3% interest compounded semi-annually. How much will she have in the account after a year?

    She will have _____ in the account.

28. A farm stand sold tomatoes 5 for $3. Max bought 12 tomatoes. How much did he pay?

    Max paid _____ for tomatoes.

29. Albert's school day lasts 7 hours 20 minutes. After 3 hours 45 minutes have gone by, how much is left in his school day?

    _____ hours _____ minutes are left.

30. Grace bought 6 loaves of bread. She spent $10.74. How much did each loaf cost?

    Each loaf cost _____.

31. Peter's cat weighs 4.21 kilograms. Pam's cat weighs 3,984 grams. Whose cat weighs more? How much more?

    _____ cat weighs _____ kilogram or _____ grams more.

32. A jacket that originally cost $78.50 was marked down to $62.80. By what percent was the jacket discounted?

    The jacket was discounted _____.

33. Justine wrote $3\frac{1}{2}$ pages of a book report on Monday and $2\frac{1}{3}$ pages on Tuesday. How much has she written in all?

    Justine has written _____ pages.

34. The Willis family traveled 820 miles in the first 2 days of their cross-country trip. At that rate, how far will they have traveled in a week?

    They will have traveled _____ miles.

27.	28.
29.	30.
31.	32.
33.	34.

CHAPTERS 1–5 MID-TEST

Mid-Test Chapters 1–5

Solve each problem.

35. Greg borrowed $1,200 for 2 years. He had to pay $132 in simple interest. What was the interest rate on the loan?

    The interest rate was _____.

36. Baby Mary weighed 9 pounds 13 ounces at her last checkup. Since then, she has gained 8 ounces. How much does she weigh now?

    She weighs _____ pounds _____ ounces now.

37. A recipe calls for $\frac{3}{4}$ of a cup of sugar. Lucy is making 3 times the normal amount. How much sugar does she need to use?

    She needs to use _____ cups.

38. A train travels 935 miles in 5 days. Assuming it travels at the same rate all the time, how far does the train travel in 9 days?

    The train travels _____ miles.

39. The Farrells' dinner cost $78.50. They left an 18% tip on this amount. How much was the tip?

    The tip was _____.

40. Martin's fish tank holds 0.1 kiloliter of water. He removed 13 liters so he could add more plants and fish. How much water is in the fish tank now?

    _____ kiloliter or _____ liters of water are in the tank.

41. Rachel's book is 316 pages long. She has read 75% of it. How many pages has she read?

    She has read _____ pages.

42. The community center had 5 gallons of milk. It served 2 gallons 3 quarts at an event. How much milk is left?

    _____ gallons _____ quart are left.

35.	36.
37.	38.
39.	40.
41.	42.

CHAPTERS 1–5 MID-TEST

Check What You Know

Probability and Statistics

Answer the questions by interpreting data from each graph.

1. What is Keith's total weekly budget? _____

2. What percentage of Keith's budget does he spend on transportation? _____ How many degrees of the circle are used to represent this percentage? _____

3. How many degrees of the circle are used to represent entertainment? _____

Keith's Weekly Budget

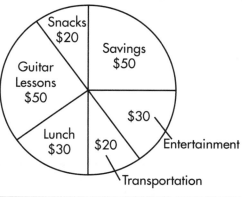

4. Who earned the most points in the contest? _____

5. How many more points did Marla earn than Dan? _____

6. How many combined points did Ali and Colin earn? _____

7. The students' goal is 20 points. How many more points does Mark need to earn? _____

Contest Points Earned

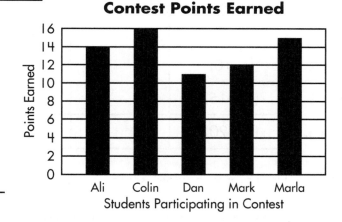

Books Read by Students over the Summer

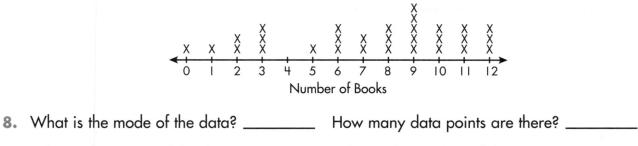

8. What is the mode of the data? _____ How many data points are there? _____

9. What is the range of the data? _____ What is the median of the data? _____

Check What You Know

Probability and Statistics

10. Alicia has 2 new pairs of shoes, white and black; 3 new skirts, red, blue, and black; and 2 new sweaters, white and red. How many different outfits can she make with her new clothing? Make a tree diagram to solve.

Fill in the missing data in the frequency table. Then, answer the questions.

Scores on Last Week's Quiz

	Score Range	Frequency	Cumulative Frequency	Relative Frequency
11.	(0–5)		3	$\frac{1}{8}$
12.	(6–10)		7	$\frac{1}{6}$
13.	(11–15)		16	$\frac{3}{8}$
14.	(16–20)		24	$\frac{1}{3}$

15. How many students' scores were included in the table? _____

16. Which score range was most frequent? _____

17. What was the relative frequency of a score between 16 and 20? _____

Use the spinner to determine the probability of the following events. Write your answer as a fraction in simplest form.

18. spinning a gray section _____

19. spinning a 3 _____

20. spinning an even number _____

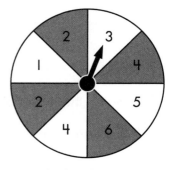

Lesson 6.1 Bar Graphs

Bar graphs are used to compare data.
This graph shows the results of an eighth grade poll that asked, "What is your favorite type of music?"

Which type of music did the most students pick? __Rock__ How many picked it? __15__

Which two types of music had the same number of fans? __R & B and Rap__

How many people in all chose either dance music or country music?
(Add the two amounts: 5 + 6) __11__

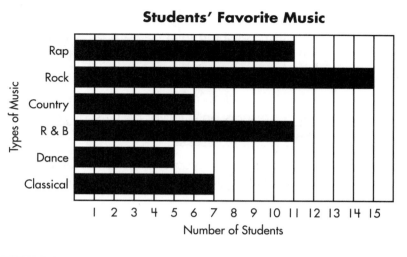

Students' Favorite Music

Answer the questions by interpreting data from the bar graphs.

Toy Store Sales for March

1. How many stuffed animals were sold, including teddy bears? _____

2. What toy was purchased twice as many times as blocks? _____

3. How many more teddy bears than cars were sold? _____

4. The store manager hoped to sell 13 dolls in March. How far short of this goal was she? _____

---

5. Which two people volunteered for the same number of hours? _____

6. Which two people have 21 combined volunteer hours? _____

7. Lisa worked 16 hours in April. Compared to to May, how many more hours did she work in April? _____

8. Sam volunteered 5 hours in April. How many more hours did he volunteer in May? _____

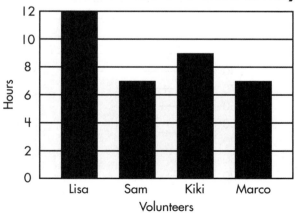

Volunteers' Hours Worked in May

Lesson 6.2 Histograms

A **histogram** is a type of bar graph. The categories are consecutive and the intervals are equal. Histograms are often used to analyze changes over a given time period.

Look at the histogram. What do the bars represent?
<u>Each bar represents an interval of 1 fiscal year. Five fiscal years are represented.</u>

Which two consecutive years saw the greatest change in tax revenues? __2000–2001__

How much did the town collect in tax revenues in 1999? (Remember that each line in the chart represents $10,000.) __$95,000__

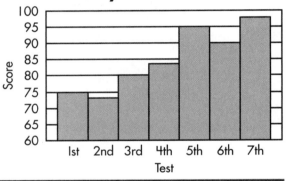

Answer the questions by interpreting data from the histograms.

1. What does each bar represent? _____

2. On which test did Wesley do best? _____

3. What was the difference between Wesley's best score and his worst score? _____

4. On which test did Wesley score 95 points?

   _____

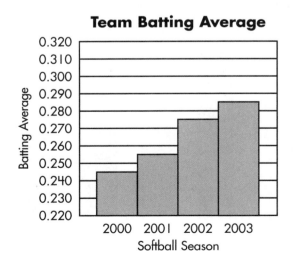

5. What is the interval represented by each bar?

   _____

6. What is the lowest batting average that can be represented on the chart? _____
   What is the highest? _____

7. What was the team batting average in 2000?

   _____

8. How much did the team batting average improve over 4 years? _____

Lesson 6.3 Line Graphs

A **line graph** shows how data changes over time. This line graph shows how the temperature changed over the course of two weeks in May.

What are the lowest and highest temperatures that could be displayed on the graph? The graph does not start at 0°. The lowest temperature that can be recorded on the graph is __40°__ . The highest temperature that can be recorded is __70°__ .

What is the highest temperature that was recorded during the two weeks? On what day was it recorded? Look for the highest point on the line. The highest temperature was __70°__ . It was recorded on May 12 .

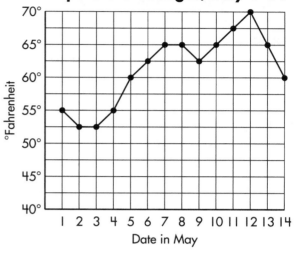

Temperature Changes, May 1–14

Answer the questions by interpreting data from the line graphs.

1. For how many weeks did Joel track his weekly running totals? _____

2. How far did Joel run during week 3? _____

3. How many more miles did Joel run in week 6 than in week 5? _____

4. How many miles in all did Joel run during weeks 5, 6, 7, and 8? _____

Joel's Weekly Running Totals

5. What was the earliest that anyone finished the marathon? _____

6. Approximately what percent of the people had finished after $3\frac{1}{2}$ hours? _____

7. Approximately what percent of the people had finished after 6 hours? _____

8. By what time had more than 50% of the people finished? _____

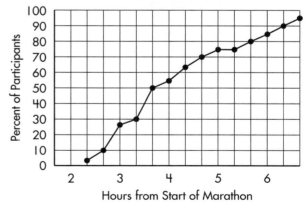

Marathon Times

Lesson 6.4 Circle Graphs

A **circle graph** is used to show how a **whole** is divided. The entire circle represents 1 whole. It is divided into **sectors** which are fractional parts of the whole.

100% of a circle is 360°.

50% or $\frac{1}{2}$ of a circle is 180°.

25% or $\frac{1}{4}$ of a circle is 90°.

12.5% or $\frac{1}{8}$ of a circle is 45°.

6.25% or $\frac{1}{16}$ of a circle is 22.5°.

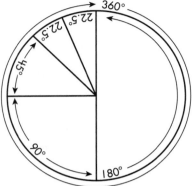

A circle graph can be divided into any number of segments of any percentage/fraction value. The total will be 100%, 1 whole, or 360°.

For the circle above, $180° + 90° + 45° + 22.5° + 22.5° = 360°$ or: $\frac{1}{2} + \frac{1}{4} + \frac{1}{8} + \frac{1}{16} + \frac{1}{16} = 1$

Determine the percentage and number of degrees for each segment. Use a protractor, if necessary.

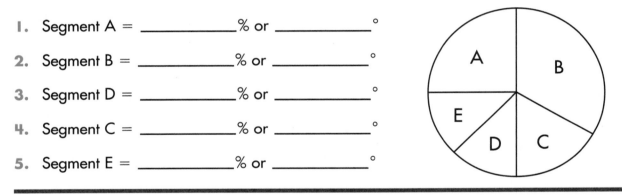

1. Segment A = _____% or _____°

2. Segment B = _____% or _____°

3. Segment D = _____% or _____°

4. Segment C = _____% or _____°

5. Segment E = _____% or _____°

Molly's Monthly Allowance Spending

The entire amount of Molly's allowance is $60 per month.

6. What percent of the whole does Molly spend on CDs?

    _____ What dollar amount is that, if the whole

    is $60? _____

7. What percent of the whole does Molly spend on snacks?

    _____

    What dollar amount is that? _____

Lesson 6.4 Circle Graphs

What percent of Jake's salary does he save each week? What fraction of 360° is 120°? _$\frac{1}{3}$_ What percent is this? _33.3%_

How Jake Spends His Weekly Salary

Jake's salary is $450. How much does he save? $\frac{1}{3}$ of $450 is __$150__ .

The *pizza* segment of the chart is 24°. How much money does Jake spend each month on pizza? Use a ratio to solve:

$$\frac{24}{360} = \frac{x}{450} \quad x = 30 \quad \text{Jake spends } \$30.$$

Answer the questions by interpreting each circle graph. Use a protractor to help you.

1. What is the total of Jenna's monthly budget? _____

2. What percentage of her monthly budget does Jenna spend on rent? _____ How many degrees of the circle are used to represent that percentage? _____

3. What percentage of her monthly budget does Jenna spend on groceries? _____ What fraction is that? _____

4. What fraction of her budget does Jenna spend on entertainment? _____ That percentage is represented by how many degrees? _____

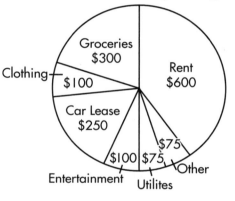

Jenna's Monthly Budget

5. What percent of each day does Ms. Perez spend teaching reading? _____ The school day is $7\frac{1}{2}$ hours. How many hours does Ms. Perez spend teaching reading? _____

6. How much time does Ms. Perez spend teaching math? _____ What fraction of the school day is that? _____

7. What percent of Ms. Perez's day is spent teaching computer skills? _____ How many minutes is this? _____

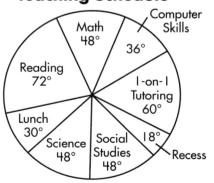

Ms. Perez's Daily Teaching Schedule

Lesson 6.5 Scattergrams

A **scattergram** is a graph that shows the relationship between two sets of data. To see the relationship clearly, a **line of best fit** can be drawn. This is drawn so that there are about the same number of data points above and below the line.

This scattergram shows the relationship between average high temperature and a family's gas use for heating fuel each month.

Is there a **positive** or **negative** relationship between gas use and temperature? As temperature increases, gas use decreases. So, the relationship is negative.

Look for the **outlier**, a data point that does not conform to the general trend. What is a reasonable explanation for this outlier? If gas use was low on one occasion even though temperature was low, perhaps the family was away for part of that month.

Monthly Gas Usage

Answer the questions by interpreting data from the scattergrams.

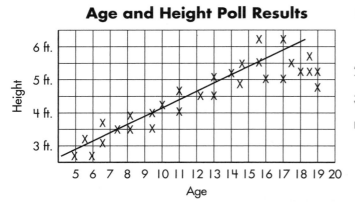

Age and Height Poll Results

1. Which two sets of data are being compared by this scattergram? _____

2. Is the correlation positive or negative? _____

3. How many people were polled? _____

4. How do you explain the data points at the end that do not follow the line of best fit? _____

5. Which two pieces of data are being compared by this scattergram? _____

6. Draw the line of best fit. Is the correlation positive or negative? _____

7. There are a few outliers for this scattergram. What do they show? _____

8. What is a possible explanation? _____

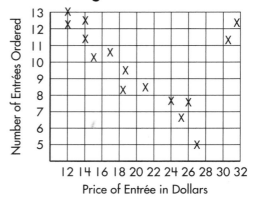

Ordering Trends at Chez Henri

Lesson 6.6 Measures of Central Tendency

When interpreting data, we look at **measures of central tendency**. These measures allow different observations about the numbers in a set of data. Each one is useful for a different reason.

Mr. Park's class received the following scores on the latest math test:

85, 88, 92, 72, 95, 84, 84, 82, 97, 67, 90, 84, 87, 90, 78, 80, 88, 90, 84, 78

What was the **mean**, or **average**, score? Add all of the scores and divide by the total number of scores: $1695 \div 20 = 84.75$.

What was the **median** score? The median is the **number in the middle**. Line up the numbers in order:

67, 72, 78, 78, 80, 82, 84, 84, 84, <u>84, 85,</u> 87, 88, 88, 90, 90, 90, 92, 95, 97

Because there are an even number of scores, the median is the average of the two middle numbers. $(84 + 85) \div 2 = 84.5$

What is the **mode**, or **most common number**? Look at the numbers in order again.

The numbers 78, 84, 88, and 90 each appear more than once, but 84 appears the most often.

What is the **range**? Subtract the lowest score from the highest: $97 - 67 = 30$.

Find the measures of central tendency for each of the following data sets.

	a		b

1. Cesar's Test Scores: 84, 80, 78, 90, 76, 88, 86, 80, 94
   How many scores are included? _____
   Rewrite them in order:
   _____

   mode: _____
   median: _____
   range: _____
   mean: _____

2. Basketball Team Scores: 78, 77, 81, 84, 67, 78, 75, 82
   How many scores are included? _____
   Rewrite them in order:
   _____

   mode: _____
   median: _____
   range: _____
   mean: _____

3. Daily Theater Attendance: 124, 127, 111, 119, 107, 99, 115
   How many days are included? _____
   Rewrite the numbers in order:
   _____

   mode: _____
   median: _____
   range: _____
   mean: _____

4. Marisa's Daily Tips: $15, $21, $18, $13, $21, $22, $25
   How many days are included? _____
   Rewrite the numbers in order:
   _____

   mode: _____
   median: _____
   range: _____
   mean: _____

Lesson 6.7 Frequency Tables

Mr. Park's class got the following scores on a recent test: 85, 88, 92, 72, 95, 84, 84, 82, 97, 67, 90, 84, 87, 90, 78, 80, 88, 90, 84, 78. He made this **frequency table** with the scores.

Score Range	Number in the Range	Cumulative Frequency	Relative Frequency
(60–69)	1	1	$\frac{1}{20}$
(70–79)	3	4	$\frac{3}{20}$
(80–89)	10	14	$\frac{10}{20}$ or $\frac{1}{2}$
(90–99)	6	20	$\frac{6}{20}$ or $\frac{3}{10}$

The chart shows that the scores ranged from the 60s to the 90s, with the most frequent scores in the 80s range. The relative frequency compares the number in each range with the total number of scores.

Complete the chart with fractions in simplest form. Then, answer the questions.

Eighth Graders' Siblings

	No. of Siblings	Frequency	Cumulative Frequency	Relative Frequency
1.	0	7	7	
2.	1	23	30	
3.	2	19	49	
4.	3+	12	61	

5. How many 8th graders were polled? _____

6. How many different options were the students given to choose from? _____

Complete the chart with the missing numbers. Then, answer the questions.

Scores on a Recent Science Test

	Score Range	Frequency	Cumulative Frequency	Relative Frequency
7.	(50–59)		2	$\frac{1}{12}$
8.	(60–69)		7	$\frac{5}{24}$
9.	(70–79)		13	$\frac{1}{4}$
10.	(80–89)		21	$\frac{1}{3}$
11.	(90–99)		24	$\frac{1}{8}$

12. In what 10-point range did the most students score? _____

13. What was the total range of points students could have received on the test? _____

Lesson 6.8 Line Plots

A **line plot** uses a number line to clearly illustrate the frequency of data. A line plot makes measures of central tendency, such as range and mode, very easy to identify. Leslie made this line plot:

Height of My Classmates

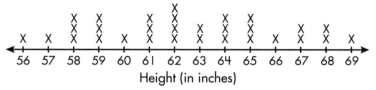

Height (in inches)

What is the **mode**, or most frequent height? (Look for the tallest stack of Xs.) The mode is 62 inches. What is the range of heights in the class? Subtract the least height from the greatest: $69 - 56 = 13$ inches.

How many students were polled? (Count the total number of Xs.) Thirty students were polled.
What is the median height of the students? Count 15 Xs in from the left and 15 Xs in from the right. The median is the average of these two numbers. Because both numbers are 62 inches, the median is 62 inches.

Interpret each line plot to answer the questions that follow.

Number of Books Read per Month

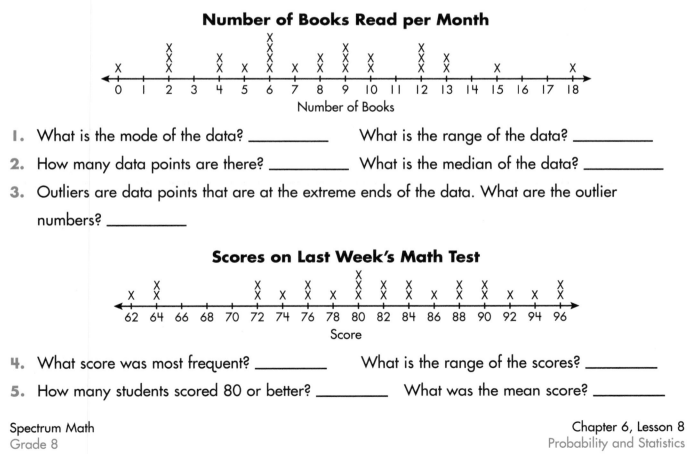

Number of Books

1. What is the mode of the data? _____   What is the range of the data? _____

2. How many data points are there? _____   What is the median of the data? _____

3. Outliers are data points that are at the extreme ends of the data. What are the outlier

   numbers? _____

Scores on Last Week's Math Test

Score

4. What score was most frequent? _____   What is the range of the scores? _____

5. How many students scored 80 or better? _____   What was the mean score? _____

Lesson 6.9 Box-and-Whisker Plots

A **box-and-whisker plot** is a specific way to represent a set of data. The middle 50% of the data set is indicated by a rectangle, divided at the median of the data set. The lowest and highest 25% are indicated by "whiskers," or lines that branch out from either side of the rectangle.

Mavis used the data she collected to create this box-and-whisker plot. It can be compared to the line plot on the previous page. A box-and-whisker plot does not show the number of data points. It cannot be used to find the mean or mode of the data.

Height of My Classmates

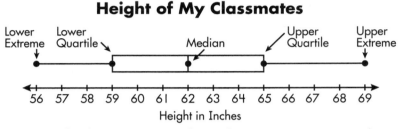

What is the range? (Subtract the lower extreme from the upper extreme.) The range is 13 inches. Between which two numbers are the middle 50% of the students' heights? Look at the two ends of the box. The middle 50% are between 59 and 65. The **interquartile range** is 65−59, or 6.

Mavis polled 6th and 7th graders on their height. She made these box-and-whisker plots with the data. Interpret each one to answer the questions.

1. What is the interquartile range in the

   6th grade data? _____

2. What is the median height in 6th grade?

   _____

3. Between which two numbers are the lowest 25%

   of students' heights in 6th grade? _____

4. What height is at the upper extreme in the

   7th grade? _____

5. What is the range of heights in 7th grade?

   _____

6. What is the interquartile range in the

   7th grade data? _____

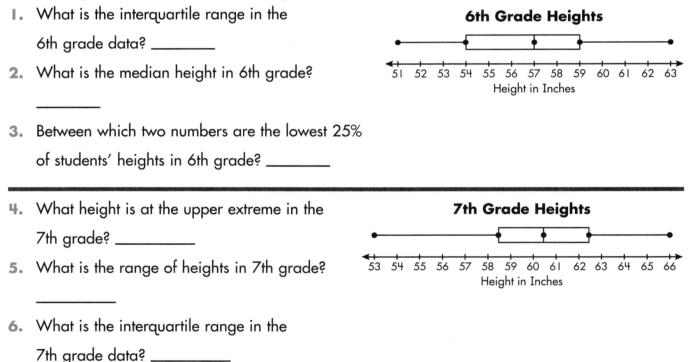

Lesson 6.10 Tree Diagrams

Sample space means **all possible outcomes of an experiment.** What is the sample space if you roll 1 die and flip 1 coin? You can show it using a chart, a list, or a **tree diagram:**

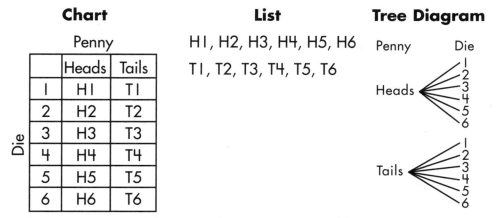

| Chart | List | Tree Diagram |

Penny

	Heads	Tails
1	H1	T1
2	H2	T2
3	H3	T3
4	H4	T4
5	H5	T5
6	H6	T6

Die

List: H1, H2, H3, H4, H5, H6
T1, T2, T3, T4, T5, T6

What is the sample space? It is 12, because there are 12 possible outcomes.

Solve each problem.

1. Juan flips a penny, a nickel, and a dime at the same time. How many different combinations of heads and tails can he get? Make a tree diagram to solve.

   _____

2. Latisha has red, blue, and black sneakers; blue, tan, and white pants; and black and gray sweatshirts. How many different outfits can she make? Make a tree

   diagram to solve. _____

3. Jonathan, Kaitlin, and Ling are trying to decide in what order they should appear during their talent show performance. They made this chart showing the possible orders. Can you show the same results using a tree diagram? (Remember, each person can appear only once in the 1, 2, 3 order.) What is the total number of possible orders?

   _____

1	2	3
J	K	L
K	L	J
L	K	J
J	L	K
K	J	L
L	J	K

Lesson 6.11 Matrices

A **matrix** is a special way of organizing data visually. It is an arrangement of rows and columns. Each row is in brackets.

A matrix compares different facets of information. This matrix compares female and male participants in 3 school activities: band, drama, and art.

	B	D	A
Female	[14	22	12]
Male	[20	16	13]

A matrix is described by its number of rows and columns. This is a **2-by-3 matrix.**

Answer the following questions about matrices.

1. Ramón researched 100 people and made this matrix showing data about them. Which of the following could be the information compiled in the chart? Circle A, B, or C.

[17 20   2   5]
[2 14 11   9]
[3   6   6   5]

   A. Whether they were left- or right-handed, and whether their favorite meal was breakfast, lunch, or dinner

   B. Whether their hair was black, brown, blond, or red, and whether their eyes were brown, blue, or other

   C. Whether they drove a car, truck, or SUV, and whether they had completed high school, college, or graduate school

---

Isabel made this matrix. It shows the results of her poll of people aged 1–10, 11–20, and 21–30 regarding whether they enjoyed any of the following activities: skiing, rollerblading, playing video games, and hiking. Respondents could choose any number of activities, including all or none.

	S	R	V	H
(1–10)	[3	5	8	5]
(11–20)	[18	15	12	13]
(21–30)	[15	12	9	13]

2. Which activity was most popular with both sets of people over 10 years old? _____

3. Which activity was most popular with people under 11? _____

4. Which activity was chosen by the same number of respondents from 2 age groups? _____

5. Can you tell from the matrix how many people were included in Isabel's poll? _____

Lesson 6.12 Calculating Probability

Probability is the likelihood of a given event happening. To find probability, compare the number of outcomes of a given event to the total number of possible outcomes.

When you spin the spinner, what is the probability that you will spin a 3?
How many equal sections of the spinner are there? __8__
How many of them say 3? __2__
The probability is 2 out of 8 or 1 out of 4.
You can also express this as $\frac{1}{4}$, 1:4, or 25%.

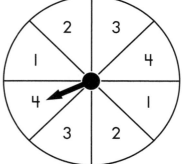

What is the probability of spinning a 1-digit number?
Because all of the numbers on the spinner are 1-digit numbers, that probability is 100% or 1.
What is the probability of spinning 6? Because 6 never appears on the spinner, that probability is 0.

Determine the probability for each of the following events. Write each answer as a fraction in simplest form.

1. drawing a gray marble _____

2. drawing a white marble _____

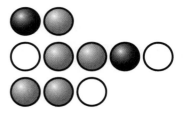

3. drawing a black marble _____

4. drawing either a gray or a black marble _____

---

5. spinning a gray section _____

6. spinning 4 _____

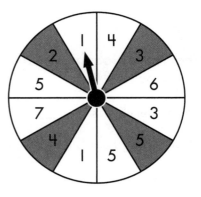

7. spinning 1 _____

8. spinning *either* 4 or 5 _____

9. spinning an even number _____

Lesson 6.12 Problem Solving

Solve each problem. Write each answer as a fraction in simplest form.

1. You roll a standard six-sided die. What is the probability that you roll a 3?

   The probability is _____.

2. What is the probability you roll an even number?

   The probability is _____.

   Your dentist wants to make an appointment for you. You tell her that any weekday is equally good. She chooses a weekday for your appointment.

3. What is the probability that your appointment will be on a Tuesday?

   The probability is _____.

4. What is the probability your appointment will be on a day beginning with the letter T?

   The probability is _____.

Twelve fish bowls at a pet store each contain one tropical fish. Three are purple, 2 are black, 2 are orange, and 5 are white. Mia picks a bowl without looking at the fish inside.

5. What is the probability that Mia chooses a purple fish?

   The probability is _____.

6. What is the probability that Mia chooses either a black or an orange fish?

   The probability is _____.

7. What is the probability that Mia chooses a red fish?

   The probability is _____.

1.	2.
3.	4.
5.	6.
7.	

Check What You Learned

Probability and Statistics

Answer the questions by interpreting data from each graph.

Advantage of Studying

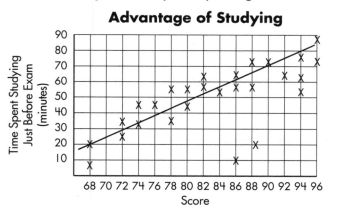

1. What two sets of data are being compared by this scattergram? _____

2. Is the correlation positive or negative? _____

3. What is a possible explanation for the outliers? _____

Page's GPA Each Semester

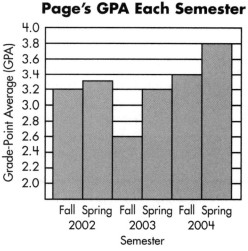

4. What is the interval represented by each bar in the histogram? _____

5. What is the lowest grade-point average (GPA) that can be represented on the histogram? _____

6. When did Page get her best GPA? _____

7. How much did Page's GPA improve from her worst semester to her best semester? _____

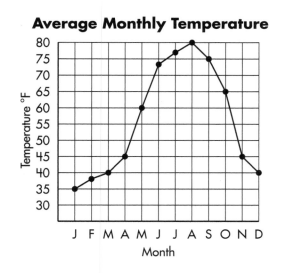

Average Monthly Temperature

8. For how long was the average temperature tracked in the line graph? _____

9. What month saw the highest average monthly temperature? _____ What was the temperature? _____

10. Between which two months did the average temperature change most sharply? _____

Check What You Learned

Probability and Statistics

Candace polled her cousins about their height. She wrote down their answers in inches. These are the results: 70, 68, 60, 63, 73, 66, 71, 66.

11. How many cousins did Candace poll? _____ What is the mode of the data? _____

12. What is the median height? _____ What is the mean height? _____

13. What is the range of the heights? _____

Candace made this box-and-whisker plot showing her cousins' ages.

My Cousins' Ages

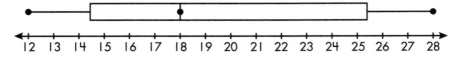

14. What is the range of their ages? _____ What is the median age? _____

15. What is the range of the middle 50% of the data? _____

16. What is the name of the highest point of the data on a box-and-whisker plot? _____

Isaac polled 6th, 7th, and 8th graders to find out if they participated in any of these activities: Sports, Theater, Volunteer Work, or Paid Work. He made this chart with the results.

```
         S     T     V     P
6th    [21    16    10    5]
7th    [25    12    12    6]
8th    [38    15     9   15]
```

17. What size matrix did Isaac make? _____

18. Which activity has the highest participation at all three grade levels? _____

19. Which two activities are equally popular with polled 7th graders? _____

20. Which of the activities has the lowest participation among all polled students? _____

Check What You Know

Geometry

Answer each question using letters to name each line or angle.

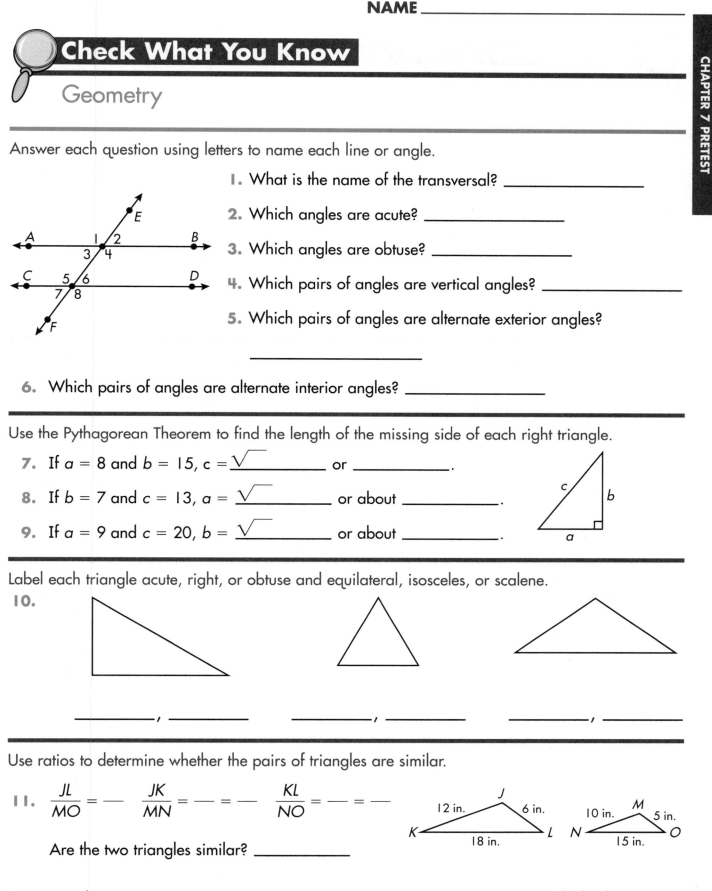

1. What is the name of the transversal? _____

2. Which angles are acute? _____

3. Which angles are obtuse? _____

4. Which pairs of angles are vertical angles? _____

5. Which pairs of angles are alternate exterior angles?

   _____

6. Which pairs of angles are alternate interior angles? _____

Use the Pythagorean Theorem to find the length of the missing side of each right triangle.

7. If $a = 8$ and $b = 15$, $c = \sqrt{}$ or _____.

8. If $b = 7$ and $c = 13$, $a = \sqrt{}$ or about _____.

9. If $a = 9$ and $c = 20$, $b = \sqrt{}$ or about _____.

Label each triangle acute, right, or obtuse and equilateral, isosceles, or scalene.

10.

_____ , _____   _____ , _____   _____ , _____

Use ratios to determine whether the pairs of triangles are similar.

11. $\dfrac{JL}{MO} = -$ $\dfrac{JK}{MN} = - = -$ $\dfrac{KL}{NO} = - = -$

   Are the two triangles similar? _____

NAME _____

Check What You Know

Geometry

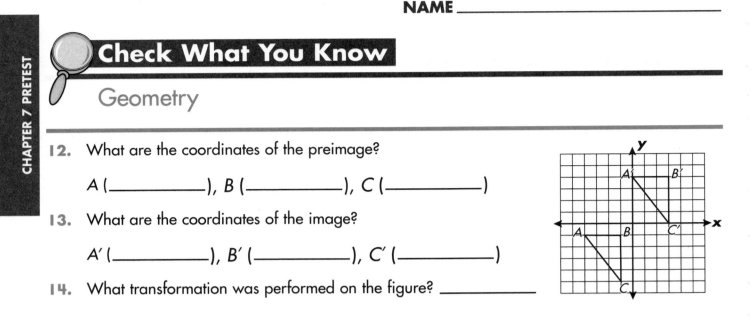

12. What are the coordinates of the preimage?

A (_____), B (_____), C (_____)

13. What are the coordinates of the image?

A' (_____), B' (_____), C' (_____)

14. What transformation was performed on the figure? _____

Use your knowledge of similar triangles and the Pythagorean Theorem to solve the following.

15.

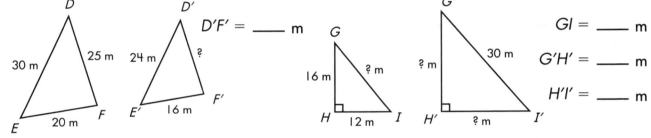

D'F' = ___ m

GI = ___ m

G'H' = ___ m

H'I' = ___ m

Solve each problem.

16. Jason and his sister Joanna cast similar shadows as shown. How tall is Joanna? How long is her shadow on the ground?

Joanna is _____ inches tall.

Her shadow is _____ inches long.

17. Two ships have similar on-ramps as shown. How long is the larger ramp? How high off the ground is the smaller ramp?

The larger ramp is _____ feet long.

The smaller ramp is _____ feet off the ground.

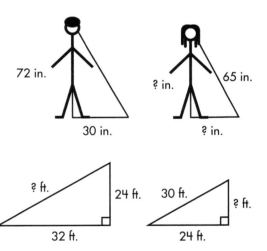

Lesson 7.1 Points and Lines

A **point** is a single location in space. It has no dimensions.
A **line** is the set of all points extending straight in both directions.
A **line segment** is the part of a line between 2 points on the line.

You can name a **point** with a letter: point B.

You can name a **line** by naming any 2 points on the line: $\overleftrightarrow{BC}$ or $\overleftrightarrow{CB}$.

You can name a **line segment** by naming its end points: $\overline{BC}$ or $\overline{CB}$.

At left is line segment DE or ED.
Write it as $\overline{DE}$ or $\overline{ED}$.
To refer to one point, just write D or E.

At left is line GH or HG. Write it as $\overleftrightarrow{GH}$ or $\overleftrightarrow{HG}$.

Tell what each symbol names. Then, draw it.

1. $\overline{PQ}$ means _____.

2. $\overleftrightarrow{ST}$ means _____.

3. P means _____.

Name each figure using letters. Name each figure in more than one way, if you can.

a	b	c

4.

U   V   L   M   Z

_____   _____   _____

5.

I   M

J   •K   L

_____   _____   _____

Lesson 7.2 Rays and Angles

A **ray** is part of a line. It has one endpoint, but extends infinitely in one direction.

•———•→   At left is ray *ST*, or $\overrightarrow{ST}$. It is *not* $\overrightarrow{TS}$.
S   T

An **angle** is the union of two rays which share a common endpoint. The endpoint is called

a **vertex.**

At left is angle *RST*. It is the union of $\overrightarrow{SR}$ and $\overrightarrow{ST}$. Angle *RST* can be written as

∠*RST* or ∠*S*. The vertex (∠*S*) stands for the angle.

At left is an angle formed by the union of $\overrightarrow{CA}$ and $\overrightarrow{CE}$. Write it ∠*ACE* or ∠*C*.

Name each figure using letters. Name each figure in more than one way, if you can.

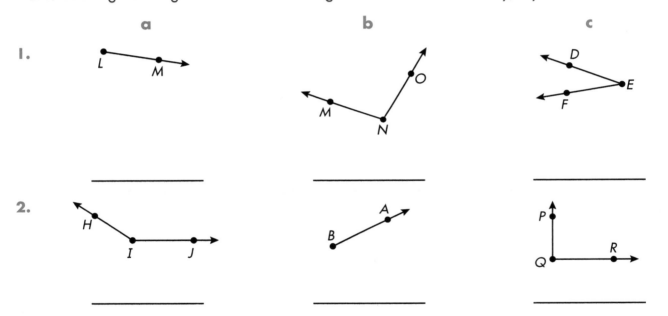

a   b   c

1.

_____   _____   _____

2.

_____   _____   _____

Tell what each symbol names. Then, draw it.

3. ∠*BCD* means _____.

4. $\overrightarrow{RS}$ means _____.

5. ∠*Q* means _____.

Lesson 7.3 Measuring Angles

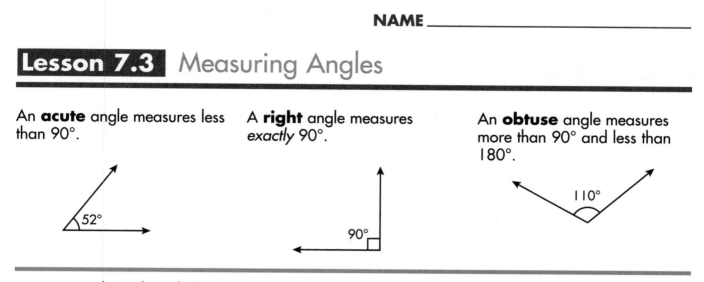

An **acute** angle measures less than 90°.

52°

A **right** angle measures *exactly* 90°.

90°

An **obtuse** angle measures more than 90° and less than 180°.

110°

Measure each angle with a protractor. Write the angle measure, then write *acute*, *right*, or *obtuse*.

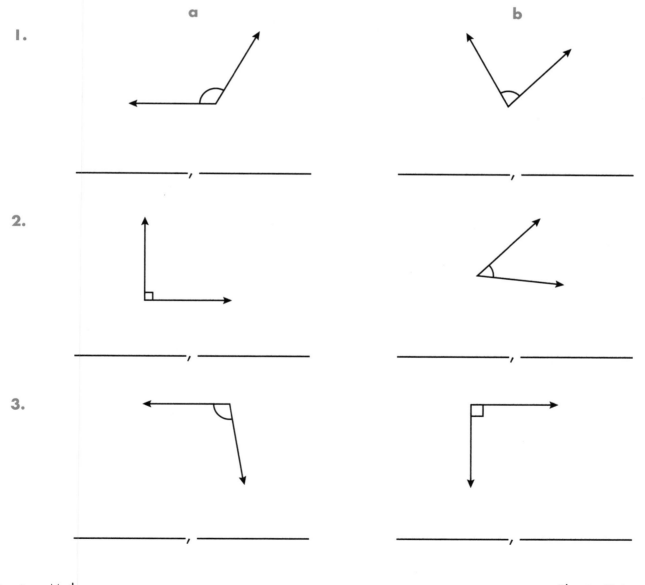

| a | b |

1.

_____ , _____   _____ , _____

2.

_____ , _____   _____ , _____

3.

_____ , _____   _____ , _____

Lesson 7.4 Vertical, Supplementary, and Complimentary Angles

Vertical angles are the 2 angles opposite each other where 2 lines meet. In the figure to the right, $\angle A$ and $\angle C$ are vertical angles. $\angle B$ and $\angle D$ are also vertical angles. Vertical angles are **congruent**. They have the same measure.

Supplementary angles are 2 angles whose measures add up to 180°. In the figure to the right, $\angle A$ and $\angle B$ are supplementary. $\angle B$ and $\angle C$ are also supplementary.

Complementary angles are 2 angles whose measures add up to 90°. In the figure to the right, $\angle E$ and $\angle F$ are complementary.

An **angle bisector** is a ray that divides an angle **exactly** in half. In the figure to the right, $\overrightarrow{IH}$ is an angle bisector of $\angle GIJ$.

Use 3 letters to name each angle in the figures below.

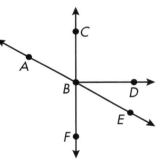 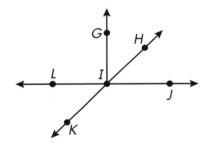

1. Which pairs of angles are complementary?

   $\angle$ _____ /$\angle$ _____ , $\angle$ _____ /$\angle$ _____

2. Which pairs of angles are supplementary?

   $\angle$ _____ /$\angle$ _____ , $\angle$ _____ /$\angle$ _____ , $\angle$ _____ /$\angle$ _____ , $\angle$ _____ /$\angle$ _____ , $\angle$ _____ /$\angle$ _____

   $\angle$ _____ /$\angle$ _____ , $\angle$ _____ /$\angle$ _____ , $\angle$ _____ /$\angle$ _____ , $\angle$ _____ /$\angle$ _____ , $\angle$ _____ /$\angle$ _____

3. Which pairs of angles are vertical angles?

   $\angle$ _____ /$\angle$ _____ , $\angle$ _____ /$\angle$ _____ , $\angle$ _____ /$\angle$ _____ , $\angle$ _____ /$\angle$ _____

4. Name a point on an angle bisector. _____

Lesson 7.5 Transversals

Parallel lines are two lines that will **never** meet. In the figure, $\overleftrightarrow{AB}$ and $\overleftrightarrow{CD}$ are parallel (∥) lines.

A **transversal** is a line that intersects 2 parallel lines. $\overleftrightarrow{EF}$ is a transversal of $\overleftrightarrow{AB}$ and $\overleftrightarrow{CD}$.

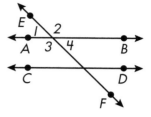

Adjacent angles are any 2 angles that are next to one another. In the figure, ∠1 and ∠2 are adjacent. ∠2 and ∠4 are also adjacent. Adjacent angles share a ray. They also form supplementary angles (180°).

---

1. Name the pairs of adjacent angles in the figure.

   ∠____/∠____ , ∠____/∠____ , ∠____/∠____ , ∠____/∠____ ,

   ∠____/∠____ , ∠____/∠____ , ∠____/∠____ , ∠____/∠____

   Alternate interior angles are those that are inside the parallel lines and opposite one another. ∠3 and ∠5 are alternate interior angles. Alternate interior angles are congruent.

2. Name another pair of alternate interior angles in the figure. ∠____/∠____

   Alternate exterior angles are those that are outside the parallel lines and opposite one another. ∠2 and ∠8 are alternate exterior angles. Alternate exterior angles are also congruent.

3. Name another pair of alternate exterior angles in the figure. ∠____/∠____

Look at the figure. List the following pairs of angles.

4. Adjacent: ∠____/∠____ , ∠____/∠____ , ∠____/∠____ , ∠____/∠____ ,

   ∠____/∠____ , ∠____/∠____ , ∠____/∠____ , ∠____/∠____

5. Alternate interior: ∠____/∠____ , ∠____/∠____

6. Alternate exterior: ∠____/∠____ , ∠____/∠____

7. Vertical: ∠____/∠____ , ∠____/∠____ ,

   ∠____/∠____ , ∠____/∠____

Lesson 7.6 Classifying Triangles (by angles)

The sum of all angles in a triangle is always 180°.

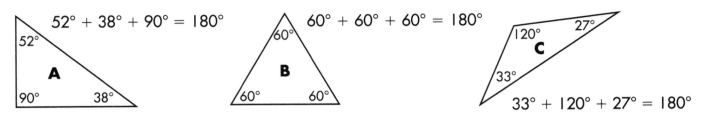

An **acute triangle** contains only acute angles; that is, angles less than 90°.

1. Which of the triangles above is acute? _____

A **right triangle** contains 1 right angle, an angle of exactly 90°.

2. Which of the triangles above is a right triangle? _____

An **obtuse triangle** contains 1 obtuse angle, an angle greater than 90°.

3. Which of the triangles above is obtuse? _____

Label each triangle acute, right, or obtuse. Check the angles with a protractor if necessary.

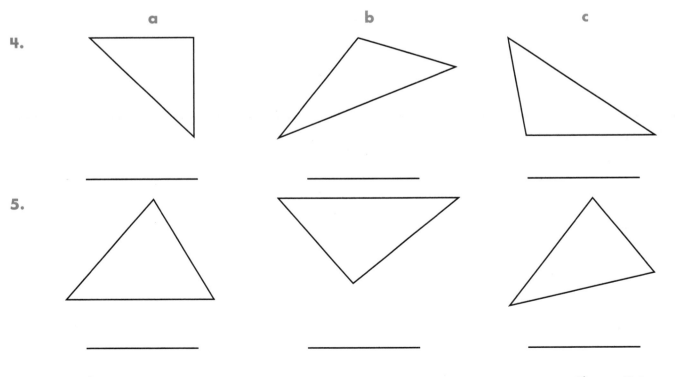

Lesson 7.7 Classifying Triangles (by sides)

An **equilateral** triangle has 3 sides of the same length.

An **isosceles** triangle has at least 2 sides of the same length.

A **scalene** triangle has no sides of the same length.

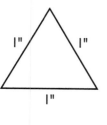

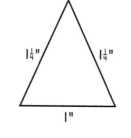

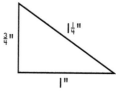

Use a ruler to measure. Label each triangle equilateral, isosceles, or scalene.

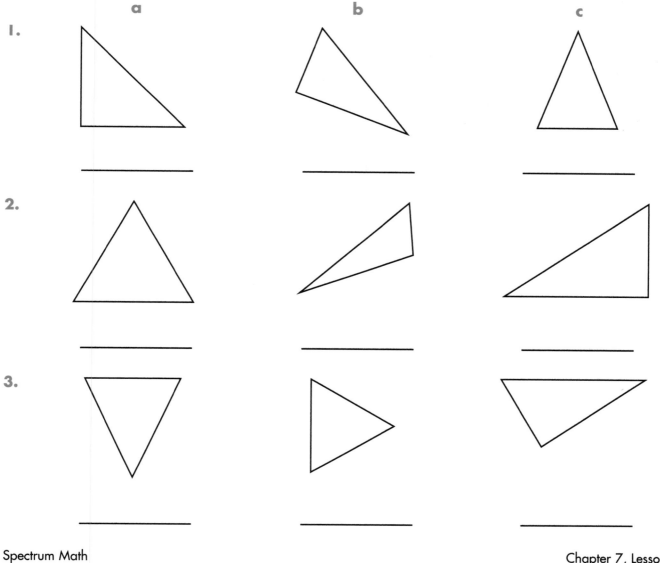

	a	b	c
1.	_____	_____	_____
2.	_____	_____	_____
3.	_____	_____	_____

Lesson 7.8 Similar Triangles

Two triangles are **similar** if their corresponding (matching) angles are congruent (have the same measure) and the lengths of their corresponding sides are proportional.

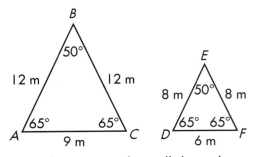

These triangles are similar. All the sides are proportional:

$$\frac{AB}{DE} = \frac{12}{8} = \frac{3}{2} \quad \frac{BC}{EF} = \frac{12}{8} = \frac{3}{2} \quad \frac{AC}{DF} = \frac{9}{6} = \frac{3}{2}$$

The angle measures are congruent.

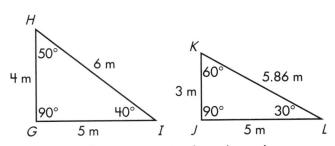

These triangles are not similar. The sides are not proportional. They do not all create the same ratio. The angle measures are not all congruent.

$$\frac{GH}{JK} = \frac{4}{3} \quad \frac{HI}{KL} = \frac{6}{5.86} \quad \frac{GI}{JL} = \frac{5}{5} = \frac{1}{1}$$

For each pair of triangles, check that their sides are all proportional. Circle *similar* or *not similar*.

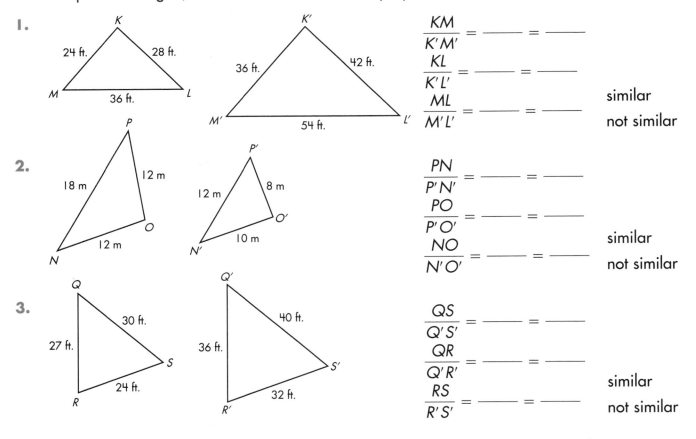

1.

$$\frac{KM}{K'M'} = \underline{\quad} = \underline{\quad}$$
$$\frac{KL}{K'L'} = \underline{\quad} = \underline{\quad}$$
$$\frac{ML}{M'L'} = \underline{\quad} = \underline{\quad}$$

similar

not similar

2.

$$\frac{PN}{P'N'} = \underline{\quad} = \underline{\quad}$$
$$\frac{PO}{P'O'} = \underline{\quad} = \underline{\quad}$$
$$\frac{NO}{N'O'} = \underline{\quad} = \underline{\quad}$$

similar

not similar

3.

$$\frac{QS}{Q'S'} = \underline{\quad} = \underline{\quad}$$
$$\frac{QR}{Q'R'} = \underline{\quad} = \underline{\quad}$$
$$\frac{RS}{R'S'} = \underline{\quad} = \underline{\quad}$$

similar

not similar

Lesson 7.8   Similar Triangles

When you know that two triangles are similar, you can use the ratio of the known lengths of the sides to figure the unknown length.

What is the length of *EF*? Use a proportion.

$$\frac{AC}{DF} = \frac{BC}{EF} \quad \frac{4}{6} = \frac{12}{n}$$

Cross multiply.
$$4n = 72 \quad n = 18$$

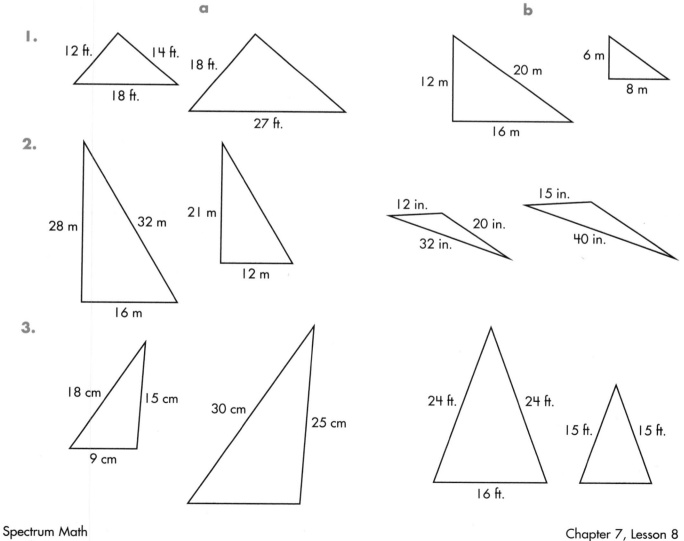

Find the length of the missing side for each pair of similar triangles. Label the side with its length.

a   **b**

1.   12 ft.   14 ft.   18 ft.   18 ft.   27 ft.   12 m   20 m   16 m   6 m   8 m

2.   28 m   32 m   16 m   21 m   12 m   12 in.   20 in.   32 in.   15 in.   40 in.

3.   18 cm   15 cm   9 cm   30 cm   25 cm   24 ft.   24 ft.   16 ft.   15 ft.   15 ft.

Lesson 7.9 Squares and Square Roots

The **square** of a number is that number times itself. A square is expressed as 6^2, which means 6×6 or 6 squared. The **square root** of a number is the number that, multiplied by itself, equals that number. The square root of 36 is 6: $\sqrt{36} = 6$

Not all square roots of numbers are whole numbers like 6. Numbers that have a whole number as their square root are called **perfect squares**.

The square root of any number that is not a perfect square is called a **radical number**. The symbol $\sqrt{}$ is called a **radical sign**. When a number is not a perfect square, you can estimate its square root by determining which perfect squares it comes between.

$\sqrt{50}$ is a little more than 7, because $\sqrt{49}$ is exactly 7. $\sqrt{60}$ is between 7 and 8 but closer to 8, because 60 is closer to 64 than to 49.

Identify the square root of these perfect squares.

	a	b	c
	$\sqrt{16} = $ _____	$\sqrt{64} = $ _____	$\sqrt{25} = $ _____
2.	$\sqrt{100} = $ _____	$\sqrt{1} = $ _____	$\sqrt{9} = $ _____
3.	$\sqrt{36} = $ _____	$\sqrt{81} = $ _____	$\sqrt{4} = $ _____

Estimate the following square roots without looking at the table on the next page.

4. $\sqrt{85}$ is between _____ and _____ but closer to _____.

5. $\sqrt{20}$ is between _____ and _____ but closer to _____.

6. $\sqrt{35}$ is between _____ and _____ but closer to _____.

7. $\sqrt{70}$ is between _____ and _____ but closer to _____.

8. $\sqrt{45}$ is between _____ and _____ but closer to _____.

Lesson 7.9 Table of Squares and Square Roots

Except in the case of perfect squares, square roots shown on the chart are not exact.

		Table of Squares and Square Roots			
n	n^2	$\sqrt{n}$	n	n^2	$\sqrt{n}$
1	1	1	51	2,601	7.14
2	4	1.41	52	2,704	7.21
3	9	1.73	53	2,809	7.28
4	16	2	54	2,916	7.35
5	25	2.24	55	3,025	7.42
6	36	2.45	56	3,136	7.48
7	49	2.65	57	3,249	7.55
8	64	2.83	58	3,364	7.62
9	81	3	59	3,481	7.68
10	100	3.16	60	3,600	7.75
11	121	3.32	61	3,721	7.81
12	144	3.46	62	3,844	7.87
13	169	3.61	63	3,969	7.94
14	196	3.74	64	4,096	8
15	225	3.87	65	4,225	8.06
16	256	4	66	4,356	8.12
17	289	4.12	67	4,489	8.19
18	324	4.24	68	4,624	8.25
19	361	4.36	69	4,761	8.31
20	400	4.47	70	4,900	8.37
21	441	4.58	71	5,041	8.43
22	484	4.69	72	5,184	8.49
23	529	4.80	73	5,329	8.54
24	576	4.90	74	5,476	8.60
25	625	5	75	5,625	8.66
26	676	5.10	76	5,776	8.72
27	729	5.20	77	5,929	8.77
28	784	5.29	78	6,084	8.83
29	841	5.39	79	6,241	8.89
30	900	5.48	80	6,400	8.94
31	961	5.57	81	6,561	9
32	1,024	5.66	82	6,724	9.06
33	1,089	5.74	83	6,889	9.11
34	1,156	5.83	84	7,056	9.17
35	1,225	5.92	85	7,225	9.22
36	1,296	6	86	7,396	9.27
37	1,369	6.08	87	7,569	9.33
38	1,444	6.16	88	7,744	9.38
39	1,521	6.24	89	7,921	9.43
40	1,600	6.32	90	8,100	9.49
41	1,681	6.40	91	8,281	9.54
42	1,764	6.48	92	8,464	9.59
43	1,849	6.56	93	8,649	9.64
44	1,936	6.63	94	8,836	9.70
45	2,025	6.71	95	9,025	9.75
46	2,116	6.78	96	9,216	9.80
47	2,209	6.86	97	9,409	9.85
48	2,304	6.93	98	9,604	9.90
49	2,401	7	99	9,801	9.95
50	2,500	7.07	100	10,000	10

Lesson 7.10 Using the Pythagorean Theorem

The **Pythagorean Theorem** states that the square of the length of the hypotenuse of a right triangle is equal to the sum of the squares of the other 2 sides. It is true for all right triangles.

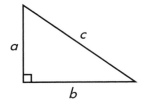

In a right triangle, the **hypotenuse** is the side opposite the right angle. The other 2 sides are called **legs**. In this figure, c is the hypotenuse and a and b are the legs.

If a, b, and c are the lengths of the sides of this triangle, $a^2 + b^2 = c^2$.

If $a = 3$ and $b = 4$, what is c?

$$a^2 + b^2 = c^2 \qquad 3^2 + 4^2 = c^2 \qquad 9 + 16 = c^2 \qquad 25 = c^2 \qquad \sqrt{25} = c \qquad 5 = c$$

If $a = 4$ and $b = 6$, what is b?

$$a^2 + b^2 = c^2 \qquad 4^2 + 6^2 = c^2 \qquad 16 + 36 = c^2 \qquad 52 = c^2 \qquad \sqrt{52} = c \quad c \text{ is } about\ 7.21.$$

Use the Pythagorean Theorem to determine the length of c. Assume that each problem describes a right triangle. Sides a and b are the legs and the hypotenuse is c. Refer to the table on page 93, if necessary.

1. If $a = 9$ and $b = 4$, $c = \sqrt{\rule{2cm}{0pt}}$ _____ or about _____.

2. If $a = 5$ and $b = 7$, $c = \sqrt{\rule{2cm}{0pt}}$ _____ or about _____.

3. If $a = 3$ and $b = 6$, $c = \sqrt{\rule{2cm}{0pt}}$ _____ or about _____.

4. If $a = 2$ and $b = 9$, $c = \sqrt{\rule{2cm}{0pt}}$ _____ or _____.

5. If $a = 5$ and $b = 6$, $c = \sqrt{\rule{2cm}{0pt}}$ _____ or about _____.

6. If $a = 3$ and $b = 5$, $c = \sqrt{\rule{2cm}{0pt}}$ _____ or about _____.

7. If $a = 7$ and $b = 6$, $c = \sqrt{\rule{2cm}{0pt}}$ _____ or about _____.

8. If $a = 8$ and $b = 6$, $c = \sqrt{\rule{2cm}{0pt}}$ _____ or _____.

9. If $a = 7$ and $b = 2$, $c = \sqrt{\rule{2cm}{0pt}}$ _____ or about _____.

10. If $a = 8$ and $b = 5$, $c = \sqrt{\rule{2cm}{0pt}}$ _____ or about _____.

Lesson 7.10 Using the Pythagorean Theorem

You can use the Pythagorean Theorem to find the unknown length of a side of a right triangle as long as the other two lengths are known.

If $a = 12$ m and $c = 13$ m, what is b?

$a^2 + b^2 = c^2$ $12^2 + b^2 = 13^2$

$144 + b^2 = 169$

$144 + b^2 - 144 = 169 - 144$

$b^2 = 25$ $b = \sqrt{25}$ $b = 5$ m

If $b = 15$ ft. and $c = 17$ ft., what is a?

$a^2 + b^2 = c^2$ $a^2 + 15^2 = 17^2$

$a^2 + 225 = 289$

$a^2 + 225 - 225 = 289 - 225$

$a^2 = 64$ $a = \sqrt{64}$ $a = 8$ ft.

Assume that each problem describes a right triangle. Use the Pythagorean Theorem to find the unknown lengths. You may wish to refer to the table of squares and square roots on page 93.

1. If $a = 12$ and $c = 20$, $b = \sqrt{\rule{2cm}{0pt}}$ _____ or _____.

2. If $b = 24$ and $c = 26$, $a = \sqrt{\rule{2cm}{0pt}}$ _____ or _____.

3. If $c = 8$ and $a = 5$, $b = \sqrt{\rule{2cm}{0pt}}$ _____ or about _____.

4. If $b = 13$ and $c = 17$, $a = \sqrt{\rule{2cm}{0pt}}$ _____ or about _____.

5. If $a = 20$ and $c = 32$, $b = \sqrt{\rule{2cm}{0pt}}$ _____ or about _____.

6. If $c = 15$ and $b = 12$, $a = \sqrt{\rule{2cm}{0pt}}$ _____ or _____.

7. If $c = 41$ and $b = 40$, $a = \sqrt{\rule{2cm}{0pt}}$ _____ or _____.

8. If $a = 36$ and $c = 85$, $b = \sqrt{\rule{2cm}{0pt}}$ _____ or _____.

9. If $c = 73$ and $b = 48$, $a = \sqrt{\rule{2cm}{0pt}}$ _____ or _____.

10. If $a = 14$ and $c = 22$, $b = \sqrt{\rule{2cm}{0pt}}$ _____ or about _____.

Lesson 7.10 Problem Solving

SHOW YOUR WORK

Use the Pythagorean Theorem to solve each problem.

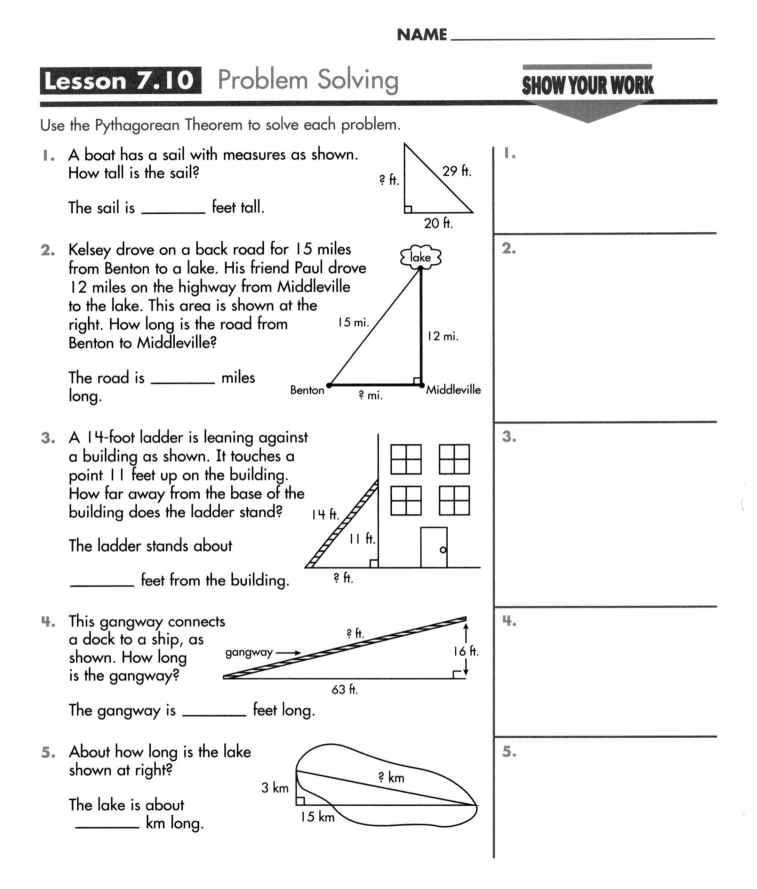

1. A boat has a sail with measures as shown. How tall is the sail?

   ? ft.   29 ft.   20 ft.

   The sail is _____ feet tall.

   1.

2. Kelsey drove on a back road for 15 miles from Benton to a lake. His friend Paul drove 12 miles on the highway from Middleville to the lake. This area is shown at the right. How long is the road from Benton to Middleville?

   15 mi.   12 mi.   Benton   ? mi.   Middleville   lake

   The road is _____ miles long.

   2.

3. A 14-foot ladder is leaning against a building as shown. It touches a point 11 feet up on the building. How far away from the base of the building does the ladder stand?

   14 ft.   11 ft.   ? ft.

   The ladder stands about

   _____ feet from the building.

   3.

4. This gangway connects a dock to a ship, as shown. How long is the gangway?

   gangway →   ? ft.   16 ft.   63 ft.

   The gangway is _____ feet long.

   4.

5. About how long is the lake shown at right?

   3 km   ? km   15 km

   The lake is about _____ km long.

   5.

Lesson 7.11 The Pythagorean Theorem and Similar Right Triangles

You can use the Pythagorean Theorem and the ratios of similar triangles to find the unknown lengths of sides.

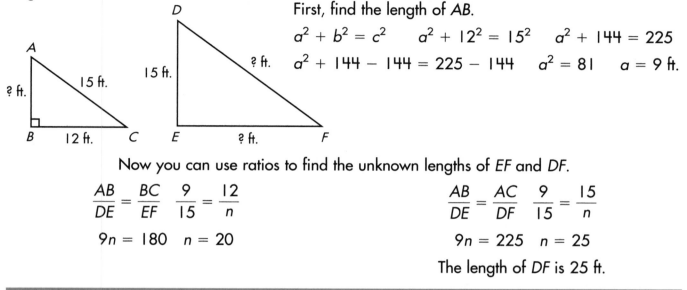

First, find the length of AB.

$a^2 + b^2 = c^2$ $a^2 + 12^2 = 15^2$ $a^2 + 144 = 225$

$a^2 + 144 - 144 = 225 - 144$ $a^2 = 81$ $a = 9$ ft.

Now you can use ratios to find the unknown lengths of EF and DF.

$\dfrac{AB}{DE} = \dfrac{BC}{EF}$ $\dfrac{9}{15} = \dfrac{12}{n}$

$9n = 180$ $n = 20$

$\dfrac{AB}{DE} = \dfrac{AC}{DF}$ $\dfrac{9}{15} = \dfrac{15}{n}$

$9n = 225$ $n = 25$

The length of DF is 25 ft.

Find the lengths of the missing sides for each pair of similar right triangles.

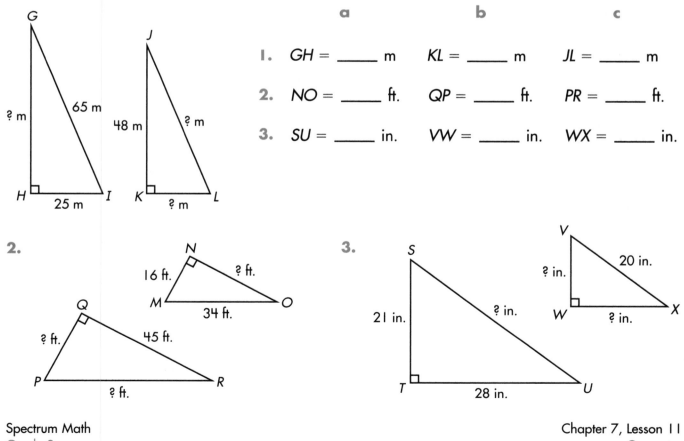

	a	b	c
1.	$GH =$ _____ m	$KL =$ _____ m	$JL =$ _____ m
2.	$NO =$ _____ ft.	$QP =$ _____ ft.	$PR =$ _____ ft.
3.	$SU =$ _____ in.	$VW =$ _____ in.	$WX =$ _____ in.

Lesson 7.11 Problem Solving

SHOW YOUR WORK

Use the Pythagorean Theorem and ratios to solve each problem.

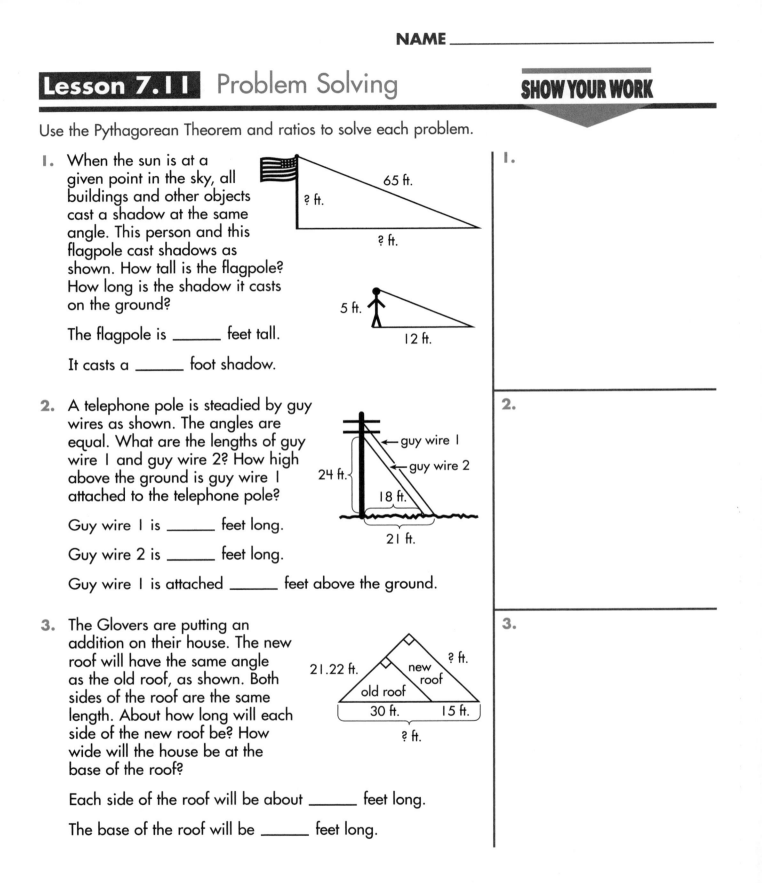

1. When the sun is at a given point in the sky, all buildings and other objects cast a shadow at the same angle. This person and this flagpole cast shadows as shown. How tall is the flagpole? How long is the shadow it casts on the ground?

The flagpole is _____ feet tall.

It casts a _____ foot shadow.

1.

2. A telephone pole is steadied by guy wires as shown. The angles are equal. What are the lengths of guy wire 1 and guy wire 2? How high above the ground is guy wire 1 attached to the telephone pole?

Guy wire 1 is _____ feet long.

Guy wire 2 is _____ feet long.

Guy wire 1 is attached _____ feet above the ground.

2.

3. The Glovers are putting an addition on their house. The new roof will have the same angle as the old roof, as shown. Both sides of the roof are the same length. About how long will each side of the new roof be? How wide will the house be at the base of the roof?

Each side of the roof will be about _____ feet long.

The base of the roof will be _____ feet long.

3.

Lesson 7.12 Transformations

Transformation is the movement of a geometric figure. There are 4 types of transformations: translation, reflection, rotation, and dilation.

Translation is a slide of the figure. The figure can be slid up, down, or sideways.

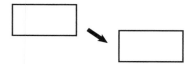

This figure has been translated down and to the right.

Reflection is a flip of the figure. It can be flipped to the side or up/down. It can flip around a point on the figure or another point.

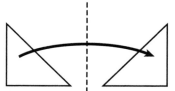

This figure has been flipped horizontally over the dotted line.

Rotation is a turn of the figure. The figure can be rotated any number of degrees.

This figure has been rotated 90° clockwise about the point. This point is called the **center of rotation.**

Dilation is an increase or decrease in the size of the figure to create a similar figure.

This figure has been dilated by a factor of 2.

Graphing figures on a coordinate plane helps show how they are translated. The original figure is called a **preimage.** The translated figure is called the **image.** Read the numbers on the x-axis and y-axis to determine the location of the figure. (**Note**: For information on plotting ordered pairs in the coordinate plane, see lesson 9.12.)

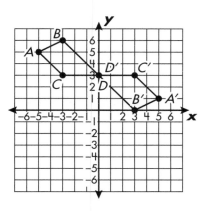

This figure has been rotated 180° about one point of the figure. As a result, the preimage and the image share a point. The 4 corners of the preimage are points A, B, C, and D. The 4 corners of the image are points A', B', C', and D'.

The coordinates of the preimage are: A(−5, 5), B(−3, 6) C(−3, 3), D(0, 3).
The coordinates of the image are: A'(5, 1), B'(3, 0), C' (3, 3), D'(0, 3).

Lesson 7.12 Transformations

The location of each figure is identified by the coordinates of its corners. The first figure, or preimage, has coordinate points labeled A, B, etc. The transformed figure, or image, has coordinate points labeled A′, B′, etc.

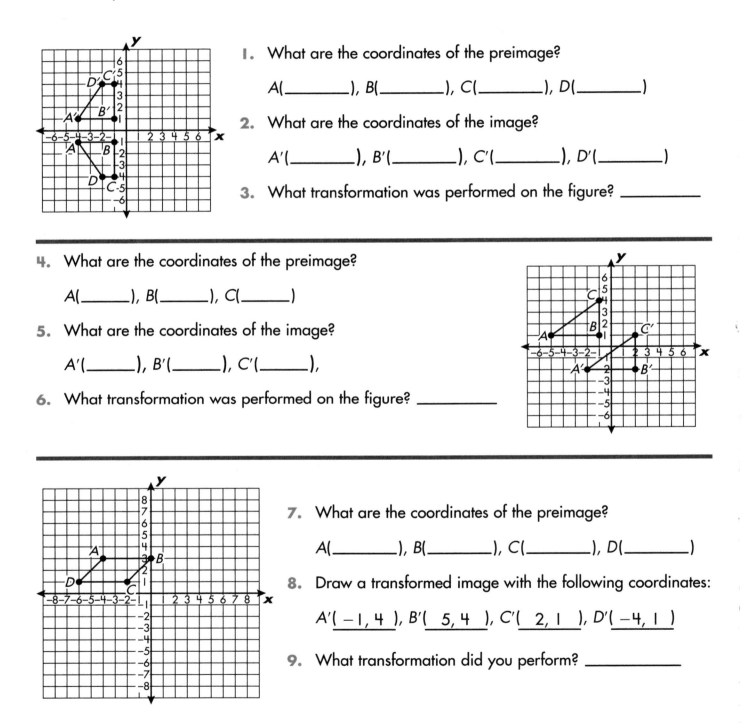

1. What are the coordinates of the preimage?

   A(_____), B(_____), C(_____), D(_____)

2. What are the coordinates of the image?

   A′(_____), B′(_____), C′(_____), D′(_____)

3. What transformation was performed on the figure? _____

4. What are the coordinates of the preimage?

   A(_____), B(_____), C(_____)

5. What are the coordinates of the image?

   A′(_____), B′(_____), C′(_____),

6. What transformation was performed on the figure? _____

7. What are the coordinates of the preimage?

   A(_____), B(_____), C(_____), D(_____)

8. Draw a transformed image with the following coordinates:

   A′(−1, 4), B′(5, 4), C′(2, 1), D′(−4, 1)

9. What transformation did you perform? _____

Check What You Learned

Geometry

Label each triangle acute, right, or obtuse and equilateral, isosceles, or scalene.

1.

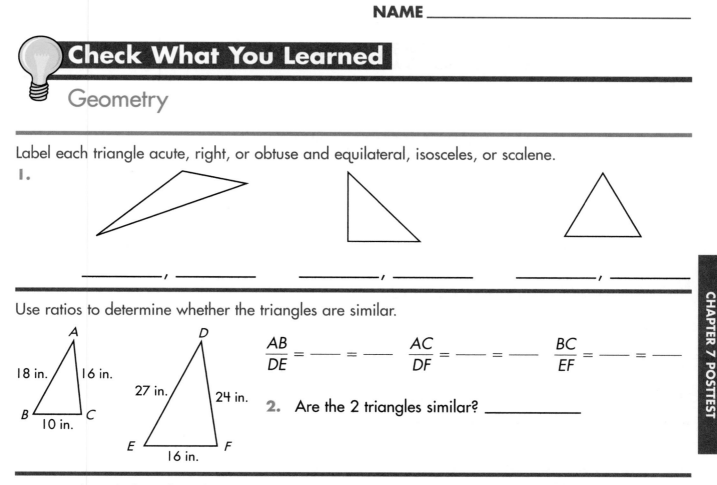

_____ , _____   _____ , _____   _____ , _____

Use ratios to determine whether the triangles are similar.

$\dfrac{AB}{DE} = $ ___ $ = $ ___ $\dfrac{AC}{DF} = $ ___ $ = $ ___ $\dfrac{BC}{EF} = $ ___ $ = $ ___

A
18 in.   16 in.
B   10 in.   C

D
27 in.   24 in.
E   16 in.   F

2. Are the 2 triangles similar? _____

Use your knowledge of similar triangles and the Pythagorean Theorem to solve the following.

a   **b**

3.

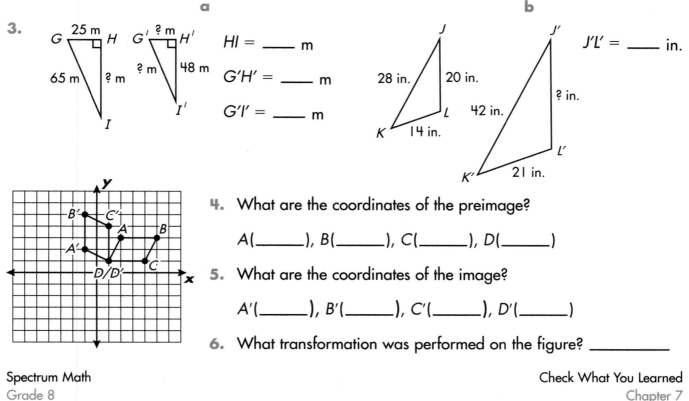

$HI = $ ___ m

$G'H' = $ ___ m

$G'I' = $ ___ m

$J'L' = $ ___ in.

4. What are the coordinates of the preimage?

A(_____), B(_____), C(_____), D(_____)

5. What are the coordinates of the image?

A'(_____), B'(_____), C'(_____), D'(_____)

6. What transformation was performed on the figure? _____

Check What You Learned

Geometry

Answer questions using letters to name each line angle.

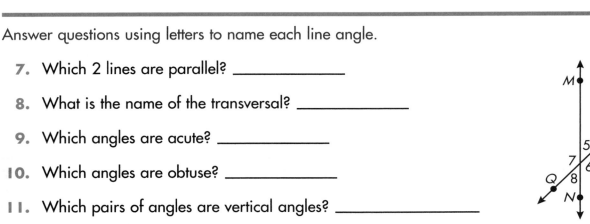

7. Which 2 lines are parallel? _____

8. What is the name of the transversal? _____

9. Which angles are acute? _____

10. Which angles are obtuse? _____

11. Which pairs of angles are vertical angles? _____

12. Which pairs of angles are alternate exterior angles? _____

13. Which pairs of angles are alternate interior angles? _____

CHAPTER 7 POSTTEST

Use the Pythagorean Theorem to find the answers to the following.

14. If $a = 7$ and $b = 10$, $c = \sqrt{\rule{2cm}{0pt}}$ or about _____.

15. If $a = 11$ and $c = 18$, $b = \sqrt{\rule{2cm}{0pt}}$ or about _____.

Solve each problem.

16. A flagpole and a telephone pole cast shadows as shown in the figure. How tall are the poles?

    The flagpole is _____ feet tall.

    The telephone pole is _____ feet tall.

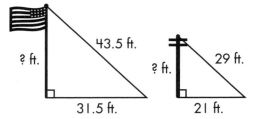

17. STU is similar to VTW. How tall is the building?

    The building is _____ m tall.

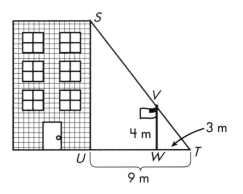

Check What You Know

Perimeter, Area, and Volume

Find the area and perimeter of each figure.

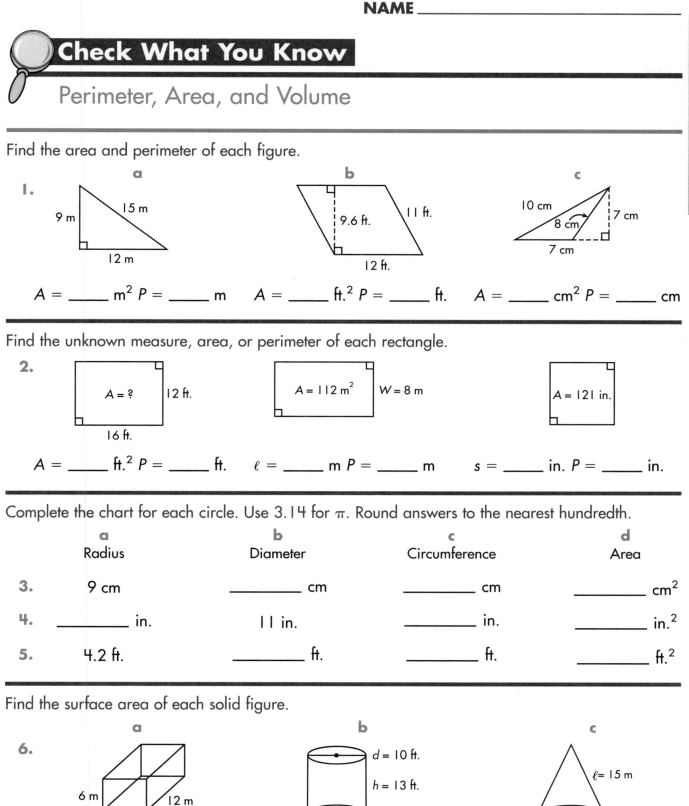

      a   **b**   **c**

1.

15 m   9 m   12 m

9.6 ft.   11 ft.   12 ft.

10 cm   8 cm   7 cm   7 cm

$A =$ _____ m^2 $P =$ _____ m $A =$ _____ $ft.^2$ $P =$ _____ ft. $A =$ _____ cm^2 $P =$ _____ cm

Find the unknown measure, area, or perimeter of each rectangle.

2.

$A = ?$ 12 ft.   16 ft.

$A = 112\ m^2$ $W = 8$ m

$A = 121$ in.

$A =$ _____ $ft.^2$ $P =$ _____ ft. $\ell =$ _____ m $P =$ _____ m $s =$ _____ in. $P =$ _____ in.

Complete the chart for each circle. Use 3.14 for π. Round answers to the nearest hundredth.

	a Radius	**b** Diameter	**c** Circumference	**d** Area
3.	9 cm	_____ cm	_____ cm	_____ cm^2
4.	_____ in.	11 in.	_____ in.	_____ $in.^2$
5.	4.2 ft.	_____ ft.	_____ ft.	_____ $ft.^2$

Find the surface area of each solid figure.

      a   **b**   **c**

6.

6 m   8 m   12 m

$d = 10$ ft. $h = 13$ ft.

$\ell = 15$ m $r = 6$ in.

$SA =$ _____ m^2 $SA =$ _____ $ft.^2$ $SA =$ _____ $in.^2$

NAME _____

Check What You Know

Perimeter, Area, and Volume

Find the volume of each solid figure. Use 3.14 for π. Round answers to the nearest hundredth.

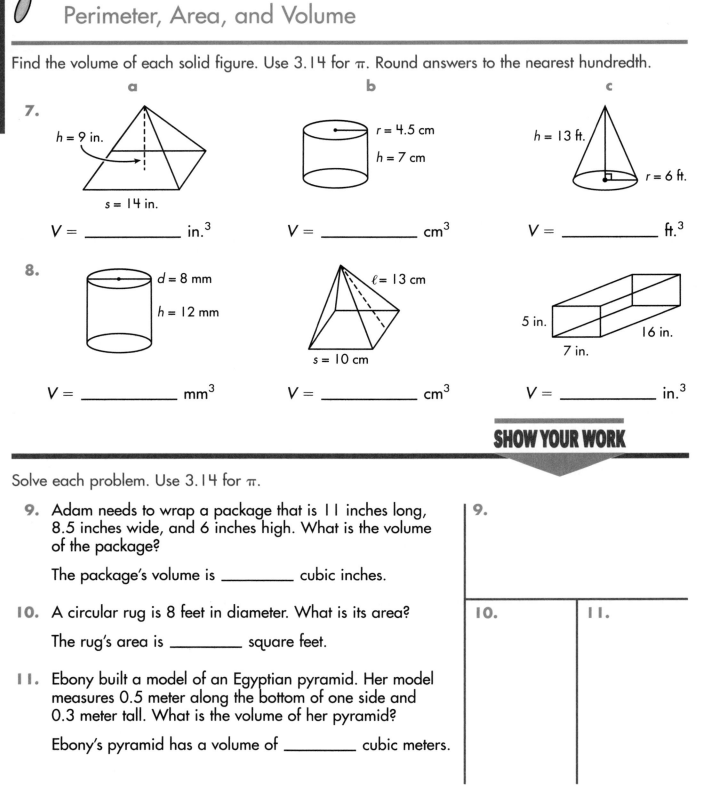

     a   b   c

7.

$h = 9$ in. $s = 14$ in.

$V =$ _____ in.^{3}

$r = 4.5$ cm $h = 7$ cm

$V =$ _____ cm^3

$h = 13$ ft. $r = 6$ ft.

$V =$ _____ ft.^{3}

8.

$d = 8$ mm $h = 12$ mm

$V =$ _____ mm^3

$\ell = 13$ cm $s = 10$ cm

$V =$ _____ cm^3

5 in.   7 in.   16 in.

$V =$ _____ in.^{3}

SHOW YOUR WORK

Solve each problem. Use 3.14 for π.

9. Adam needs to wrap a package that is 11 inches long, 8.5 inches wide, and 6 inches high. What is the volume of the package?

The package's volume is _____ cubic inches.

9.

10. A circular rug is 8 feet in diameter. What is its area?

The rug's area is _____ square feet.

10.   **11.**

11. Ebony built a model of an Egyptian pyramid. Her model measures 0.5 meter along the bottom of one side and 0.3 meter tall. What is the volume of her pyramid?

Ebony's pyramid has a volume of _____ cubic meters.

Lesson 8.1 Perimeter

The **perimeter** of a figure is the distance around it.

When all side lengths are known, you can just add them.

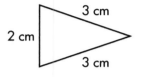

3 cm
2 cm
3 cm

When you know that certain sides are equal, you can calculate missing side lengths.

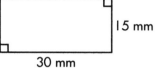

15 mm
30 mm

If a polygon is **regular**, meaning that all sides are equal in length, you can multiply the length of one side by the number of sides.

15 mm

$P = s + s + s = 2 + 3 + 3$
$P = 8$ cm

$P = 2\ell + 2W$ or $2(\ell + W)$
$P = 2(15 + 30)$
$P = 90$ mm

$P = 4s$ $P = 4 \times 15 = 60$ mm

Find the perimeter of each figure. Unless shown otherwise, assume each figure is regular.

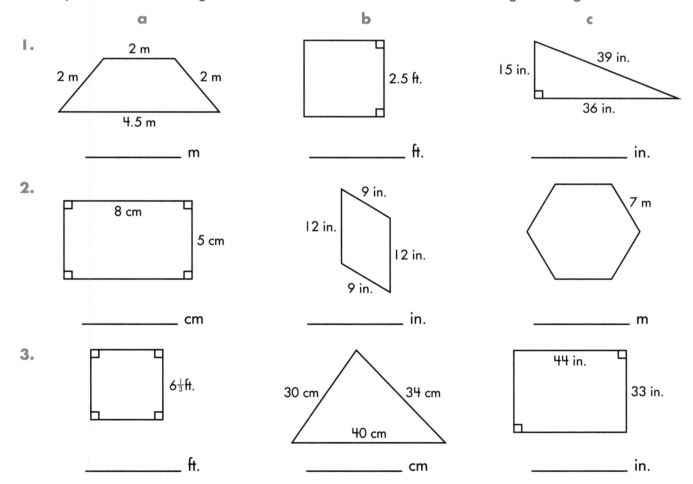

	a	b	c
1.	2 m, 2 m, 2 m, 4.5 m _____ m	2.5 ft. _____ ft.	39 in., 15 in., 36 in. _____ in.
2.	8 cm, 5 cm _____ cm	9 in., 12 in., 12 in., 9 in. _____ in.	7 m _____ m
3.	$6\frac{1}{3}$ ft. _____ ft.	30 cm, 34 cm, 40 cm _____ cm	44 in., 33 in. _____ in.

Lesson 8.2 Area of a Rectangle

The **area** of a figure is the number of square units inside that figure. Area is expressed in **square units** or **units^2**.

The area of a rectangle is the product of its length and its width.

5 cm ▭ 10 cm

$A = \ell \times w$
$A = 5 \times 10 = 50 \text{ cm}^2$

5 cm ☐

$A = 5 \times 5$
$A = 5 \times 5 \text{ or } 5^2$
$A = 25 \text{ cm}^2$

If you know the area of a rectangle and either its length or its width, you can determine the unknown measure.

$A = 24 \text{ m}^2$ 6 m

$A = \ell \times w$
$24 = 6 \times w$
$\frac{24}{6} = \frac{6w}{6}$ $4 = w$
The width is 4 meters.

Find the unknown measure for each rectangle below.

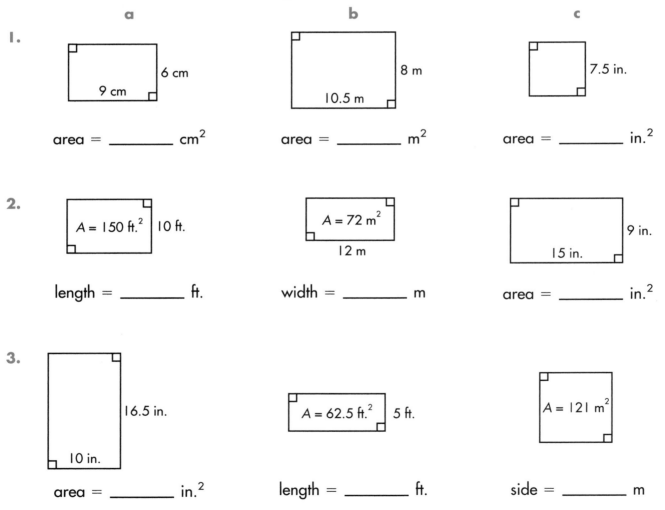

	a	**b**	**c**

1.

a. 6 cm, 9 cm — area = _____ cm^2

b. 8 m, 10.5 m — area = _____ m^2

c. 7.5 in. — area = _____ in.^{2}

2.

a. $A = 150 \text{ ft.}^2$, 10 ft. — length = _____ ft.

b. $A = 72 \text{ m}^2$, 12 m — width = _____ m

c. 9 in., 15 in. — area = _____ in.^{2}

3.

a. 16.5 in., 10 in. — area = _____ in.^{2}

b. $A = 62.5 \text{ ft.}^2$, 5 ft. — length = _____ ft.

c. $A = 121 \text{ m}^2$ — side = _____ m

Lesson 8.3 Area of a Triangle

To find the area of a triangle, find $\frac{1}{2}$ the product of the measure of its base and its height.

$$A = \frac{1}{2} \times b \times h$$

$b = 6$ in. and $h = 8$ in.

Find A.

$A = \frac{1}{2} \times b \times h$

$A = \frac{1}{2} \times 6 \times 8$

$A = 24$ in.^{2}

The height is the distance from the base to the highest point on the triangle, using a line perpendicular to the base.

Find the area of each triangle.

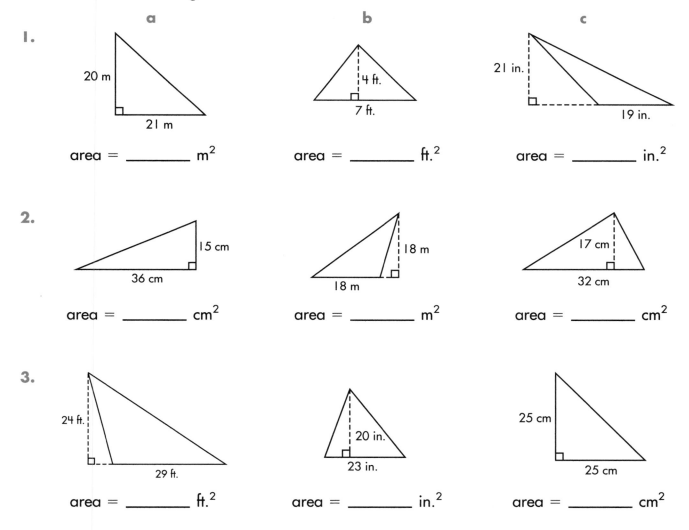

	a	b	c
1.	20 m, 21 m	4 ft., 7 ft.	21 in., 19 in.
	area = _____ m^2	area = _____ ft.^{2}	area = _____ in.^{2}
2.	15 cm, 36 cm	18 m, 18 m	17 cm, 32 cm
	area = _____ cm^2	area = _____ m^2	area = _____ cm^2
3.	24 ft., 29 ft.	20 in., 23 in.	25 cm, 25 cm
	area = _____ ft.^{2}	area = _____ in.^{2}	area = _____ cm^2

Lesson 8.4 Circumference of a Circle

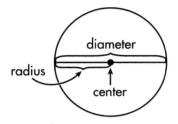

The **center** of a circle is the point from which all points on the circle are an equal distance.

The **radius** of a circle is the distance from its center to its outer edge.

The **diameter** of a circle is the distance straight across the circle, through the center. It is twice as long as the radius.

The **circumference** of a circle is the distance around the outside of the circle. The formula for finding circumference is πd or $2\pi r$. It is the diameter of the circle, or 2 times the radius, times π. π represents about $3\frac{1}{7}$ or 3.14.

If the diameter of a circle is 4 cm, the circumference is 4π cm, or about 12.56 cm.

If the radius of a circle is 5 cm, the circumference is $2\pi 5$ cm, or about 31.4 cm.

Complete the chart for each circle described below. Use 3.14 for π. When necessary, round to the nearest hundredth.

	a Radius	b Diameter	c Circumference
1.	2 m	_____ m	_____ m
2.	_____ cm	18 cm	_____ cm
3.	_____ mm	9.2 mm	_____ mm
4.	5.5 in.	_____ in.	_____ in.
5.	12.2 cm	_____ cm	_____ cm
6.	_____ ft.	5 ft.	_____ ft.
7.	17 mm	_____ mm	_____ mm
8.	$3\frac{1}{2}$ ft.	_____ ft.	_____ ft.
9.	_____ cm	13 cm	_____ cm
10.	_____ yd.	3.8 yd.	_____ yd.

Lesson 8.5 Area of a Circle

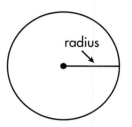

radius

The **area** of a circle is the number of square units it contains. Like circumference, area is calculated using π, which represents about $3\frac{1}{7}$ or 3.14.

The formula for finding the area of a circle is:

Area = $\pi \times$ radius $\times$ radius $A = \pi r^2$

If a circle has a **radius** of 3 in., its area is $\pi \times 3 \times 3$ or about 28.26 in.^{2}

If a circle has a **diameter** of 7 in., its **radius** is $\frac{1}{2}$ of 7 in., or 3.5 in.

Its area is $\pi \times 3.5 \times 3.5$ in., or about 38.465 in.^{2}

Complete the chart for each circle described below. Use 3.14 for π. When necessary, round to the nearest hundredth.

	a Radius	**b** Diameter	**c** Area
1.	4 in.	_____ in.	_____ in.^{2}
2.	_____ ft.	12 ft.	_____ ft.^{2}
3.	1.5 m	_____ m	_____ m^2
4.	11 in.	_____ in.	_____ in.^{2}
5.	_____ km	0.8 km	_____ km^2
6.	90 mm	_____ mm	_____ mm^2
7.	5 ft.	_____ ft.	_____ ft.^{2}
8.	_____ in.	9 in.	_____ in.^{2}
9.	_____ cm	8.2 cm	_____ cm^2
10.	_____ m	11 m	_____ m^2

Lesson 8.6 Area of a Parallelogram

A parallelogram is a polygon with 2 sets of parallel sides. To find the **area** of a parallelogram, multiply the measure of its base by the measure of its height: $A = b \times h$ or $A = bh$.

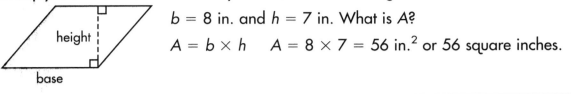

$b = 8$ in. and $h = 7$ in. What is A?

$A = b \times h$ $A = 8 \times 7 = 56$ in.^{2} or 56 square inches.

Find the area of each parallelogram.

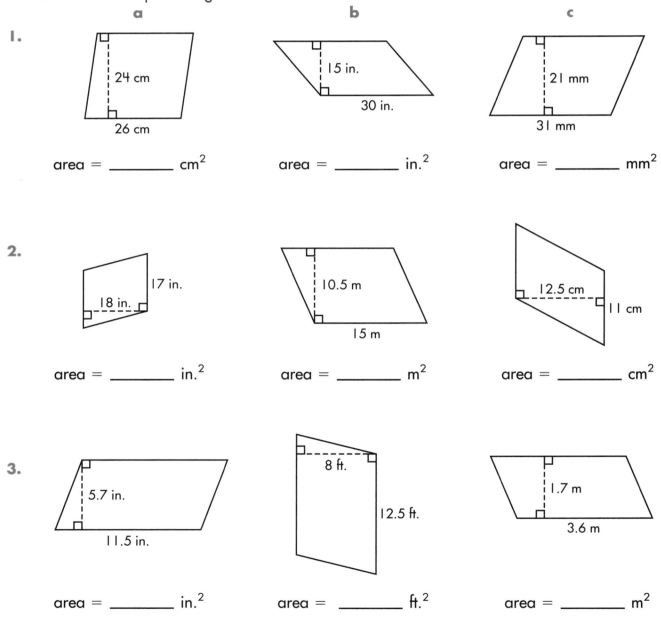

	a	b	c
1.	24 cm, 26 cm	15 in., 30 in.	21 mm, 31 mm
	area = _____ cm^2	area = _____ in.^{2}	area = _____ mm^2
2.	17 in., 18 in.	10.5 m, 15 m	12.5 cm, 11 cm
	area = _____ in.^{2}	area = _____ m^2	area = _____ cm^2
3.	5.7 in., 11.5 in.	8 ft., 12.5 ft.	1.7 m, 3.6 m
	area = _____ in.^{2}	area = _____ ft.^{2}	area = _____ m^2

Lesson 8.7 Problem Solving

Solve each problem. Use $3\frac{1}{7}$ for π. When necessary, round answers to the nearest hundredth.

1. The Longs are building a fenced-in area for their dog. The area will be 15 feet long and 18 feet wide. How much fencing will they need? How much space will the dog have to play?

   The Longs will need _____ feet of fencing.

   The dog will have _____ square feet to play.

2. Bertha is making a braided rug in the shape of a circle. Its diameter, when finished, will be 7 feet. What will the rug's circumference be? How large will the rug be in square feet?

   The rug will measure _____ feet in circumference.

   The rug will be _____ square feet.

3. A canvas sail forms a right triangle. It is 21 meters high and 20 meters long at its base. How many square meters of canvas were needed to make the sail?

   21 m

   20 m

   _____ square meters of canvas were needed.

4. The sail described in **problem 3** needs to be restitched all around its perimeter. How many meters of sail need to be restitched? (Hint: Use the Pythagorean Theorem to calculate the length of the unknown side.)

   _____ meters of sail need to be restitched.

5. The Rincons fenced in their rectangular yard. The area of their yard is 700 square feet. The length of the yard is 25 feet. What is the width of the yard?

   The yard is _____ feet wide.

1.	
2.	
3.	
4.	
5.	

Lesson 8.8 Surface Area of a Rectangular Solid

The **surface area** of a solid is the sum of the areas of all surfaces of the solid. A rectangular solid has 6 surfaces.

The area of each surface is determined by a finding:

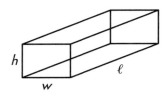

length × width, length × height, width × height

The total surface area is found using this formula:

$SA = 2\ell w + 2\ell h + 2wh$

If $\ell = 10\ m^2$, $w = 6\ m^2$, and $h = 4\ m^2$, the surface area is found as follows:

$SA = 2(10 \times 6) + 2(10 \times 4) + 2(6 \times 4)$

$SA = 2(60) + 2(40) + 2(24) = 120 + 80 + 48 = 248\ m^2$

Find the surface area of each rectangular solid.

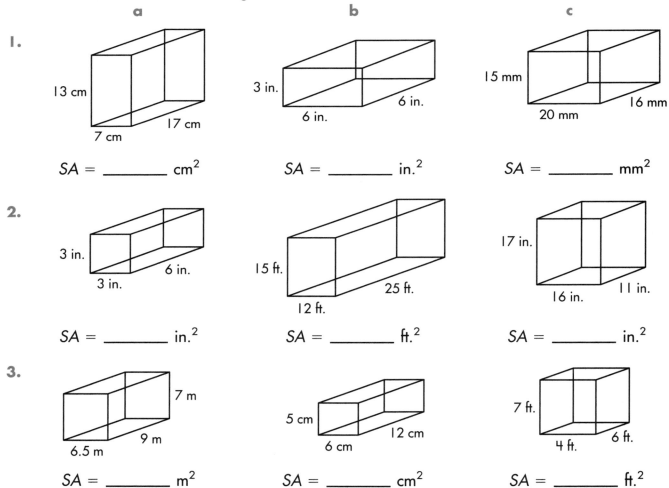

	a	b	c
1.	13 cm, 7 cm, 17 cm	3 in., 6 in., 6 in.	15 mm, 20 mm, 16 mm
	SA = _____ cm²	SA = _____ in.²	SA = _____ mm²
2.	3 in., 3 in., 6 in.	15 ft., 12 ft., 25 ft.	17 in., 16 in., 11 in.
	SA = _____ in.²	SA = _____ ft.²	SA = _____ in.²
3.	7 m, 6.5 m, 9 m	5 cm, 6 cm, 12 cm	7 ft., 4 ft., 6 ft.
	SA = _____ m²	SA = _____ cm²	SA = _____ ft.²

Lesson 8.9 Volume of a Rectangular Solid

Volume is the amount of space a solid (three-dimensional) figure occupies. You can calculate the volume of a rectangular solid by multiplying the area of its base by its height: $V = Bh$

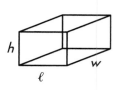

The area of the base is found by multiplying length and width. $B = \ell \times w$, so the volume can be found by using the formula $V = \ell \times w \times h$.

If $\ell = 10$ m, $w = 11$ m, and $h = 7$ m, what is the volume of the solid?

$V = 10 \times 11 \times 7$ $V = 770$ m^3 or 770 cubic meters.

Because the measure is in 3 dimensions, it is measured in **cubic units** or **units^3**.

Find the volume of each rectangular solid.

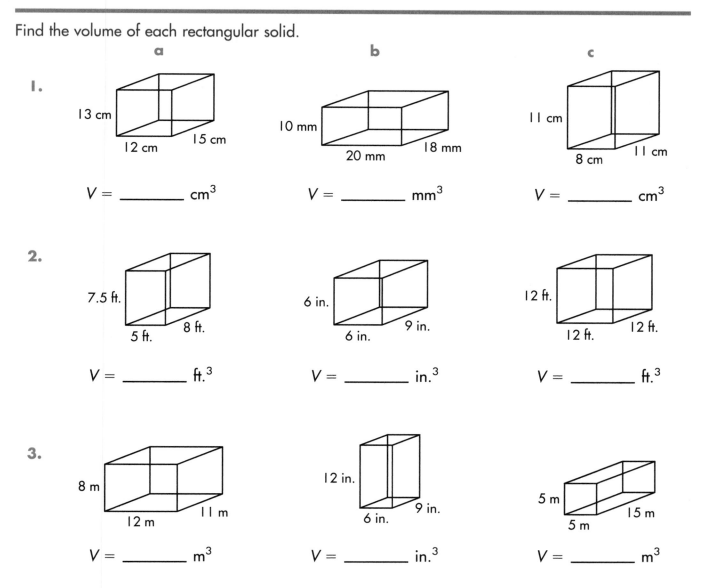

	a	b	c

1.

13 cm 12 cm 15 cm

$V =$ _____ cm^3

10 mm 20 mm 18 mm

$V =$ _____ mm^3

11 cm 8 cm 11 cm

$V =$ _____ cm^3

2.

7.5 ft. 5 ft. 8 ft.

$V =$ _____ ft.^{3}

6 in. 6 in. 9 in.

$V =$ _____ in.^{3}

12 ft. 12 ft. 12 ft.

$V =$ _____ ft.^{3}

3.

8 m 12 m 11 m

$V =$ _____ m^3

12 in. 6 in. 9 in.

$V =$ _____ in.^{3}

5 m 5 m 15 m

$V =$ _____ m^3

Lesson 8.10 Problem Solving

Solve each problem. Round answers to the nearest hundredth.

1. Ilia wants to wrap some books to mail as a present. She has measured the stack and finds that it is 5.5 inches tall, 8 inches wide, and 9 inches long. What is the total volume of her books? What is the minimum amount of paper she will need to cover the surface area of the package?

   The books' volume is _____ cubic inches.

   Ilia will need at least _____ square inches of paper.

2. Manuel has a moving box measuring 1.2 meters in length, 0.9 meter in height, and 0.9 meter in width. What volume can his box hold?

   The box can hold _____ cubic meter of items.

3. Clara has two boxes of tissues to choose from at the store. She wants the one with the greatest volume of tissues. Box A has a measure of 6 inches by 6 inches by 7.5 inches. Box B has a measure of 11 inches by 5 inches by 4.5 inches. What volume of tissues does each box contain?

   Box A has a volume of _____ cubic inches.

   Box B has a volume of _____ cubic inches.

4. Marcus has a rectangular fish tank measuring 1.8 meters long, 0.5 meter tall, and 0.75 meter wide. It is made entirely of glass, including its top. How much glass was used to make the tank? How much water could the tank hold if it were filled completely?

   The fish tank is made of _____ square meters of glass.

   It could hold _____ cubic meters of water.

5. Gloria is repainting a room measuring 8 yards long, $7\frac{1}{3}$ yards wide, and 4 yards high. She will repaint all four walls, the floor, and the ceiling. How much surface area will she be painting?

   Gloria will be painting _____ square yards.

1.

2.

3.

4.   5.

Lesson 8.11 Surface Area of a Cylinder

Surface area is the sum of all areas of a figure. For a **cylinder**, the surface area is the area of the circles at the top and bottom, plus the area of the round section in the middle.

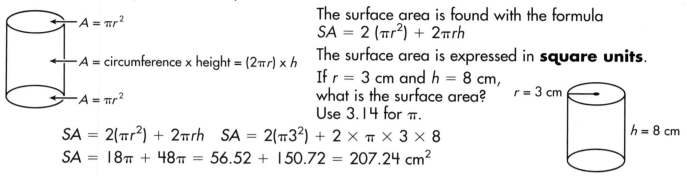

$A = \pi r^2$

$A = \text{circumference} \times \text{height} = (2\pi r) \times h$

$A = \pi r^2$

The surface area is found with the formula
$SA = 2(\pi r^2) + 2\pi rh$

The surface area is expressed in **square units**.
If $r = 3$ cm and $h = 8$ cm, what is the surface area? Use 3.14 for π.

$r = 3$ cm

$h = 8$ cm

$SA = 2(\pi r^2) + 2\pi rh$ $SA = 2(\pi 3^2) + 2 \times \pi \times 3 \times 8$
$SA = 18\pi + 48\pi = 56.52 + 150.72 = 207.24$ cm^2

Find the surface area of each cylinder. Use 3.14 for π. Remember that $d = 2r$.

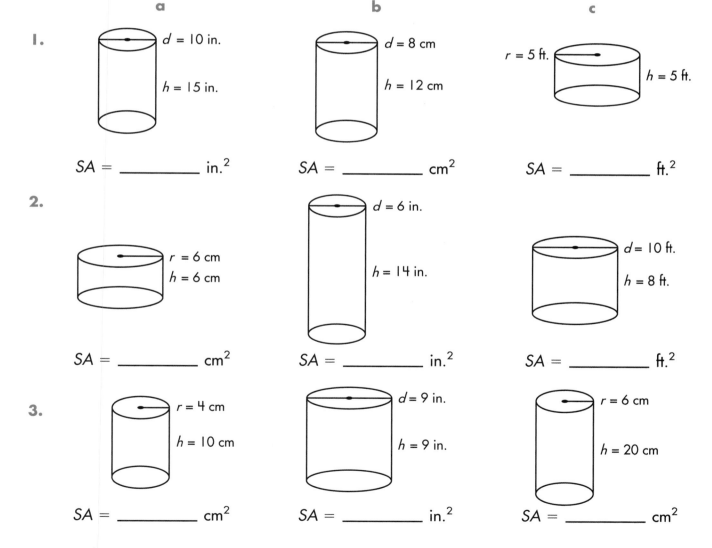

a	b	c

1.

a. $d = 10$ in. $h = 15$ in.   SA = _____ in.^{2}

b. $d = 8$ cm $h = 12$ cm   SA = _____ cm^2

c. $r = 5$ ft. $h = 5$ ft.   SA = _____ ft.^{2}

2.

a. $r = 6$ cm $h = 6$ cm   SA = _____ cm^2

b. $d = 6$ in. $h = 14$ in.   SA = _____ in.^{2}

c. $d = 10$ ft. $h = 8$ ft.   SA = _____ ft.^{2}

3.

a. $r = 4$ cm $h = 10$ cm   SA = _____ cm^2

b. $d = 9$ in. $h = 9$ in.   SA = _____ in.^{2}

c. $r = 6$ cm $h = 20$ cm   SA = _____ cm^2

Lesson 8.12 Volume of a Cylinder

Volume is the amount of space a solid (three-dimensional) figure occupies. You can calculate the **volume of a cylinder** by multiplying the area of the base by the height (Bh).

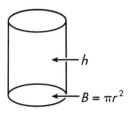

The area of the base is the area of the circle, πr^2, so volume can be found using the formula: $V = \pi r^2 h$

The volume is expressed in **cubic units**, or **units^3**.

If $r = 3$ cm and $h = 10$ cm, what is the volume? Use 3.14 for π.

$V = \pi r^2 h \quad V = \pi(3^2 \times 10) \quad V = \pi \times 90 \quad V = 282.6$ cm^3

Find the volume of each cylinder. Use 3.14 for π. Remember that $d = 2r$. Round answers to the nearest hundredth.

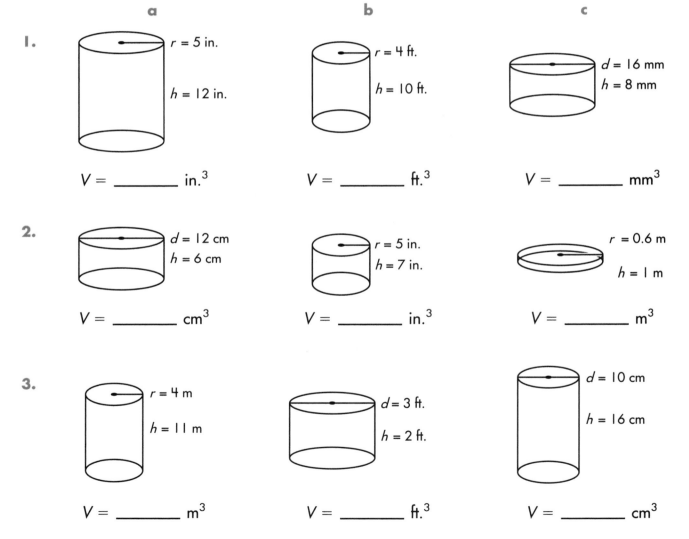

           a   b   c

1. $r = 5$ in. $r = 4$ ft. $d = 16$ mm
        $h = 12$ in. $h = 10$ ft. $h = 8$ mm

   $V = $ _____ in.^{3} $V = $ _____ ft.^{3} $V = $ _____ mm^3

2. $d = 12$ cm $r = 5$ in. $r = 0.6$ m
        $h = 6$ cm $h = 7$ in. $h = 1$ m

   $V = $ _____ cm^3 $V = $ _____ in.^{3} $V = $ _____ m^3

3. $r = 4$ m $d = 3$ ft. $d = 10$ cm
        $h = 11$ m $h = 2$ ft. $h = 16$ cm

   $V = $ _____ m^3 $V = $ _____ ft.^{3} $V = $ _____ cm^3

Lesson 8.13 Problem Solving

SHOW YOUR WORK

Solve each problem. Use 3.14 for π.

1. Jermaine has a mailing cylinder for posters that measures 18 inches long and 6 inches in diameter. What is the surface area of the cylinder? What volume can it hold?

   The cylinder's surface area is _____ square inches.

   The cylinder can hold _____ cubic inches.

2. An oatmeal container is a cylinder measuring 16 centimeters in diameter and 32 centimeters tall. How much oatmeal can the container hold? What is the surface area of the container?

   The container can hold _____ cubic centimeters of oatmeal.

   Its surface area is _____ square centimeters.

3. Trina is using 2 glasses in an experiment. Glass A measures 8 centimeters in diameter and 18 centimeters tall. Glass B measures 10 centimeters in diameter and 13 centimeters tall. Which one can hold more liquid? How much more?

   Glass _____ can hold _____ more cubic centimeters of liquid.

4. Stacy is wrapping 24 cylindrical candles as party favors. Each candle is 2 inches in diameter and 3 inches tall. What is the minimum amount of wrapping paper she will need to cover the surface area of all of the candles?

   Stacy will need a minimum of _____ square inches of wrapping paper.

5. Paul completely filled a glass with water. The glass was 10 centimeters in diameter and 17 centimeters tall. He drank the water. What volume of water did he drink?

   Paul drank _____ cubic centimeters of water.

1.

2.

3.

4.

5.

Lesson 8.14 Surface Area of a Cone

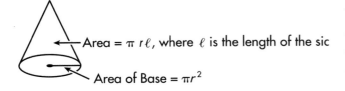

Area = $\pi r\ell$, where ℓ is the length of the sic

Area of Base = πr^2

The surface area of a solid is the sum of the areas of all surfaces of the solid. The **surface area of a cone** is the sum of the area of the base plus the area of the top portion of the cone.

$$SA = \pi r\ell + \pi r^2 \text{ or } \pi r(\ell + r)$$

If $\ell = 9$ in. and $r = 4$ in., what is the surface area of the cone? Use 3.14 for π.

$$SA = \pi r(\ell + r) = \pi 4(9 + 4) = \pi 52 = 163.28 \text{ in.}^2$$

If you do not know the length of the side but do know the height of the cone, you can use the Pythagorean Theorem to find the length:

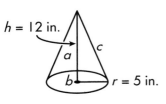

$h = 12$ in.

$r = 5$ in.

$$a^2 + b^2 = c^2 \quad 12^2 + 5^2 = c^2 \quad 169 = c^2 \quad c = 13 = \text{length}$$

$$SA = \pi r(\ell + r) = \pi 5(13 + 5) = \pi 90 = 282.6 \text{ in.}^2$$

Find the surface area of each cone. Use 3.14 for π. Round answers to the nearest hundredth.

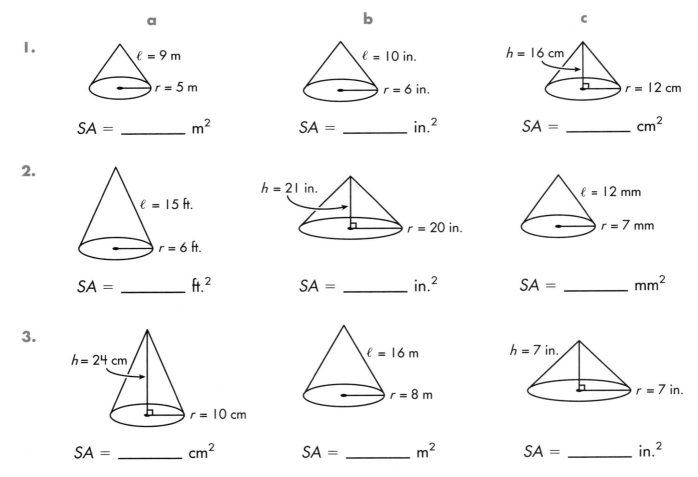

       a   b   c

1.
$\ell = 9$ m $r = 5$ m   SA = _____ m²

$\ell = 10$ in. $r = 6$ in.   SA = _____ in.²

$h = 16$ cm $r = 12$ cm   SA = _____ cm²

2.
$\ell = 15$ ft. $r = 6$ ft.   SA = _____ ft.²

$h = 21$ in. $r = 20$ in.   SA = _____ in.²

$\ell = 12$ mm $r = 7$ mm   SA = _____ mm²

3.
$h = 24$ cm $r = 10$ cm   SA = _____ cm²

$\ell = 16$ m $r = 8$ m   SA = _____ m²

$h = 7$ in. $r = 7$ in.   SA = _____ in.²

Lesson 8.15 Volume of a Cone

Volume is the amount of space a solid figure occupies. The **volume of a cone** is calculated as $\frac{1}{3}$ base × height.

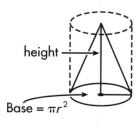

height

Base = πr^2

This is because a cone occupies $\frac{1}{3}$ of the volume of a cylinder of the same height. Base is the area of the circle, πr^2.

$$V = \tfrac{1}{3}\pi r^2 h \quad \text{Volume is given in \textbf{cubic units}, or \textbf{units}}^3.$$

If the height of a cone is 7 cm and radius is 3 cm, what is the volume?

Use 3.14 for π. $V = \tfrac{1}{3}\pi 3^2 7$ $V = \frac{\pi 63}{3}$ $V = \pi 21$ $V = 65.94$ cm^3

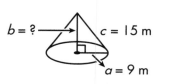

b = ?   c = 15 m

a = 9 m

If you do not know the height but you do know the radius and the length of the side, you can use the Pythagorean Theorem to find the height.
What is b? $a^2 + b^2 = c^2$ $81 + b^2 = 225$ $b^2 = 144$ $b = 12$ m

$$V = \tfrac{1}{3}\pi r^2 h = \tfrac{1}{3}\pi \times 81 \times 12 = 324\pi = 1017.36 \text{ m}^3$$

Find the volume of each cone. Use 3.14 for π. Remember that $d = 2r$.

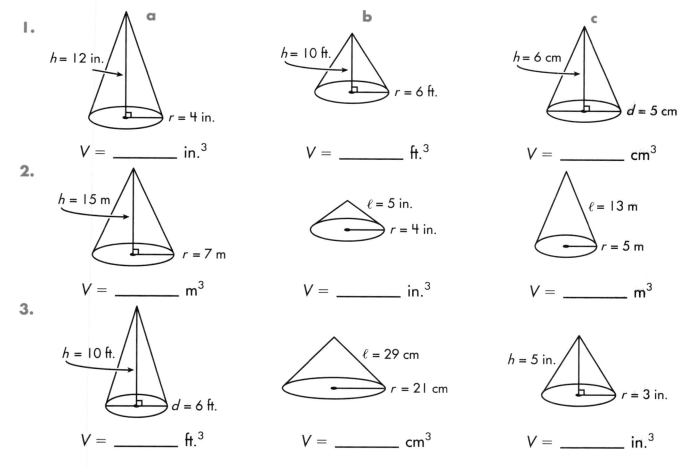

1.

a
h = 12 in.
r = 4 in.
V = _____ in.^{3}

b
h = 10 ft.
r = 6 ft.
V = _____ ft.^{3}

c
h = 6 cm
d = 5 cm
V = _____ cm^3

2.
h = 15 m
r = 7 m
V = _____ m^3

ℓ = 5 in.
r = 4 in.
V = _____ in.^{3}

ℓ = 13 m
r = 5 m
V = _____ m^3

3.
h = 10 ft.
d = 6 ft.
V = _____ ft.^{3}

ℓ = 29 cm
r = 21 cm
V = _____ cm^3

h = 5 in.
r = 3 in.
V = _____ in.^{3}

Lesson 8.16 Surface Area of a Pyramid

The surface area of a solid is the sum of the areas of all surfaces of the solid. The **surface area of a square pyramid** is the sum of the area of the square base and each of the 4 triangular sides.

Each triangle's area is $\frac{1}{2}$ base × height. In a pyramid, base is the **side** length and height is the slant height, or length. So surface area or

$SA = (\text{side} \times \text{side}) + 4(\frac{1}{2} \text{side} \times \text{length}).$

$SA = s^2 + 2s\ell$ SA is given in **square units**, or **units²**.

If $s = 6$ cm and $\ell = 10$ cm, what is the surface area?

$SA = 5^2 + 2s\ell$

$SA = 6^2 + 2 \times 6 \times 10 = 36 + 120 = 156$ cm²

side

slant height, or *length* (ℓ) of the side

Find the surface area of each square pyramid.

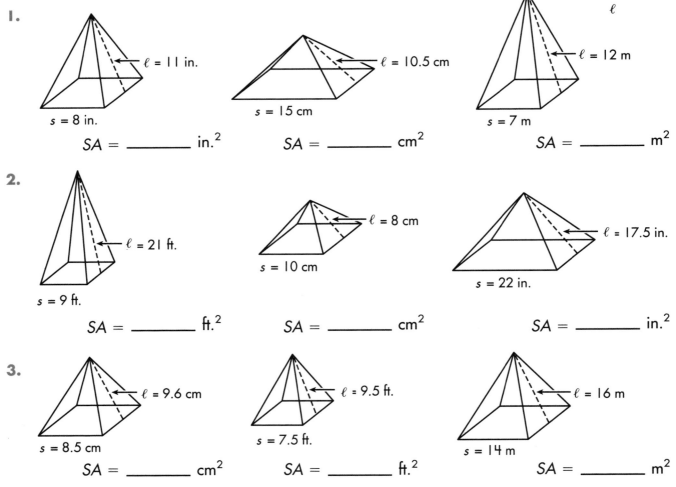

	a	b	c
1.	$\ell = 11$ in. $s = 8$ in. SA = _____ in.²	$\ell = 10.5$ cm $s = 15$ cm SA = _____ cm²	ℓ $\ell = 12$ m $s = 7$ m SA = _____ m²
2.	$\ell = 21$ ft. $s = 9$ ft. SA = _____ ft.²	$\ell = 8$ cm $s = 10$ cm SA = _____ cm²	$\ell = 17.5$ in. $s = 22$ in. SA = _____ in.²
3.	$\ell = 9.6$ cm $s = 8.5$ cm SA = _____ cm²	$\ell = 9.5$ ft. $s = 7.5$ ft. SA = _____ ft.²	$\ell = 16$ m $s = 14$ m SA = _____ m²

Lesson 8.17   Volume of a Pyramid

Volume is the amount of space a solid figure occupies. The **volume of a pyramid** is calculated as $\frac{1}{3}$ base × height. This is because a pyramid occupies $\frac{1}{3}$ of the volume of a rectangular prism of the same height. Because the base of a square pyramid is square, $B = s^2$.

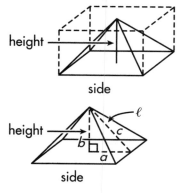

So, $V = \frac{1}{3}Bh$ or $\frac{1}{3}s^2h$. Volume is given in **cubic units**, or **units^3**.

If $s = 10$ cm and $h = 9$ cm, what is the volume?

$V = \frac{1}{3}s^2h$ $V = \frac{1}{3}10^2 \times 9$ $V = \frac{900}{3}$ $V = 300$ cm^3

If you do not know the height but you do know the slant height or **length** of a triangle, you can use the Pythagorean Theorem to find the height. $a = \frac{1}{2}$ of the side length, $b =$ the height of the pyramid, $c =$ length

If $s = 6$ m and $\ell = 5$ m what is h? $a^2 + b^2 = c^2$ $3^2 + b^2 = 25$ m $b^2 = 16$ $b = 4$ m

Find the volume of each pyramid. Round answers to the nearest hundredth.

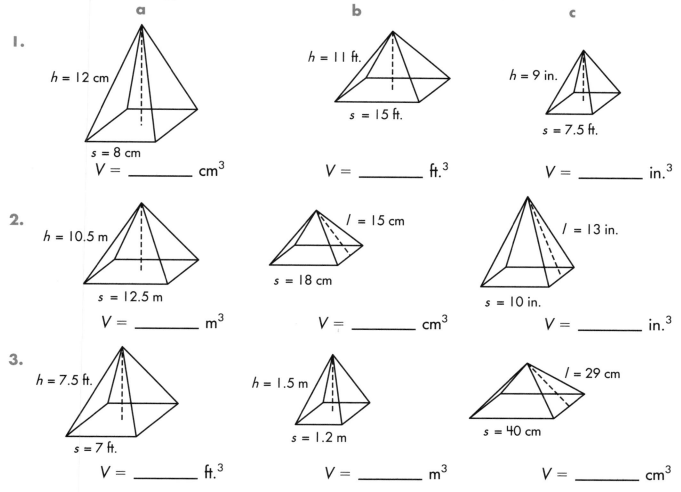

a

1. $h = 12$ cm, $s = 8$ cm $V =$ _____ cm^3

2. $h = 10.5$ m, $s = 12.5$ m $V =$ _____ m^3

3. $h = 7.5$ ft., $s = 7$ ft. $V =$ _____ ft.^{3}

b

1. $h = 11$ ft., $s = 15$ ft. $V =$ _____ ft.^{3}

2. $l = 15$ cm, $s = 18$ cm $V =$ _____ cm^3

3. $h = 1.5$ m, $s = 1.2$ m $V =$ _____ m^3

c

1. $h = 9$ in., $s = 7.5$ ft. $V =$ _____ in.^{3}

2. $l = 13$ in., $s = 10$ in. $V =$ _____ in.^{3}

3. $l = 29$ cm, $s = 40$ cm $V =$ _____ cm^3

Lesson 8.18 Problem Solving

Solve each problem. Use 3.14 for π. Round answers to the nearest hundredth.

1. Tom and Maura built a square pyramid out of sand at the beach. Each side was 1.2 meters at its base, and the height of the pyramid was 0.8 meter. What was the volume of the pyramid?

   The pyramid's volume was _____ cubic meters.

2. An ice-cream cone has a side length of 6.5 inches and a diameter at the top of 3 inches. What is the surface area of the cone? (The cone does not have a top.)

   The cone's surface area is _____ square inches.

3. Another ice-cream cone has a height of 6 inches and a diameter of 3 inches. How much ice cream can this cone hold?

   The cone can hold _____ cubic inches of ice cream.

4. Alison is making 12 cone-shaped party hats out of paper. Each one will have a side length of 10 inches and an opening of 6 inches in diameter. How much paper will she need, at a minimum, to make all 12 hats? (Remember that the circular openings will not be covered.)

   Alison will need a minimum of _____ square inches of paper.

5. The Great Pyramid of Giza was about 160 yards high when originally built. Each side was about 250 yards at its base. What was the volume of the pyramid?

   The pyramid's volume was about _____ cubic yards.

1.

2.

3.

4.

5.

Check What You Learned

Perimeter, Area, and Volume

Find the unknown measure, area, or perimeter for each figure.

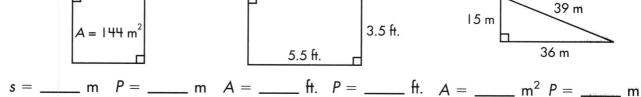

    a   b   c

1.

$A = 144 \text{ m}^2$ 3.5 ft.   39 m, 15 m, 36 m

5.5 ft.

$s =$ _____ m $P =$ _____ m $A =$ _____ ft. $P =$ _____ ft. $A =$ _____ m² $P =$ _____ m

Complete the chart for each circle described below. Use 3.14 for π. Round answers to the nearest hundredth.

	a Radius	b Diameter	c Circumference	d Area
2.	2.5 ft.	_____ ft.	_____ ft.	_____ ft.²
3.	_____ in.	9 in.	_____ in.	_____ in.²
4.	1.5 m	_____ m	_____ m	_____ m²

Find the volume of each solid figure. Use 3.14 for π. Round answers to the nearest hundredth.

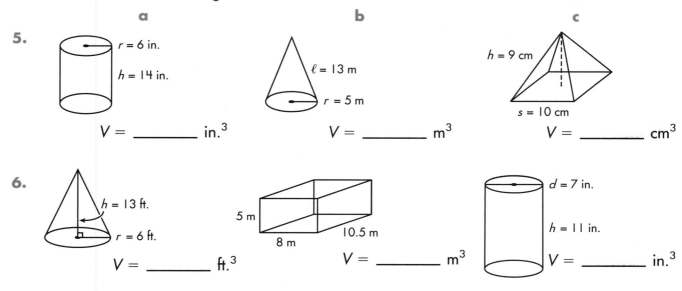

    a   b   c

5. $r = 6$ in., $h = 14$ in. $\ell = 13$ m, $r = 5$ m $h = 9$ cm, $s = 10$ cm

$V =$ _____ in.³ $V =$ _____ m³ $V =$ _____ cm³

6. $h = 13$ ft., $r = 6$ ft.   5 m, 8 m, 10.5 m $d = 7$ in., $h = 11$ in.

$V =$ _____ ft.³ $V =$ _____ m³ $V =$ _____ in.³

Check What You Learned

Perimeter, Area, and Volume

Find the surface area of each solid figure. Use 3.14 for π.

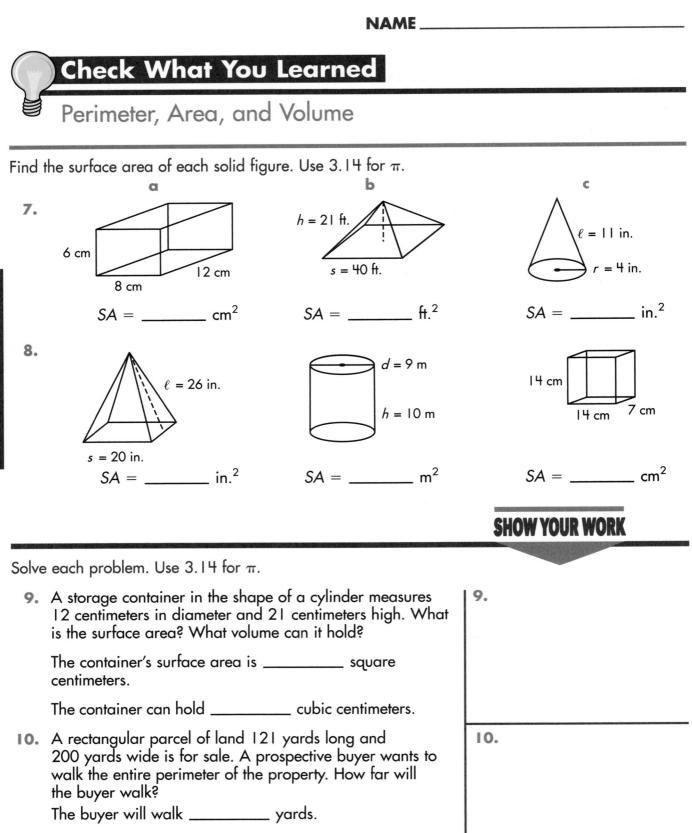

| a | b | c |

7.

SA = _____ cm^2 SA = _____ ft.^{2} SA = _____ in.^{2}

8.

SA = _____ in.^{2} SA = _____ m^2 SA = _____ cm^2

SHOW YOUR WORK

Solve each problem. Use 3.14 for π.

9. A storage container in the shape of a cylinder measures 12 centimeters in diameter and 21 centimeters high. What is the surface area? What volume can it hold?

The container's surface area is _____ square centimeters.

The container can hold _____ cubic centimeters.

9.

10. A rectangular parcel of land 121 yards long and 200 yards wide is for sale. A prospective buyer wants to walk the entire perimeter of the property. How far will the buyer walk?

The buyer will walk _____ yards.

10.

Spectrum Math
Grade 8
124

CHAPTER 8 POSTTEST

Check What You Learned
Chapter 8

Check What You Know

Preparing for Algebra

Translate each sentence into an equation. Use n for an unknown number.

1. A number decreased by 7 is 13. _____
2. Eight times a number, decreased by 5, is 27. _____
3. The product of a number and 6 is 42. _____

Write an equation to illustrate each property.

4. The Identity Property of Multiplication _____
5. The Distributive Property _____
6. The Commutative Property of Addition _____

Evaluate each expression if $a = 9$ and $b = 5$. Underline the step completed first.

a	b	c

7. $3a + 2(b - 1) =$ _____ $b + 9 \times a \div 3 =$ _____ $a \times (b - 3) + 6 =$ _____
8. $9(a + b) \div 7 =$ _____ $6 \times b \div 10 + 3 =$ _____ $13 + a \div 3 \times 2 =$ _____

Rewrite each multiplication or division expression using a base and an exponent.

9. $4^5 \div 4^2 =$ _____ $6^{-5} \times 6^3 =$ _____ $8^{-4} \div 8^{-2} =$ _____
10. $9^{11} \div 9^6 =$ _____ $5^{-3} \times 5^{-1} =$ _____ $3^{-6} \div 3^4 =$ _____

Rewrite each number in scientific notation.

11. 320.4 _____   0.0046 _____   1306 _____
12. 0.017 _____   53842 _____   0.0007 _____

Find the value of the variable in each equation.

13. $a + 13 = 27$ _____ $2n - 2 = 10$ _____ $\frac{x}{4} + 4 = 12$ _____
14. $18 - 2p = 10$ _____ $\frac{n}{24} = 3$ _____ $n - 33 = 19$ _____
15. $f + 22 = 45$ _____ $\frac{r}{16} + 3 = 6$ _____ $s \times 4 + 2 = 46$ _____

Check What You Know

Preparing for Algebra

16. Tell where each lettered point is located on Grid 1.

A(_____), B(_____), C(_____), D(_____)

17. Plot each ordered pair on Grid 1.

E(5, −2)   F(1, 5)   G(−5, 2)   H(1, −3)

18. Complete the function table. Then, graph the function.

y = 2x − 3

x	y

Grid 1

Grid 2

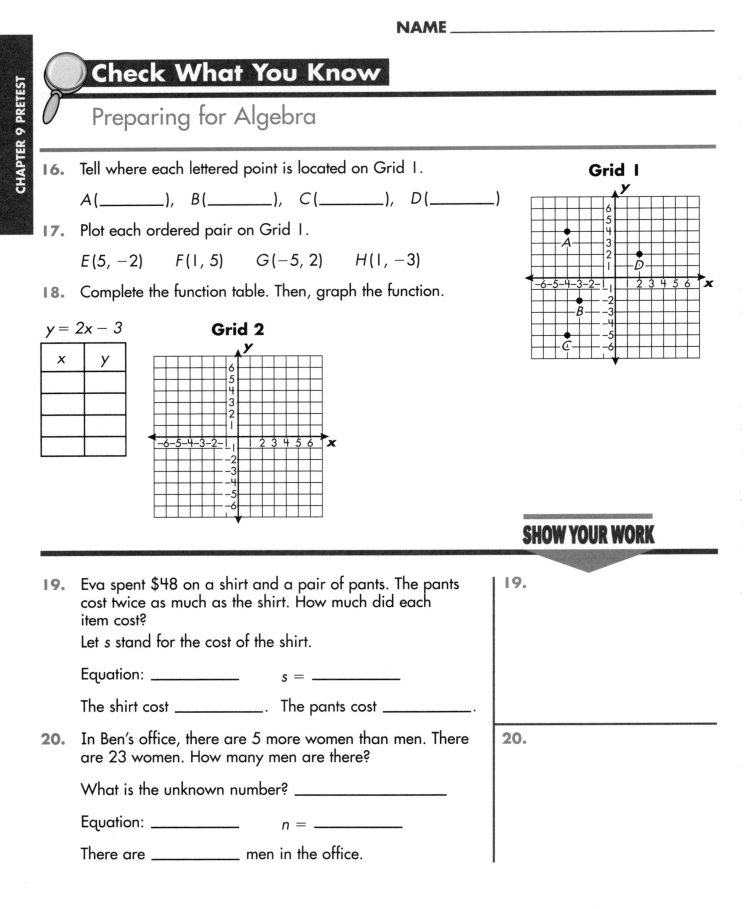

SHOW YOUR WORK

19. Eva spent $48 on a shirt and a pair of pants. The pants cost twice as much as the shirt. How much did each item cost?

Let s stand for the cost of the shirt.

Equation: _____   s = _____

The shirt cost _____. The pants cost _____.

19.

20. In Ben's office, there are 5 more women than men. There are 23 women. How many men are there?

What is the unknown number? _____

Equation: _____   n = _____

There are _____ men in the office.

20.

Lesson 9.1 Multiplying and Dividing Powers

A number multiplied by itself can be written as follows:

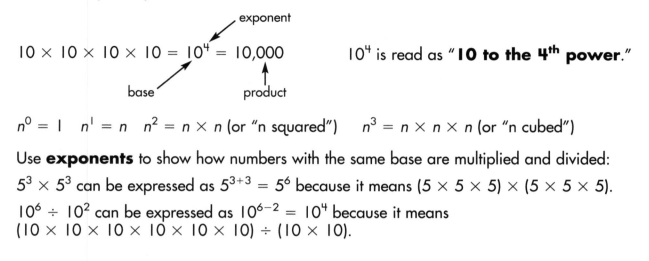

$10 \times 10 \times 10 \times 10 = 10^4 = 10,000$ 10^4 is read as "**10 to the 4th power**."

exponent, base, product

$n^0 = 1$ $n^1 = n$ $n^2 = n \times n$ (or "n squared") $n^3 = n \times n \times n$ (or "n cubed")

Use **exponents** to show how numbers with the same base are multiplied and divided:

$5^3 \times 5^3$ can be expressed as $5^{3+3} = 5^6$ because it means $(5 \times 5 \times 5) \times (5 \times 5 \times 5)$.

$10^6 \div 10^2$ can be expressed as $10^{6-2} = 10^4$ because it means
$(10 \times 10 \times 10 \times 10 \times 10 \times 10) \div (10 \times 10)$.

Rewrite each multiplication or division expression using a base and an exponent.

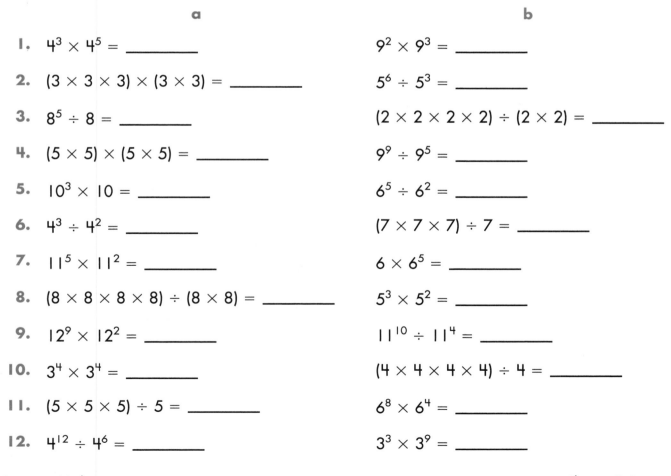

	a	b
1.	$4^3 \times 4^5 =$ _____	$9^2 \times 9^3 =$ _____
2.	$(3 \times 3 \times 3) \times (3 \times 3) =$ _____	$5^6 \div 5^3 =$ _____
3.	$8^5 \div 8 =$ _____	$(2 \times 2 \times 2 \times 2) \div (2 \times 2) =$ _____
4.	$(5 \times 5) \times (5 \times 5) =$ _____	$9^9 \div 9^5 =$ _____
5.	$10^3 \times 10 =$ _____	$6^5 \div 6^2 =$ _____
6.	$4^3 \div 4^2 =$ _____	$(7 \times 7 \times 7) \div 7 =$ _____
7.	$11^5 \times 11^2 =$ _____	$6 \times 6^5 =$ _____
8.	$(8 \times 8 \times 8 \times 8) \div (8 \times 8) =$ _____	$5^3 \times 5^2 =$ _____
9.	$12^9 \times 12^2 =$ _____	$11^{10} \div 11^4 =$ _____
10.	$3^4 \times 3^4 =$ _____	$(4 \times 4 \times 4 \times 4) \div 4 =$ _____
11.	$(5 \times 5 \times 5) \div 5 =$ _____	$6^8 \times 6^4 =$ _____
12.	$4^{12} \div 4^6 =$ _____	$3^3 \times 3^9 =$ _____

Lesson 9.2 Negative Exponents

A **negative exponent** may be written with the base as the denominator in a fraction where the numerator is 1. The exponent then becomes positive.

$$5^{-3} \text{ means } \frac{1}{5^3} = \frac{1}{125} = 0.008 \qquad 10^{-2} \text{ means } \frac{1}{10^2} = \frac{1}{100} = 0.01$$

It is possible to multiply and divide numbers with positive and negative exponents that have the same base.

$$5^{-3} \times 5^{-2} = 5^{-3 + (-2)} = 5^{-5} \qquad 4^{-3} \div 4^{-2} = 4^{-3 - (-2)} = 4^{-3 + 2} = 4^{-1}$$

$$6^{-4} \times 6^2 = 6^{-4 + 2} = 6^{-2} \qquad\qquad 8^4 \div 8^{-3} = 8^{4 - (-3)} = 8^{4 + 3} = 8^7$$

Rewrite each multiplication or division expression using a base and an exponent.

a	b
1. $3^{-4} \times 3^{-6} =$ _____	$9^{-3} \div 9^{-5} =$ _____
2. $4^3 \div 4^{-2} =$ _____	$5^5 \times 5^{-6} =$ _____
3. $12^{-3} \times 12^{-4} =$ _____	$4^{-6} \times 4^4 =$ _____
4. $7^6 \div 7^{-3} =$ _____	$2^{-3} \div 2^3 =$ _____
5. $11^4 \times 11^{-3} =$ _____	$6^{-5} \times 6^{-4} =$ _____
6. $8^{-5} \div 8^3 =$ _____	$12^{-4} \div 12 =$ _____
7. $7^5 \times 7^{-4} =$ _____	$5^{-3} \times 5^2 =$ _____
8. $2^5 \div 2^{-3} =$ _____	$3^{-12} \times 3^{-4} =$ _____
9. $6^3 \div 6^{-4} =$ _____	$7^{-3} \div 7^4 =$ _____
10. $9^{-3} \times 9^4 =$ _____	$10^{-5} \times 10^{-2} =$ _____
11. $8^{-4} \div 8^{-2} =$ _____	$2^{-2} \times 2^{-12} =$ _____
12. $3^{-6} \times 3^{-3} =$ _____	$8^{-6} \div 8^4 =$ _____

Lesson 9.3 Scientific Notation

Scientific notation is most often used as a concise way of writing very large and small numbers. It is written as a number between 1 and 10 multiplied by a power of 10. Any number can be written in scientific notation.

$$1{,}503 = 1.503 \times 10^3 \qquad 0.0376 = 3.76 \times 10^{-2} \qquad 85 = 8.5 \times 10$$
$$+3 \qquad\qquad\qquad -2 \qquad\qquad\qquad +1$$

Translate numbers written in scientific notation into standard form by reading the exponent.

$$7.03 \times 10^5 = 703000 \qquad\qquad 5.4 \times 10^{-4} = 0.00054$$
$$\text{Add 5 places.} \qquad\qquad\qquad \text{Subtract 4 places.}$$

Write each number in scientific notation.

	a	b	c
1.	0.013 = _____	4105 = _____	27.3 = _____
2.	810.4 = _____	0.684 = _____	0.017 = _____
3.	0.0006 = _____	427.5 = _____	36,054 = _____
4.	50,210 = _____	0.0005 = _____	256.21 = _____
5.	36.25 = _____	0.892 = _____	0.00065 = _____
6.	0.027 = _____	1,416.3 = _____	0.0049 = _____

Write each number in standard form.

	a	b	c
7.	2.6×10^{-3} = _____	8.46×10^5 = _____	4.65×10^{-1} = _____
8.	9.02×10^4 = _____	5.15×10^{-2} = _____	8.45×10^3 = _____
9.	7.25×10^{-4} = _____	1.06×10^3 = _____	9.06×10^{-5} = _____
10.	9.7×10^{-3} = _____	3.02×10^4 = _____	1.56×10^4 = _____

Lesson 9.4 Variables, Equations, and Inequalities

An **equation** is a number sentence that contains an equals sign.
An **expression** is a number phrase without an equals sign.
An **inequality** shows how 2 numbers or phrases compare to one another.
Equations, expressions, and inequalities may contain only numerals, or they also may contain variables. A **variable** is a symbol, usually a letter, that stands for an unknown number.

	Equation	Expression	Inequality
Numerical	$3 \times 5 = 15$	$9 + 2$	$17 < 20$
Variable	$2n + 2 = 18$	$a - 5$	$12 > 3d$

All equations, expressions, and inequalities express an idea.

3×4 means "three 4s." $6 \div 3 = 2$ means "6 divided by 3 is 2."

$n - 7$ means "n decreased by 7" or "a number decreased by 7."

$4n + 2 = 6$ means "four times a number, plus 2, is 6" or "4ns, plus 2, is 6."

Translate each phrase into an algebraic expression, equation, or inequality.

a **b**

1. x increased by 5 _____ 12 divided by a number _____

2. seven ns _____ c less than 7 _____

3. a number that is less than 23 _____ one fourth of x _____

4. p added to 6 _____ the product of 15 and m _____

Translate each sentence into an equation. Use n for an unknown number.

5. 11 decreased by a number is 7. _____

6. 8 times a number, plus 4, is 84. _____

7. A number divided by 5 is 6. _____

Write each expression in words.

8. $n - 5$ _____

9. $3n \div 6$ _____

Lesson 9.5 Order of Operations

To evaluate an expression, simplify and solve it in this order:

1. Simplify expressions in parentheses and/or brackets (innermost first).

2. Simplify expressions with exponents.

3. Perform multiplication and/or division operations, in order from left to right.

4. Perform addition and/or subtraction operations, in order from left to right.

Underline the operation that should be performed first. Then, complete each equation.

	a	**b**

1. $4 + 3(9 + 1) =$ _____ $2 \times 3^2 - (3 + 4) =$ _____

2. $13 \times 6 - 18 \div 2 =$ _____ $45 \div (5 + 8 \div 2) =$ _____

3. $4 \times [12 \div (10 - 6)] =$ _____ $28 + 10^3 \div 40 - 13 =$ _____

4. $44 - 3 \times (6 + 5) + 5 =$ _____ $81 - 24 \times 2 \div 3 =$ _____

Evaluate each expression if $a = 9$, $b = 4$, and $c = 5$.

5. $2a + 7 - 5$ _____ $(c - 1) \times 3b - 8$ _____

6. $(4b + 3)a - 25$ _____ $(6a + 2b) \div 4$ _____

7. $4^3 - 6c$ _____ $11b + a^2$ _____

8. $(15 - 2b)^2 - a \times 2$ _____ $(c^2 + 15) \div b$ _____

9. $2a + 12c \div 3$ _____ $(2a + 7) \div 5$ _____

10. $c^3 - (2ab)$ _____ $c - 1 \times (3b - 8)$ _____

11. $6a + 2b \div 4$ _____ $4b + (3a - 25)$ _____

12. $(2a + 12c) \div 3$ _____ $11(b + a^2)$ _____

Lesson 9.6 Number Properties

The **Commutative Properties of Addition and Multiplication** state:

$$a + b = b + a \quad a \times b = b \times a$$

The **Associative Properties of Addition and Multiplication** state:

$$(a + b) + c = a + (b + c) \quad (a \times b) \times c = a \times (b \times c)$$

The **Identity Properties of Addition, Multiplication, and Exponents** state:

$$a + 0 = a \quad a \times 1 = a \quad a^1 = a$$

The **Properties of Zero** are:

$$a \times 0 = 0 \quad 0 \div a = 0 \quad a^0 = 1 \text{ unless } a = 0$$

Complete or rewrite the equation using your knowledge of number properties.

a	b
1. $17 + n =$ _____	$n + 0 =$ _____
2. _____ $= (x + y) + 2$	_____ $= q^0$
3. $m \times n \times p =$ _____	$r + s =$ _____
4. $a \times 0 =$ _____	$p^1 =$ _____

Solve each equation. Use the number properties to help.

5. $(5 \times 7)^1 =$ _____	$6 \times 5 \times 4 =$ _____
6. $11 + 18 + 12 =$ _____	$4 \times 3 + 0 =$ _____
7. $(5 + 3) \times 0 =$ _____	$(5 \times 4 - 1)^0 =$ _____
8. $8 \times 2 \times 5 =$ _____	$(9 \times 1) \div 3 =$ _____
9. $22^1 - 11 \times 1 =$ _____	$36 + 5 \times 0 =$ _____
10. $2 \times 9 \times 15 =$ _____	$14 + 15 + 16 =$ _____

Lesson 9.7 The Distributive Property

The **Distributive Property** states: $a \times (b + c) = (a \times b) + (a \times c)$

The same property also means that: $a \times (b - c) = (a \times b) - (a \times c)$

This can help solve complex multiplication problems:

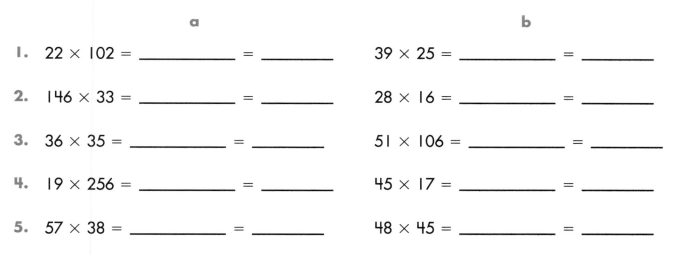

$26 = 20 + 6$ $17 \times 26 = (17 \times 20) + (17 \times 6) = 340 + 102 = 442$

$18 = 20 - 2$ $47 \times 18 = (47 \times 20) - (47 \times 2) = 940 - 94 = 846$

Using the Distributive Property, rewrite each expression in a way that will help solve it (choices may vary). Then, solve.

	a	**b**
1.	$22 \times 102 = $ _____ = _____	$39 \times 25 = $ _____ = _____
2.	$146 \times 33 = $ _____ = _____	$28 \times 16 = $ _____ = _____
3.	$36 \times 35 = $ _____ = _____	$51 \times 106 = $ _____ = _____
4.	$19 \times 256 = $ _____ = _____	$45 \times 17 = $ _____ = _____
5.	$57 \times 38 = $ _____ = _____	$48 \times 45 = $ _____ = _____

Rewrite each expression using the Distributive Property.

6. $5 \times (m + n) = $ _____ $(f \times 12) + (f \times 15) = $ _____

7. $(p \times 16) + (p \times q) = $ _____ $12 \times (4 + e) = $ _____

8. $16 \times (9 - r) = $ _____ $17 \times b - 17 \times c = $ _____

9. $(11 \times 2) + (11 \times n) = $ _____ $15(p - q) = $ _____

10. $14 \times (17 - p) = $ _____ $12 \times n + 12 \times m = $ _____

11. $p \times r + p \times s = $ _____ $14t - 14v = $ _____

12. $st + sv = $ _____ $9(f - e) = $ _____

Lesson 9.8 Solving Addition and Subtraction Equations

The **Addition and Subtraction Properties of Equality** state that when the same number is added to both sides of an equation, the two sides remain equal:

$$4 + 17 = 21 \quad 4 + 17 + 5 = 21 + 5 \quad (26 = 26)$$

When the same number is subtracted from both sides of an equation, the two sides remain equal:

$$32 = 16 + 16 \quad 32 - 4 = 16 + 16 - 4 \quad (28 = 28)$$

Use these properties to determine the value of variables:

$x + 17 = 23$	$40 - n = 19$	$y - 14 = 3$
$x + 17 - 17 = 23 - 17$	$40 - n - 40 = 19 - 40$	$y - 14 + 14 = 3 + 14$
$x + 0 = 6 \quad x = 6$	$0 - n = -29 \quad n = 29$	$y + 0 = 17 \quad y = 17$

Find the value of the variable in each equation.

	a	**b**	**c**
1.	$a + 12 = 25$ _____	$48 + d = 60$ _____	$y - 19 = 18$ _____
2.	$31 - x = 16$ _____	$11 + n = 25$ _____	$m - 21 = 34$ _____
3.	$28 + b = 50$ _____	$p - 16 = 32$ _____	$t + 22 = 57$ _____
4.	$33 + c = 54$ _____	$e + 19 = 37$ _____	$16 + r = 40$ _____
5.	$52 - n = 24$ _____	$y - 15 = 18$ _____	$21 + n = 49$ _____
6.	$m - 5 = 18$ _____	$36 + s = 45$ _____	$21 - a = 7$ _____
7.	$17 + d = 29$ _____	$x - 23 = 9$ _____	$27 + f = 35$ _____
8.	$r - 15 = 24$ _____	$27 - p = 3$ _____	$34 - x = 18$ _____
9.	$y + 12 = 20$ _____	$n - 24 = 31$ _____	$16 + p = 38$ _____
10.	$18 + q = 25$ _____	$m + 17 = 32$ _____	$e + 29 = 36$ _____
11.	$39 - r = 34$ _____	$42 + x = 56$ _____	$q - 21 = 35$ _____
12.	$18 + p = 22$ _____	$s - 32 = 9$ _____	$43 + n = 49$ _____

Lesson 9.9 Solving Multiplication and Division Equations

The **Multiplication and Division Properties of Equality** state that when each side of the equation is multiplied by the same number, the two sides remain equal:

$$3 + 4 = 7 \quad (3 + 4) \times 5 = 7 \times 5 \quad (35 = 35)$$

When each side of the equation is divided by the same number, the two sides remain equal:

$$2 \times 6 = 12 \quad \frac{(2 \times 6)}{3} = \frac{12}{3} \quad (4 = 4)$$

Use these properties to determine the value of variables:

$n \div 5 = 4$	$3n = 18$	$\frac{60}{n} = 4$
$n \div 5 \times 5 = 4 \times 5$	$\frac{3n}{3} = \frac{18}{3}$	$\frac{60n}{n} = 4n$ or $60 = 4n$
$n = 20$	$n = 6$	$\frac{60}{4} = \frac{4n}{4} \quad 15 = n$

Find the value of the variable in each equation.

	a	b	c
1.	$5b = 35$ _____	$\frac{a}{4} = 16$ _____	$f \times 12 = 72$ _____
2.	$x \div 4 = 7$ _____	$3k = 33$ _____	$\frac{42}{b} = 7$ _____
3.	$9 \times n = 72$ _____	$44 \div m = 22$ _____	$12a = 60$ _____
4.	$\frac{n}{20} = 4$ _____	$a \times 12 = 60$ _____	$6p = 90$ _____
5.	$x \div 7 = 11$ _____	$t \div 25 = 8$ _____	$\frac{x}{15} = 6$ _____
6.	$b \times 16 = 64$ _____	$11d = 132$ _____	$\frac{65}{m} = 5$ _____
7.	$\frac{n}{14} = 3$ _____	$f \times 9 = 99$ _____	$4n = 60$ _____
8.	$e \times 5 = 120$ _____	$\frac{120}{m} = 10$ _____	$b \div 9 = 7$ _____
9.	$8t = 104$ _____	$\frac{b}{9} = 6$ _____	$m \times 18 = 54$ _____
10.	$\frac{e}{6} = 12$ _____	$7m = 84$ _____	$a \div 4 = 18$ _____

Lesson 9.10 Problem Solving

Write an equation to represent the problem, using the variable *n* for the unknown number. Then, solve for the value of the variable. Look at the following problem as an example.

Hanna bought some peaches. Kevin bought 12 peaches. He bought 2 times as many as Hanna. How many did Hanna buy?

What is the unknown number? the number of peaches Hanna bought

(If *n* stands for that, what stands for the number of peaches Kevin bought? 2*n*
What number is that? 12)

Equation: 2*n* = 12   *n* = 6

SHOW YOUR WORK

Solve each problem.

1. Jaden has a number of baseball cards. He has 35 more than his brother, who has 52. How many cards does Jaden have?

   What is the unknown number? _____

   Equation: _____   *n* = _____

1.

2. Orlando paid $55.60 for a number of tickets to a hockey game. If each ticket was $6.95, how many tickets did Orlando buy?

   What is the unknown number? _____

   Equation: _____   *n* = _____

2.

3. Erica's room is 1.5 times longer than it is wide. It is 18 feet long. How wide is it?

   What is the unknown number? _____

   Equation: _____   *n* = _____

3.

4. In a recent basketball game, the Grizzlies lost by 11 points. The Palominos beat them with a score of 92 points. How many points did the Grizzlies score?

   What is the unknown number? _____

   Equation: _____   *n* = _____

4.

Lesson 9.11 Solving Two-Step Equations

Some problems with variables require more than one step to solve. Use the properties of equality to undo each step and find the value of the variable.

$$2n - 7 = 19$$

First, undo the subtraction by adding.

$$2n - 7 + 7 = 19 + 7 \quad 2n = 26$$

Then, undo the multiplication by dividing.

$$\frac{2n}{2} = \frac{26}{2} \quad n = 13$$

$$\frac{n}{3} + 5 = 11$$

First, undo the addition by subtracting.

$$\frac{n}{3} + 5 - 5 = 11 - 5 \quad \frac{n}{3} = 6$$

Then, undo the division by multiplying.

$$\frac{n}{3} \times 3 = 6 \times 3 \quad n = 18$$

Find the value of the variable in each equation.

	a	b	c
1.	$2n + 2 = 16$ _____	$\frac{a}{3} - 1 = 4$ _____	$\frac{b}{4} + 2 = 11$ _____
2.	$11p - 5 = 28$ _____	$8b + 12 = 52$ _____	$\frac{r}{20} - 3 = 3$ _____
3.	$\frac{m}{16} + 7 = 10$ _____	$6n + 4 = 64$ _____	$4s - 5 = 39$ _____
4.	$\frac{a}{9} - 3 = 6$ _____	$5d + 6 = 71$ _____	$\frac{m}{8} + 5 = 14$ _____
5.	$9a - 11 = 61$ _____	$\frac{e}{12} - 7 = 3$ _____	$\frac{i}{4} + 5 = 73$ _____
6.	$3p + 12 = 54$ _____	$\frac{n}{3} + 12 = 27$ _____	$5b - 7 = 93$ _____
7.	$\frac{s}{15} + 1 = 5$ _____	$6x + 25 = 73$ _____	$\frac{a}{3} - 3 = 11$ _____
8.	$3r - 11 = 43$ _____	$\frac{x}{7} + 14 = 22$ _____	$5m + 13 = 68$ _____
9.	$\frac{n}{5} - 5 = 8$ _____	$\frac{a}{6} + 4 = 20$ _____	$3p - 15 = 48$ _____

Lesson 9.11 Problem Solving

Write an equation to represent the problem, using the variable n for the unknown number. Then, solve for the value of the variable. Look at the following problem as an example.

George and Cindy are saving for bicycles. Cindy has saved $15 less than twice as much as George has saved. Together, they have saved $120. How much did each of them save?

Let n stand for the amount George has saved. What stands for the amount Cindy has saved? __$2n - 15$__ What equals the total amount? __$n + (2n - 15) = 120$__

Simplify: ___$3n - 15 = 120$___ Solve.

How much has George saved? __$45__
How much has Cindy saved? __$75__

SHOW YOUR WORK

Solve each problem.

1. Nate and Laura picked apples. Laura picked $\frac{1}{2}$ as many as Nate picked. Together they picked 90 apples. How many did each of them pick?

   Let n stand for the number Nate picked.
   Equation: _____
   How many apples did Nate pick? _____
   How many apples did Laura pick? _____

2. Jordan travels $\frac{3}{4}$ of a mile longer to school each day than Harrison does. Combined, they travel $5\frac{1}{4}$ miles to school. How far does each travel?

   Let n stand for the distance Jordan travels.
   Equation: _____
   How far does Jordan travel? _____
   How far does Harrison travel? _____

3. Two jackets have a combined cost of $98. Jacket A costs $12 less than Jacket B. How much does each jacket cost?

   Let n stand for the cost of Jacket A.
   Equation: _____
   Jacket A costs _____.
   Jacket B costs _____.

1.

2.

3.

Lesson 9.12 Plotting Ordered Pairs

A coordinate plane is formed by two intersecting number lines. The **x-axis** is the horizontal line. The **y-axis** is the vertical line. A relation is any set of ordered pairs. Ordered pairs are listed as (x, y). This shows the distance the point is from the **origin** $(0, 0)$, in the domain (the set of x coordinates) and the range (the set of y coordinates). Point A is located at $(4, 2)$. Point B is located at $(-5, -3)$.

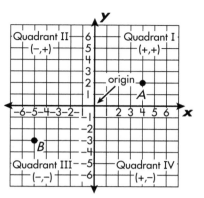

Plot each ordered pair on Grid 1.

Grid 1

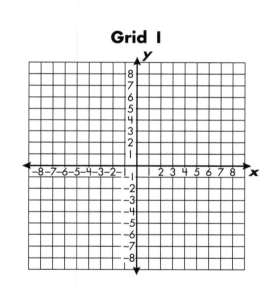

1. $A(-5, 3)$ $B(-2, 4)$

2. $C(-2, -5)$ $D(3, -3)$

3. $E(1, 7)$ $F(2, 3)$

4. $G(4, 5)$ $H(5, -2)$

5. $I(8, -3)$ $J(-4, -4)$

Write where each lettered point is located on Grid 2.

Grid 2

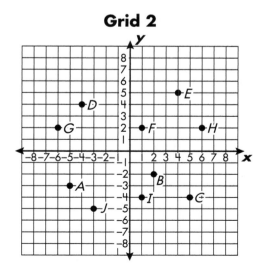

6. $A(\_\_\_\_\_)$ $B(\_\_\_\_\_)$

7. $C(\_\_\_\_\_)$ $D(\_\_\_\_\_)$

8. $E(\_\_\_\_\_)$ $F(\_\_\_\_\_)$

9. $G(\_\_\_\_\_)$ $H(\_\_\_\_\_)$

10. $I(\_\_\_\_\_)$ $J(\_\_\_\_\_)$

Lesson 9.12 Plotting Ordered Pairs

Write where each lettered point is located on Grid 1.

Grid 1

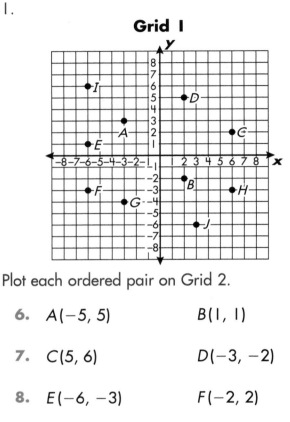

1. A(_____)   B(_____)

2. C(_____)   D(_____)

3. E(_____)   F(_____)

4. G(_____)   H(_____)

5. I(_____)   J(_____)

Grid 2

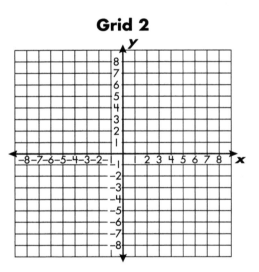

Plot each ordered pair on Grid 2.

6. A(−5, 5)   B(1, 1)

7. C(5, 6)   D(−3, −2)

8. E(−6, −3)   F(−2, 2)

9. G(5, −2)   H(1, −5)

10. I(2, 5)   J(−4, −5)

In the following problems, each set of points forms a shape.
Graph the set of points on Grid 3. Name the shape.

Grid 3

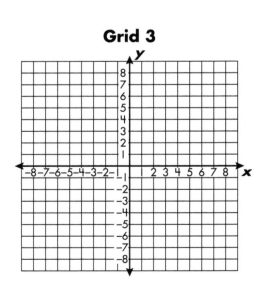

11. A(−6, 5), B(−2, 5), C(−3, 2), D(−7, 2)

   What is the shape? _____

12. E(1, 3), F(4, 7), G(7, 3)

   What is the shape? _____

13. H(−3, −2), I(3, −2), J(3, −8), K(−3, −8)

   What is the shape? _____

Lesson 9.13 Creating Function Tables

A **function** is a rule for how two variables relate. For each value of **x** (the domain), there is only one value of **y** (the range). For example, if $y = x + 6$, whatever x is, y **must** be greater than x by the number 6.

A **function table** shows the values for each pair of variables as the result of the particular function.

Complete each function table for the given functions.

1.

$y = x + 6$

x	y
−10	−4
−2	4
−0	
3	
5	
8	

$y = 2x − 2$

x	y
0	
1	
3	
5	
8	
10	

$y = x − 7$

x	y
0	
2	
5	
7	
10	
15	

2.

$y = x^2 − 3$

x	y
−3	
−2	
−1	
0	
3	

$y = \frac{x}{4}$

x	y
−8	
−4	
4	
8	
12	

$y = \frac{x}{2} − 1$

x	y
−10	
−6	
−2	
2	
4	

3.

$y = 3x + 2$

x	y
−3	
−2	
0	
2	
5	

$y = (2 + x) ÷ 3$

x	y
−8	
−5	
1	
4	
7	

$y = \frac{x}{3} + 3$

x	y
−9	
−6	
−3	
3	
6	

Lesson 9.13 Creating Function Tables

Read each function. Experiment with values of x. Look for whole number values of x that create a whole number value for y (positive or negative). Once you find 5 numbers for x, fill in the function table for x and for y. Put the values of x in numerical order.

1. $y = \frac{x}{2} - 7$ $y = \frac{x}{3} - 7$ $y = \frac{x + 4}{5}$

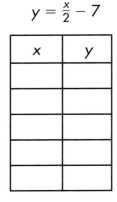 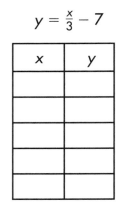 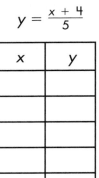

x	y

x	y

x	y

2. $y = 9x - 3$ $y = \frac{x^2}{2}$ $y = 2 - \frac{x}{6}$

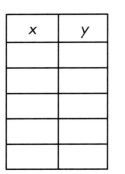 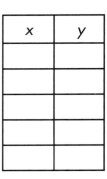

x	y

x	y

x	y

Read each function table. See if you can identify the function it represents.

3.

x	y
−2	−3
−1	−2
0	−1
1	0
2	1

$y = $ _____

x	y
0	0
1	−3
2	−6
3	−9
5	−15

$y = $ _____

x	y
−4	−1
−2	0
0	1
2	2
4	3

$y = $ _____

x	y
−3	9
−2	4
0	0
1	1
2	4

$y = $ _____

Lesson 9.14 Graphing Linear Equations

A **linear equation** is an equation that creates a straight line when graphed on a coordinate plane. To graph a linear function, create a function table with at least 3 ordered pairs. Then, plot these ordered pairs on a coordinate plane. Draw a line through the points. In the table are some points for this linear function:

$$y = \frac{x}{2} + 1$$

These points are plotted on the line graph at the far right.

x	y
-2	0
0	1
2	2
4	3

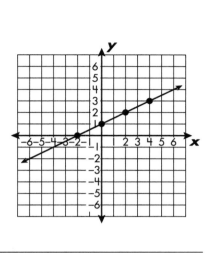

Complete the function table for each function. Then, graph the function.

a

b

1. $y = x - 3$

x	y

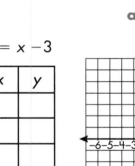

$y = 2x + 1$

x	y

2. $y = \frac{x}{2} - 2$

x	y

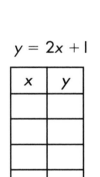

$y = \frac{x - 2}{3}$

x	y

Lesson 9.14 Graphing Linear Equations

Graph each linear function.

	a	b

1.
$y = 2x - 4$

$y = \frac{2x}{3}$

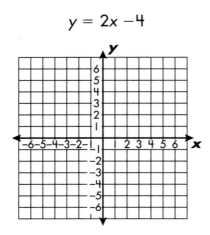
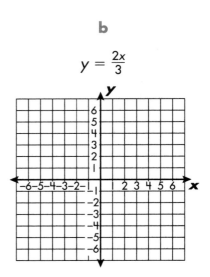

2.
$y = \frac{x}{4} + 2$

$y = 3x - 3$

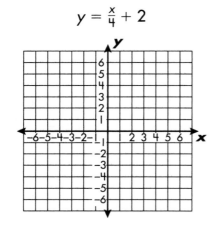
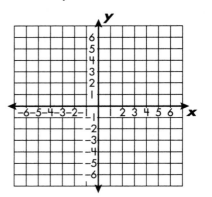

3.
$y = 2x + 1$

$y = 3 - \frac{x}{2}$

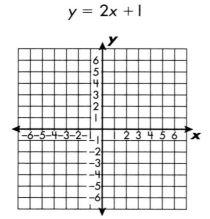
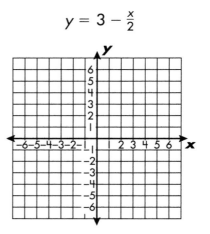

Check What You Learned

Preparing for Algebra

Rewrite each number in standard notation.

	a	b	c

1. 3.04×10^{-3} _____ 4.26×10^2 _____ 8.1×10^{-4} _____

2. 6.5×10^5 _____ 2.4×10^{-2} _____ 7.15×10 _____

Evaluate each expression if $a = 6$ and $b = 8$. Underline the step you did first.

3. $a^2 + b(3 + a)$ ____ $3 \times b \div 2 + 4$ ____ $8a \div 3 - 2b$ ____

4. $8b \div (a + 10)$ ____ $2 + 3 \times a - b$ ____ $18 - a \div 2 \times 3$ ____

Find the value of the variable in each expression.

5. $12 + n = 37$ _____ $\frac{a}{3} = 15$ _____ $3x + 2 = 56$ _____

6. $p - 17 = 26$ _____ $9 - \frac{m}{4} = 4$ _____ $q + 27 = 35$ _____

7. $7b - 5 = 44$ _____ $n \times 4 = 52$ _____ $\frac{e}{8} + 4 = 11$ _____

Rewrite each multiplication or division expression using a base and an exponent.

8. $8^2 \times 8^3 = $ _____ $5^{-6} \times 5^{-2} = $ _____ $6^2 \times 6^4 = $ _____

9. $4^{-1} \times 4^3 = $ _____ $3^4 \div 3^{-3} = $ _____ $12^{-2} \div 12^4 = $ _____

Complete the table for each function. Then, graph the function.

	a		b

10. $y = \frac{x}{4}$

x	y

$y = 3x - 2$

x	y

Check What You Learned

Preparing for Algebra

Write an equation to illustrate each property.

11. The Commutative Property of Multiplication: _____

12. The Associative Property of Addition: _____

13. The Distributive Property: _____

14. Write where each lettered point is located on Grid 1.

    A(_____), B(_____)
    C(_____), D(_____)

15. Plot each ordered pair on Grid 1.

    E(5, 2)   F(3, −2)
    G(−2, 3)   H(1, −3)

Grid 1

Translate each sentence into an equation. Use n for an unknown number.

16. Nine less than a number is 23. _____

17. Eight times a number, increased by 3, is 28. _____

SHOW YOUR WORK

Solve each problem by writing a variable equation.

18. Patrick paid $72.60 for some computer games. Each game cost $24.20. How many games did Patrick buy? What is the unknown number? _____
    Equation: _____ n = _____

    18.

19. Noelle and Gina have a combined height of 130 inches. Noelle is 4 inches taller than Gina. How tall is each girl? Let n stand for Noelle's height.
    Equation: _____
    Noelle is _____ inches tall. Gina is _____ inches tall.

    19.

Final Test Chapters 1-9

Answer each question using letters to name each line or angle.

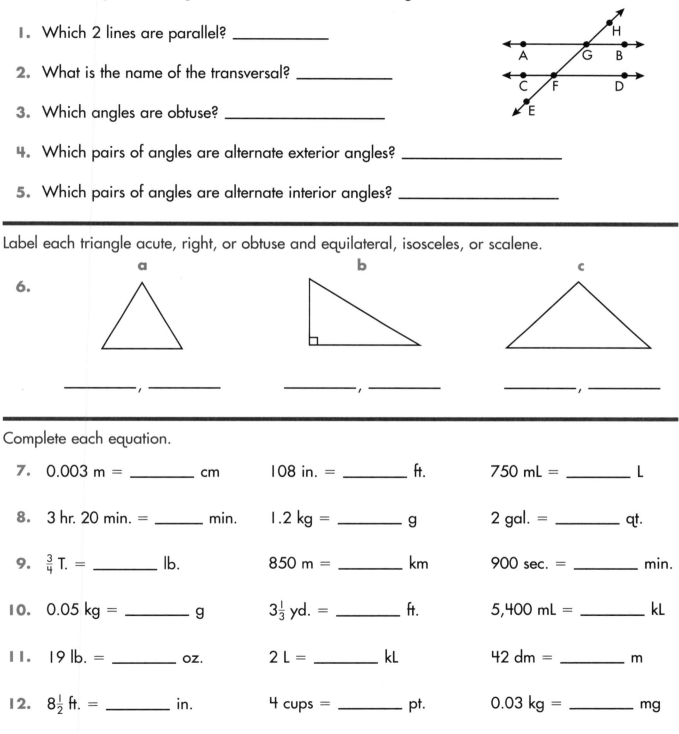

1. Which 2 lines are parallel? _____

2. What is the name of the transversal? _____

3. Which angles are obtuse? _____

4. Which pairs of angles are alternate exterior angles? _____

5. Which pairs of angles are alternate interior angles? _____

Label each triangle acute, right, or obtuse and equilateral, isosceles, or scalene.

         a   b   c

6.

_____ , _____   _____ , _____   _____ , _____

Complete each equation.

7.   0.003 m = _____ cm   108 in. = _____ ft.   750 mL = _____ L

8.   3 hr. 20 min. = _____ min.   1.2 kg = _____ g   2 gal. = _____ qt.

9. $\frac{3}{4}$ T. = _____ lb.   850 m = _____ km   900 sec. = _____ min.

10.   0.05 kg = _____ g $3\frac{1}{3}$ yd. = _____ ft.   5,400 mL = _____ kL

11.   19 lb. = _____ oz.   2 L = _____ kL   42 dm = _____ m

12. $8\frac{1}{2}$ ft. = _____ in.   4 cups = _____ pt.   0.03 kg = _____ mg

Spectrum Math
Grade 8

Final Test
Chapters 1-9
147

CHAPTERS 1-9 FINAL TEST

Final Test   Chapters 1–9

Find the area and perimeter of each figure.

a	b	c

13.

$A =$ _____ in.^{2} $P =$ _____ in. $A =$ _____ m^2 $P =$ _____ m $A =$ _____ ft.^{2} $P =$ _____ ft.

Complete the chart for each circle. Use 3.14 for π. Round to the nearest hundredth.

	a Radius	b Diameter	c Circumference	d Area
14.	_____ cm	9 cm	_____ cm	_____ cm^2
15.	5 in.	_____ in.	_____ in.	_____ in.^{2}
16.	_____ m	1.4 m	_____ m	_____ m^2

Complete each sentence.

	a	b
17.	25 is 125% of _____.	44% of 76 is _____.
18.	106 is _____% of 53.	14 is 5% of _____.
19.	68% of 120 is _____.	87 is _____% of 116.

Fill in the missing information about each loan. Round to cents.

	Principal	Rate	Time	Compounded	Interest	Total Amount
20.	$600	_____	2 yr.	no	$72	$672
21.	_____	7.5%	1 yr.	no	$90	_____
22.	$850	7%	_____ yr.	no	$178.50	$1,028.50
23.	$1,000	8%	1 yr.	quarterly	_____	_____
24.	$1,200	6%	3 mo.	monthly	_____	_____

Final Test Chapters 1-9

Each pair of triangles is similar. Find the missing side lengths.

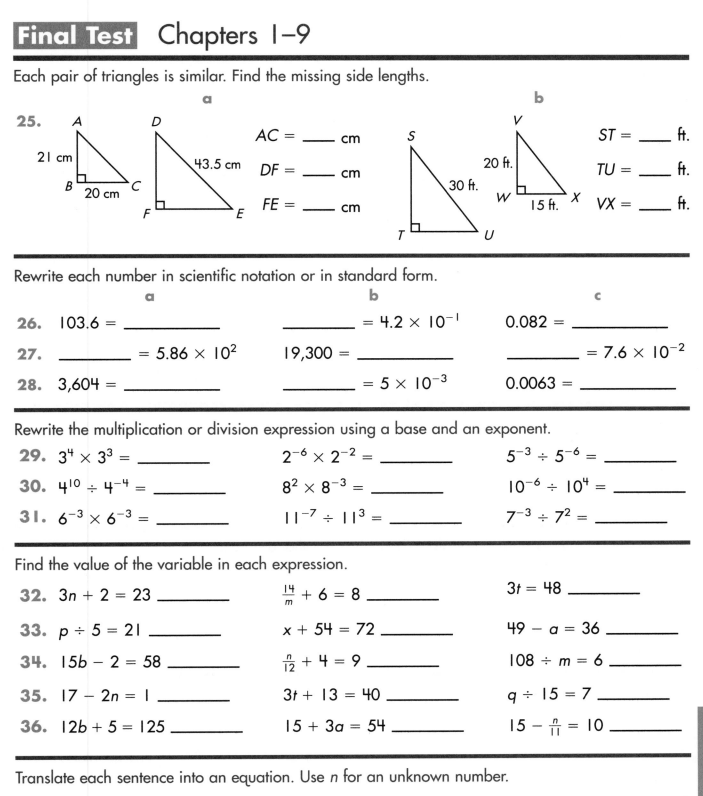

a

25.

$AC =$ _____ cm

$DF =$ _____ cm

$FE =$ _____ cm

b

$ST =$ _____ ft.

$TU =$ _____ ft.

$VX =$ _____ ft.

Rewrite each number in scientific notation or in standard form.

a	b	c

26. $103.6 =$ _____   _____ $= 4.2 \times 10^{-1}$ $0.082 =$ _____

27. _____ $= 5.86 \times 10^2$ $19,300 =$ _____   _____ $= 7.6 \times 10^{-2}$

28. $3,604 =$ _____   _____ $= 5 \times 10^{-3}$ $0.0063 =$ _____

Rewrite the multiplication or division expression using a base and an exponent.

29. $3^4 \times 3^3 =$ _____ $2^{-6} \times 2^{-2} =$ _____ $5^{-3} \div 5^{-6} =$ _____

30. $4^{10} \div 4^{-4} =$ _____ $8^2 \times 8^{-3} =$ _____ $10^{-6} \div 10^4 =$ _____

31. $6^{-3} \times 6^{-3} =$ _____ $11^{-7} \div 11^3 =$ _____ $7^{-3} \div 7^2 =$ _____

Find the value of the variable in each expression.

32. $3n + 2 = 23$ _____ $\frac{14}{m} + 6 = 8$ _____ $3t = 48$ _____

33. $p \div 5 = 21$ _____ $x + 54 = 72$ _____ $49 - a = 36$ _____

34. $15b - 2 = 58$ _____ $\frac{n}{12} + 4 = 9$ _____ $108 \div m = 6$ _____

35. $17 - 2n = 1$ _____ $3t + 13 = 40$ _____ $q \div 15 = 7$ _____

36. $12b + 5 = 125$ _____ $15 + 3a = 54$ _____ $15 - \frac{n}{11} = 10$ _____

Translate each sentence into an equation. Use *n* for an unknown number.

37. Half of a number, decreased by 7, is 3. _____

38. A number increased by 13 is 24. _____

Spectrum Math
Grade 8

Final Test
Chapters 1-9

149

CHAPTERS 1-9 FINAL TEST

Final Test Chapters 1–9

Add or subtract.

	a	b	c	d
39.	$\begin{array}{r} 4\,3\,7\,1\,0\,5 \\ 5\,2\,1\,0\,7\,6 \\ 1\,0\,3\,9\,4\,9 \\ 7\,1\,2\,3\,0\,6 \\ +\,5\,2\,3\,0\,3\,6 \\ \hline \end{array}$	$\begin{array}{r} 12\frac{2}{3} \\ 9\frac{3}{4} \\ +13\frac{5}{6} \\ \hline \end{array}$	$\begin{array}{r} 1\,2.0\,5\,7\,4 \\ 3\,6.7\,0\,1 \\ 4\,2.1\,0\,1\,7 \\ 3\,3.5\,2 \\ +\,8\,1.8\,2\,5 \\ \hline \end{array}$	$\begin{array}{r} 11\frac{1}{3} \\ 5\frac{1}{4} \\ +\ 6\frac{3}{5} \\ \hline \end{array}$
40.	$\begin{array}{r} 12\frac{1}{3} \\ -\ 8\frac{7}{9} \\ \hline \end{array}$	$\begin{array}{r} 1\,2\,0.9\,6 \\ -\ \ 9\,8.8\,7\,2 \\ \hline \end{array}$	$\begin{array}{r} 4\,4\,7\,6\,1\,3\,2 \\ -\,4\,3\,8\,1\,0\,8\,5 \\ \hline \end{array}$	$\begin{array}{r} 3\,8.0\,5\,6 \\ -\,1\,9.7\,2\,3\,1 \\ \hline \end{array}$

Multiply or divide.

41. $\begin{array}{r} 2\,3.7\,2\,5 \\ \times\ \ \ \ 1.3\,6 \\ \hline \end{array}$ $\qquad 0.2\,3\overline{)\,2.8\,9\,8}$ $\qquad 2\frac{1}{8} \times 12\frac{1}{3} =$ $\qquad 3\frac{1}{4} \div \frac{7}{9} =$

Cross-multiply to check each proportion. Circle the ones that are true.

42. $\frac{14}{16} = \frac{21}{24}$ $\qquad \frac{16}{18} = \frac{20}{24}$ $\qquad \frac{15}{18} = \frac{25}{30}$ $\qquad \frac{18}{21} = \frac{42}{49}$

43. $\frac{7}{9} = \frac{21}{30}$ $\qquad \frac{8}{6} = \frac{20}{15}$ $\qquad \frac{9}{12} = \frac{20}{25}$ $\qquad \frac{16}{10} = \frac{20}{14}$

Solve for n in each proportion.

	a	b	c
44.	$\frac{n}{6} = \frac{30}{36}$ _____	$\frac{15}{n} = \frac{45}{42}$ _____	$\frac{10}{15} = \frac{n}{12}$ _____
45.	$\frac{12}{10} = \frac{30}{n}$ _____	$\frac{n}{12} = \frac{8}{48}$ _____	$\frac{14}{n} = \frac{84}{144}$ _____

Spectrum Math
Grade 8
150

CHAPTERS 1–9 FINAL TEST

Final Test
Chapters 1-9

Final Test   Chapters 1–9

Complete the frequency table with the missing data. Then, answer the questions.

Number of Pets My Classmates Have

	No. of Pets	Frequency	Cumulative Frequency	Relative Frequency
46.	0	5		5/28
47.	1	10		5/14
48.	2	7		1/4
49.	3	5		5/28
50.	4 or more	1		1/28

51. How many students were polled? _____

52. What was the most frequent response? _____ How many gave that response? _____

Answer the questions by interpreting the data.

Science Test Scores

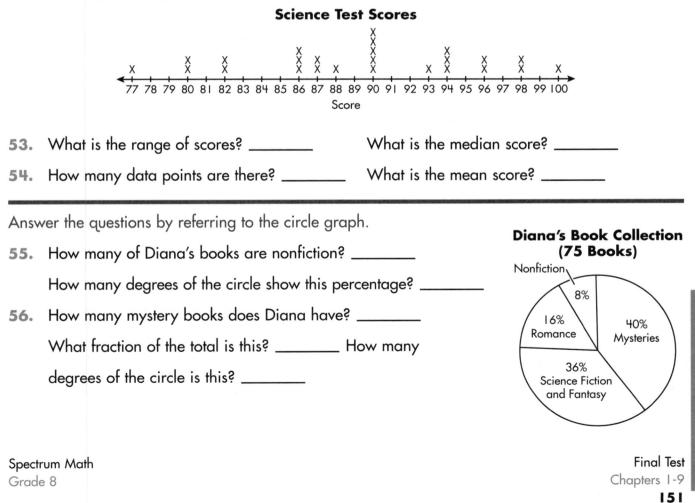

Score

53. What is the range of scores? _____   What is the median score? _____

54. How many data points are there? _____   What is the mean score? _____

Answer the questions by referring to the circle graph.

55. How many of Diana's books are nonfiction? _____

How many degrees of the circle show this percentage? _____

56. How many mystery books does Diana have? _____

What fraction of the total is this? _____ How many

degrees of the circle is this? _____

Diana's Book Collection (75 Books)

Nonfiction
8%
16% Romance
40% Mysteries
36% Science Fiction and Fantasy

Spectrum Math
Grade 8

Final Test
Chapters 1-9

CHAPTERS 1-9 FINAL TEST

151

Final Test Chapters 1–9

Complete the function table for each function. Then, graph the function.

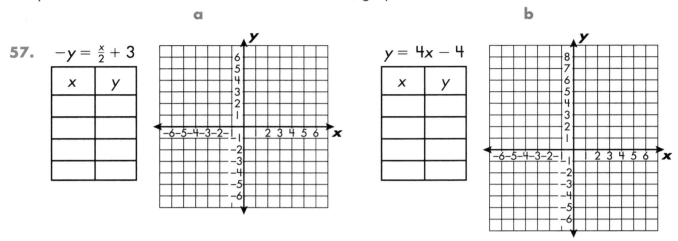

a

57. $-y = \frac{x}{2} + 3$

x	y

b

$y = 4x - 4$

x	y

Find the surface area or volume of each solid figure. Use 3.14 for π. Round to the nearest hundredth.

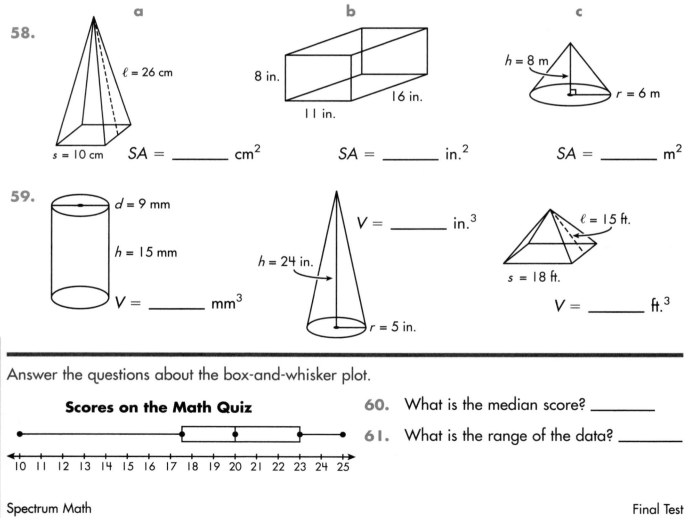

a

58.

$\ell = 26$ cm

$s = 10$ cm $SA = $ _____ cm^2

b

8 in.

16 in.

11 in.

$SA = $ _____ in.^{2}

c

$h = 8$ m

$r = 6$ m

$SA = $ _____ m^2

59.

$d = 9$ mm

$h = 15$ mm

$V = $ _____ mm^3

$h = 24$ in.

$r = 5$ in.

$V = $ _____ in.^{3}

$\ell = 15$ ft.

$s = 18$ ft.

$V = $ _____ ft.^{3}

Answer the questions about the box-and-whisker plot.

Scores on the Math Quiz

10 11 12 13 14 15 16 17 18 19 20 21 22 23 24 25

60. What is the median score? _____

61. What is the range of the data? _____

Spectrum Math
Grade 8
152

CHAPTERS 1-9 FINAL TEST

Final Test
Chapters 1-9

Scoring Record for Posttests, Mid-Test, and Final Test

Chapter Posttest	Your Score	Performance			
		Excellent	Very Good	Fair	Needs Improvement
1	____ of 30	29–30	25–28	19–24	18 or fewer
2	____ of 32	31–32	27–30	20–26	19 or fewer
3	____ of 45	43–45	37–42	28–36	27 or fewer
4	____ of 51	48–51	42–47	32–41	31 or fewer
5	____ of 46	44–46	38–43	29–37	28 or fewer
6	____ of 24	23–24	20–22	15–19	14 or fewer
7	____ of 40	38–40	33–37	25–32	24 or fewer
8	____ of 30	29–30	25–28	19–24	18 or fewer
9	____ of 70	66–70	57–65	43–56	42 or fewer
Mid-Test	____ of 104	98–104	84–97	63–83	62 or fewer
Final Test	____ of 174	162–174	140–161	105–139	104 or fewer

Record your test score in the Your Score column. See where your score falls in the Performance columns. Your score is based on the total number of required responses. If your score is fair or needs improvement, review the chapter material.

Grade 8 Answers

Chapter 1

Pretest, page 1

	a	b	c	d	e
1.	2000525	$11\frac{1}{12}$	202.483	$1\frac{11}{14}$	372915
2.	615946	0.312	$2\frac{5}{8}$	9.747	6.6341
3.	27.442	$2\frac{11}{24}$	106992	$10\frac{17}{20}$	24.5256
4.	$7\frac{2}{9}$	$3\frac{1}{5}$	$3\frac{1}{21}$	3.508	
5.	7.8	11.955051	1322592	903r381	
6.	1630146	4.27	$2\frac{19}{48}$	1884r2	

Pretest, page 2

7. $59.15 8. $6\frac{23}{60}$ 9. $11\frac{1}{4}$ 10. $7,563.83

11. $6,045 12. $7.75 13. 595; 4

Lesson 1.1, page 3

	a	b	c	d	e
1.	46	539	13299	58181	1327514
2.	150	1297	8034	111263	1934919
3.	202	1452	12671	128336	1533361
4.	136	2169	23443	179402	2777762
5.	195	2700	28736	296992	2424707

Lesson 1.2, page 4

	a	b	c	d	e
1.	3	538	2383	14179	334598
2.	67	355	546	78719	144663
3.	38	833	2803	7466	461278
4.	48	563	6883	38954	72159
5.	10	183	6367	11678	508147
6.	39	172	951	47620	647975

Lesson 1.3, page 5

	a	b	c	d	e
1.	174	456	1855	3332	12888
2.	1386	7728	26892	1926	18816
3.	1539	329680	27459	219232	169750
4.	149513	170847	2065308	4308032	1830904

Lesson 1.4, page 6

	a	b	c	d
1.	79r5	17r22	7r32	212r3
2.	114r3	18r38	4r172	532r5
3.	13668	2459r3	443r12	509r33
4.	29r29	112r4	506r91	475r4

Lesson 1.5, page 7

	a	b	c	d	e
1.	55	0.307	191.65	7.239	171.406
2.	1.75	8.367	38.292	4.3385	66.6285
3.	2.54	6.25	393.87	5.0478	705.365
4.	5.8	50.31	14.3214	22.88	2.6335
5.	66.7	4.84	70.576	126.413	548.343

Lesson 1.6, page 8

	a	b	c	d	e
1.	38.15	126.44	9.272	69.495	0.6808
2.	25.284	114.1	57.648	4.095	7.242
3.	3.094	137.268	5.17935	0.9016	207.225
4.	223.17	191.557	1.1607	7086.1	2.06988
5.	1.0863	233.5	0.1182	8.449	0.71816

Lesson 1.7, page 9

	a	b	c	d
1.	35	148	1.4	36
2.	9.75	1.12	8.80	512
3.	456	257	1.26	65
4.	1.06	0.89	4.36	5.36

Lesson 1.8, page 10

	a	b	c
1.	$\frac{1}{5}$	$3\frac{1}{6}$	$\frac{5}{7}$
2.	$\frac{7}{9}$	$\frac{3}{5}$	$3\frac{3}{8}$
3.	$7\frac{5}{8}$	$\frac{2}{3}$	$\frac{3}{7}$
4.	$\frac{3}{5}$	$4\frac{2}{5}$	$\frac{4}{9}$
5.	$\frac{2}{3}$	$\frac{8}{9}$	$6\frac{1}{4}$
6.	$5\frac{6}{7}$	$\frac{3}{5}$	$\frac{1}{2}$

Lesson 1.9, page 11

	a	b	c	d
1.	$\frac{38}{7}$	$9\frac{1}{5}$	$4\frac{1}{5}$	$\frac{26}{9}$
2.	$\frac{43}{9}$	$2\frac{2}{5}$	$\frac{11}{3}$	$1\frac{11}{12}$
3.	$\frac{27}{45}, \frac{20}{45}$	$\frac{21}{36}, \frac{20}{36}$	$\frac{45}{50}, \frac{36}{50}$	
4.	$\frac{8}{14}, \frac{7}{14}$	$\frac{8}{36}, \frac{15}{36}$	$\frac{15}{40}, \frac{28}{40}$	

Lesson 1.10, page 12

	a	b	c	d
1.	$10\frac{1}{24}$	$1\frac{5}{18}$	$1\frac{17}{20}$	$1\frac{11}{16}$
2.	$6\frac{29}{40}$	$1\frac{19}{48}$	$1\frac{7}{30}$	$\frac{19}{36}$
3.	$5\frac{1}{12}$	$7\frac{7}{8}$	$\frac{17}{40}$	$1\frac{49}{60}$
4.	$8\frac{9}{40}$	$2\frac{1}{20}$	$7\frac{17}{18}$	$3\frac{37}{40}$

Lesson 1.11, page 13

	a	b	c
1.	$\frac{20}{21}$	$\frac{24}{77}$	$27\frac{11}{15}$
2.	$24\frac{4}{15}$	$\frac{1}{5}$	$\frac{1}{84}$
3.	$\frac{2}{3}$	$5\frac{1}{7}$	$4\frac{23}{30}$
4.	$3\frac{45}{49}$	$\frac{7}{54}$	$1\frac{1}{10}$
5.	$1\frac{1}{2}$	$\frac{55}{78}$	$3\frac{1}{9}$
6.	$2\frac{7}{9}$	$\frac{17}{80}$	$\frac{16}{105}$

Grade 8 Answers

Lesson 1.12, page 14

	a	b	c
1.	$1\frac{1}{3}$	60	$2\frac{5}{8}$
2.	3	$5\frac{2}{5}$	$\frac{3}{5}$
3.	$\frac{5}{18}$	$\frac{5}{21}$	$\frac{17}{24}$
4.	$\frac{8}{9}$	$5\frac{1}{2}$	$7\frac{1}{2}$
5.	$10\frac{2}{3}$	$\frac{16}{49}$	$2\frac{1}{42}$
6.	$\frac{13}{16}$	6	$\frac{7}{32}$

Posttest, page 15

	a	b	c	d	e
1.	1109548	172.061	162305	233.793	$3\frac{23}{24}$
2.	44.187	112966	42.985	101.435	49489
3.	$13\frac{1}{4}$	$9\frac{11}{12}$	$6\frac{5}{8}$	$1\frac{13}{15}$	$2\frac{2}{15}$
4.	$6\frac{9}{14}$	$13\frac{3}{10}$	$\frac{36}{49}$	$3\frac{3}{4}$	
5.	8697r14	12950574	709.6	3776.4975	

Posttest, page 16

6. $117.25   7. 30   8. $1\frac{1}{30}$ gal.   9. $55.97

10. $6,277.90   11. $\frac{5}{9}$ 12. 42 hr.

Chapter 2

Chapter 2 Pretest, page 17

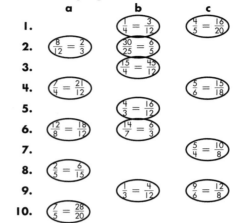

	a	b	c
1.	$\frac{4}{7} = \frac{12}{21}$	$\frac{15}{9} = \frac{10}{6}$	
2.			$\frac{9}{7} = \frac{27}{21}$
3.	$\frac{8}{6} = \frac{12}{9}$	$\frac{9}{6} = \frac{15}{10}$	$\frac{14}{12} = \frac{21}{18}$
4.			$\frac{9}{12} = \frac{15}{20}$
5.	$n = 20$	$n = 14$	$n = 8$
6.	$n = 7$	$n = 12$	$n = 39$
7.	$n = 30$	$n = 48$	$n = 3$
8.	$n = 15$	$n = 25$	$n = 6$

Chapter 2 Pretest, page 18

9. $8
10. 20
11. $3
12. 9
13. 18
14. $3
15. 28
16. $6

Lesson 2.1, page 19

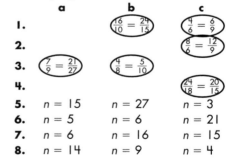

	a	b	c
1.		$\frac{1}{4} = \frac{3}{12}$	$\frac{4}{5} = \frac{16}{20}$
2.	$\frac{8}{12} = \frac{2}{3}$	$\frac{30}{25} = \frac{6}{5}$	
3.		$\frac{15}{4} = \frac{45}{12}$	
4.	$\frac{7}{4} = \frac{21}{12}$		$\frac{5}{6} = \frac{15}{18}$
5.		$\frac{4}{3} = \frac{16}{12}$	
6.	$\frac{12}{8} = \frac{18}{12}$	$\frac{14}{7} = \frac{6}{3}$	
7.			$\frac{5}{4} = \frac{10}{8}$
8.	$\frac{2}{5} = \frac{6}{15}$		
9.		$\frac{1}{3} = \frac{4}{12}$	$\frac{9}{6} = \frac{12}{8}$
10.	$\frac{7}{5} = \frac{28}{20}$		

Lesson 2.2, page 20

	a	b	c
1.	$n = 12$	$n = 15$	$n = 4$
2.	$n = 18$	$n = 10$	$n = 3$
3.	$n = 12$	$n = 4$	$n = 15$
4.	$n = 6$	$n = 20$	$n = 50$
5.	$n = 15$	$n = 9$	$n = 77$
6.	$n = 12$	$n = 35$	$n = 4$

Lesson 2.3, page 21

1. 35 min.   2. 16 mi.   3. 91 min.   4. 15 mi.
5. 42 min.

Lesson 2.4, page 22

1. 6 gal.   2. 3 gal.   3. 270 mi.   4. 54 mi.
5. 36 gal.   6. 15 gal.

Posttest, page 23

	a	b	c
1.		$\frac{16}{10} = \frac{24}{15}$	$\frac{4}{6} = \frac{6}{9}$
2.			$\frac{8}{6} = \frac{12}{9}$
3.	$\frac{7}{9} = \frac{21}{27}$	$\frac{4}{8} = \frac{5}{10}$	
4.			$\frac{24}{18} = \frac{20}{15}$
5.	$n = 15$	$n = 27$	$n = 3$
6.	$n = 5$	$n = 6$	$n = 21$
7.	$n = 6$	$n = 16$	$n = 15$
8.	$n = 14$	$n = 9$	$n = 4$

Posttest, page 24

9. 4   10. $45   11. 6
12. $24   13. $180   14. 15
15. $132   16. $50

Grade 8 Answers

Chapter 3

Pretest, page 25
1. $157.50; $857.50   **2.** 6%   **3.** $900; $990
4. $92.73; $1,092.73   **5.** $2\frac{1}{2}$ yrs.
6. $65.95; $865.95

	a	b	c	d
7.	0.15	$\frac{3}{20}$	0.22	$\frac{11}{50}$
8.	1.2	$1\frac{1}{5}$	0.54	$\frac{27}{50}$
9.	0.36	$\frac{9}{25}$	2.05	$2\frac{1}{20}$
10.	12%	1%	40%	
11.	406%	12.5%	60%	
12.	108; 45	**13.** 72; 25%	**14.** 24; 140	
15.	75%; 20.8	**16.** 60.5; 140%		

Pretest, page 26
17. $750   **18.** 198   **19.** $1368   **20.** 70 in.
21. $538.44   **22.** 87.5%   **23.** $0.60

Lesson 3.1, page 27

	a	b	c	d
1.	0.19	$\frac{19}{100}$	0.44	$\frac{11}{25}$
2.	0.36	$\frac{9}{25}$	3.45	$3\frac{9}{20}$
3.	0.55	$\frac{11}{20}$	1.1	$1\frac{1}{10}$
4.	0.2	$\frac{1}{5}$	0.56	$\frac{14}{25}$
5.	0.38	$\frac{19}{50}$	0.4	$\frac{2}{5}$
6.	0.86	$\frac{43}{50}$	2.75	$2\frac{3}{4}$
7.	0.15	$\frac{3}{20}$	2.05	$2\frac{1}{20}$
8.	0.27	$\frac{27}{100}$	0.95	$\frac{19}{20}$
9.	2.3	$2\frac{3}{10}$	0.8	$\frac{4}{5}$
10.	1.5	$1\frac{1}{2}$	1.54	$1\frac{27}{50}$
11.	0.18	$\frac{9}{50}$	0.3	$\frac{3}{10}$
12.	0.16	$\frac{4}{25}$	1.08	$1\frac{2}{25}$

Lesson 3.2, page 28

	a	b	c
1.	$\frac{1}{10}$	125%	$\frac{17}{50}$
2.	80%	$\frac{19}{20}$	$1\frac{3}{10}$
3.	$\frac{3}{8}$	260%	$\frac{13}{20}$
4.	40%	$1\frac{3}{4}$	15%
5.	$2\frac{1}{4}$	17%	20%
6.	12%	$\frac{1}{8}$	110%
7.	$\frac{9}{20}$	60%	$\frac{12}{25}$
8.	$1\frac{1}{20}$	209%	108%
9.	$87\frac{1}{2}$%	$4\frac{1}{2}$	$\frac{4}{25}$
10.	$1\frac{7}{50}$	75%	290%

Lesson 3.3, page 29

	a	b	c
1.	0.195	7%	1.2
2.	45%	0.115	22.5%
3.	0.2475	140%	0.08
4.	62.5%	1.1%	0.11
5.	3.65	0.04	0.025
6.	190%	4.6%	0.36
7.	0.0875	180%	0.023
8.	125%	0.5	0.675
9.	4.36%	1.15%	3.6%
10.	50%	0.1875	102%

Lesson 3.4, page 30

	a	b
1.	20	9.9
2.	10.24	12.32
3.	11.4	6.6
4.	2.1	3.15
5.	6.3	4.255
6.	69.12	36
7.	8	28
8.	53.55	84
9.	31.05	30
10.	20.79	0.54

Lesson 3.4, page 31

	a	b
1.	60%	20%
2.	15%	64%
3.	15%	40%
4.	10%	90%
5.	75%	40%
6.	20%	150%
7.	30%	200%
8.	37.5%	125%
9.	50%	25%
10.	120%	80%

Lesson 3.4, page 32

	a	b
1.	12	60
2.	48	100
3.	312.5	150
4.	50	96
5.	48	140
6.	100	60
7.	180	10
8.	56	50
9.	2,000	6
10.	50	400

Grade 8 Answers

Lesson 3.5, page 33
1. 17% 2. $35.75 3. 15% 4. 1,150 5. 18%
6. 69 7. 4.8 8. 280

Lesson 3.6, page 34
1. $262.50 2. $165 3. $30 4. $481.25
5. $337.50 6. $784 7. $68 8. $247.50
9. $253 10. $204.75

Lesson 3.6, page 35
1. 7% 2. 2 yrs. 3. $1,450 4. $2,117.50
5. $1\frac{1}{2}$ yrs. 6. $9,000 7. $7\frac{1}{2}$% 8. $8,31.25
9. $1,200 10. $6\frac{1}{2}$%

Lesson 3.7, page 36
1. $1,349.84 2. $842.70 3. $2,311.25
4. $1,823.26 5. $655.64 6. $749.86
7. $1,192.52 8. $449.95

Lesson 3.7, page 37
1. $1,125.51 2. $526.71 3. $765.10
4. $2,154.27 5. $1,518.83 6. $893.42
7. $1,236.27 8. $632.82

Lesson 3.8, page 38
1. $256; $1,856
2. 8%
3. $650
4. $476.41; $484; 7%
5. $212.28
6. $1

Posttest, page 39

	a	b	c	d
1.	0.24	$\frac{6}{25}$	1.1	$1\frac{1}{10}$
2.	0.37	$\frac{37}{100}$	0.55	$\frac{11}{20}$
3.	0.06	$\frac{3}{50}$	2.35	$2\frac{7}{20}$
4.	16%	5%	60%	
5.	80%	$87\frac{1}{2}$%	130%	

6. 80; 84% 7. 15; 160 8. 5%; 27.2
9. 72; $12\frac{1}{2}$% 10. 60; 4.4 11. 16%; 94.5
12. $270; $1,470 13. $500; $600 14. 2 yrs.
15. $71.87; 1,071.87 16. 8%

Posttest, page 40
17. 87.5%
18. $701.92
19. 155
20. $858
21. 7%
22. 70
23. $0.93

Chapter 4

Pretest, page 41

	a	b	c
1.	115 oz.	84 in.	12 c.
2.	135 min.	3 qt.	$4\frac{1}{2}$ lb.
3.	$9\frac{3}{4}$ ft.	$3\frac{1}{2}$ hr.	62 in.
4.	2 qt.	148 oz.	84 min.
5.	1,500 lb.	$1\frac{2}{3}$ hr.	10 c.
6.	28 ft.	5 lb.	545 sec.
7.	$4\frac{1}{2}$ qt.	120 in.	58 oz.
8.	$10\frac{1}{2}$ min.	20 c.	152 in.

9a. 6 oz. 9b. 39 min.
9c. 6 yd. 9d. 5 qt. 1 pt.
10a. 2 ft. 8 in. 10b. 8 qt. or 2 gal.
10c. 12 min. 5 sec. 10d. 8 lb.
11a. 12 ft. 2 in. 11b. 1 lb. 9 oz.
11c. 2 qt. 1 pt. 11d. 1 hr. 5 min.
12a. 16 min. 12b. 2 pt.
12c. 8 lb. 7 oz. 12d. 3 ft. 8. in.

Pretest, page 42
13. 2 gal. 1 qt. 14. 270 min. 15. 7 lb. 4 oz.
16. $5\frac{1}{3}$ yd. 17. 1 hr. 25 min. 18. 1 pt. 1 c. or 3 c.
19. 5 ft. 10 in.

Lesson 4.1, page 43

	a	b	c
1.	2 yd.	$3\frac{1}{3}$ yd.	33 in.
2.	880 yd.	$19\frac{1}{2}$ ft.	$1\frac{1}{2}$ mi.
3.	108 in.	$8\frac{1}{4}$ ft.	$\frac{1}{10}$ mi.
4.	$4\frac{1}{2}$ ft.	76 in.	3,960 ft.
5.	2 mi.	11 yd.	120 in.
6.	$10\frac{1}{2}$		
7.	4 yd.		
8.	$\frac{1}{3}$ mi.		
9.	$1173\frac{1}{3}$ yd.		

Lesson 4.2, page 44

	a	b	c
1.	8 qt.	$1\frac{1}{2}$ qt.	8 pt.
2.	20 c.	$1\frac{1}{4}$ gal.	2 qt.
3.	7 c.	12 c.	10 pt.
4.	$4\frac{1}{2}$ pt.	$\frac{3}{4}$ gal.	$1\frac{1}{2}$ gal.
5.	14 c.	$5\frac{1}{2}$ pt.	8 qt.
6.	3 c.		
7.	12 qt.		
8.	12 c.		
9.	6 qt.		

Grade 8 Answers

Lesson 4.3, page 45

	a	b	c
1.	5 lb.	210 min.	$\frac{1}{2}$ T.
2.	3 days	101 oz.	$3\frac{1}{3}$ hr.
3.	7,000 lb.	570 sec.	$1\frac{1}{4}$ T.
4.	272 oz.	$4\frac{1}{2}$ days	840 sec.
5.	3,000 lb.	1,440 min.	$6\frac{1}{4}$ lb.

6. $8\frac{1}{2}$ lbs.   7. 48 hrs.   8. $2\frac{1}{2}$ T.   9. 225 sec.

Lesson 4.4, page 46

1a. 10 lb. 2 oz.   **1b.** 8 min. 45 sec.
1c. 4 pt. or 2 qt.   **1d.** 5 yd. 1 ft.
2a. 4 pt. or 2 qt.   **2b.** 5 ft. 4 in.
2c. 3 hr. 10 min.   **2d.** 6 lb. 3 oz.
3a. 20 min.   **3b.** 32 lb. 8 oz.
3c. 4 yd.   **3d.** 5 qt. or 1 gal. 1 qt.
4a. 12 ft. 2 in.   **4b.** 4 gal. 2 qt.
4c. 26 oz. or 1 lb. 10 oz.   **4d.** 16 hr. 30 min.
5a. 12 lb. 4 oz.   **5b.** 3 min. 25 sec.
5c. 5 qt. or 1 gal. 1 qt.   **5d.** 7 yd.
6a. 4 qt. or 1 gal.   **6b.** 2 ft. 8 in.
6c. 6 pt. or 3 qt.   **6d.** 5 hr. 40 min.
7a. 8 min. 20 sec.   **7b.** 16 lb. 1 oz.
7c. 6 yd. 1 ft.   **7d.** 4 gal. 1 qt.

Lesson 4.5, page 47

1a. 1 qt.   **1b.** 2 yd. 2 ft.
1c. 3 lb. 14 oz.   **1d.** 1 min. 40 sec.
2a. 2 lb. 10 oz.   **2b.** 2 hr. 38 min.
2c. 1 gal. 1 qt.   **2d.** 9 in.
3a. 2 yd. 1 ft.   **3b.** 1 pt. 1 c.
3c. 2 min. 50 sec.   **3d.** 5 lb. 6 oz.
4a. 1 hr. 30 min.   **4b.** 1 lb. 8 oz.
4c. 4 ft. 8 in.   **4d.** 2 qt. 1 pt.
5a. 2 qt.   **5b.** 3 ft. 10 in.
5c. 10 lb. 10 oz.   **5d.** 2 min. 46 sec.
6a. 4 lb. 2 oz.   **6b.** 7 hr. 56 min.
6c. 1 qt.   **6d.** 3 yd. 1 ft.
7a. 5 ft. 9 in.   **7b.** 2 pt. 1 c.
7c. 5 min. 7 sec.   **7d.** 7 lb. 2 oz.

Lesson 4.6, page 48

1. 2 ft. 4 in. or $2\frac{1}{3}$ ft.
2. 1 gal. 3 qt.
3. 2 hr. 15 min.
4. 1 lb. 14 oz.
5. 20 ft.
6. 35 min.
7. 2 lb.

Posttest, page 49

	a	b	c
1.	$2\frac{1}{2}$ lb.	192 min.	60 in.
2.	1 qt.	$4\frac{1}{3}$ yd.	133 oz.
3.	$3\frac{1}{3}$ min.	10 pt.	56 in.
4.	$4\frac{1}{2}$ lb.	253 min.	7 pt.
5.	11 ft.	5 c.	98 oz.
6.	$7\frac{1}{2}$ min.	110 in.	1 gal.
7.	6 pt.	162 min.	$12\frac{1}{2}$ lb.
8.	$5\frac{2}{3}$ yd.	85 oz.	564 sec.

9a. 6 lb. 14 oz.   **9b.** 3 min. 48 sec.
9c. 1 yd. 1 ft.   **9d.** 1 qt. 1 pt.
10a. 7 hr. 5 min.   **10b.** 6 gal. 1 qt.
10c. 13 oz.   **10d.** 8 ft. 4 in.
11a. 7 yd. 1 ft.   **11b.** 2 lb. 11 oz.
11c. 1 pt. 1 c.   **11d.** 6 min. 33 sec.
12a. 4 qt. or 1 gal.   **12b.** 2 hr. 37 min.
12c. 4 lb. 4 oz.   **12d.** 7 ft. 10 in.

Posttest, page 50

13. 13 lb. 13 oz.   14. $12\frac{1}{2}$ ft.   15. 1 qt. 1 pt.
16. 40 min.   17. 7 in.   18. 3 pt. or 1 qt. 1 pt.
19. 4,500 lb.

Chapter 5

Pretest, page 51

	a	b	c
1.	1,260 g	4.62 m	4,200 mL
2.	0.016 kL	70 mg	70 m
3.	0.345 L	0.0044 kg	0.00231 km
4.	0.92 dm	0.000926 kL	250 g
5.	0.055 g	2060 m	450 kg
6.	0.77 kL	0.42 m	0.425 km
7.	140 mm	290 mL	0.96 dm
8.	1,250 g	4.28 L	12,300 m
9.	9.8 mm	48 mg	43 L
10.	0.33 kg	40.2 mm	9,200 kg
11.	0.0035 L	372,000 m	0.024 g
12.	920,000 mL	3,620,000 mg	0.3 dm

Pretest, page 52

13. 0.03 m or 3 cm
14. 1 L or 1,000 mL
15. $16.25
16. 1.8 km or 1,800 m
17. 0.36 g or 360 mg
18. 0.035 L or 35 mL
19. 531.75 km

Grade 8 Answers

Lesson 5.1, page 53

	a	b	c
1.	20,000 cm	1.3 m	60 cm
2.	890 m	0.45 dm	1,040 mm
3.	0.0132 km	8.8 m	750 dm
4.	9.72 m	0.023 km	6.72 dm
5.	35,000 cm	0.0908 km	1,050 mm
6.	36 m		
7.	4.5 cm		
8.	2.43 km		

Lesson 5.2, page 54

	a	b	c
1.	0.873 L	12,300 mL	20,000 mL
2.	0.056 kL	7.29 L	0.03655 kL
3.	391,000 mL	6040 L	0.205 kL
4.	5.073 L	9 mL	0.0046 kL
5.	15,000 mL	0.078 L	0.00303 kL
6.	1.5 L		
7.	5600		
8.	20 mL		

Lesson 5.3, page 55

	a	b	c
1.	0.067 g	40,000 g	0.856 kg
2.	0.00365 MT	6,700 mg	0.045 kg
3.	860,000 mg	0.52 MT	2,4000 g
4.	1,200 kg	40,000 mg	0.000782 MT
5.	90 g	0.0248 MT	3,300 mg
6.	850 mg		
7.	4.825 kg		

Lesson 5.4, page 56

1. 0.125 kg or 125 g 2. 1.1 L 3. Sam; 5 cm
4. 0.93 MT or 930 kg 5. 1.7 m or 170 cm
6. 1,850 L or 1.85 kL 7. 5.932 km or 5,932 m
8. 800 mL or .8 L

Posttest, page 57

	a	b	c
1.	106 cm	42,000 g	30 L
2.	0.29 L	0.429 m	0.196 kg
3.	0.24 km	4.46 g	83 cm
4.	92.5 cm	7.6 kL	50 mg
5.	0.025 kg	1.02 km	1,200 mL
6.	4,750 L	14,200 mg	500 dm
7.	20 mL	31 mm	0.071 g
8.	203 cm	0.05 kg	0.038 kL
9.	3,000 mg	5 L	0.18 km
10.	7.5 dm	460 cm	163 g
11.	4.69 kL	0.075 kg	12 mm
12.	1.9 m	720 mL	2,040 mg

Posttest, page 58

13. 14.25 L 14. 8.1 km or 8,100 m 15. $5.45
16. 10.2 cm or 102 mm 17. 3.5 g or 3,500 mg
18. 5.25 L 19. 9.4 kg

Mid-Test

Page 59

	a	b	c	d
1.		$\frac{6}{9} = \frac{10}{15}$	$\frac{14}{18} = \frac{35}{45}$	$\frac{4}{12} = \frac{6}{18}$
2.				$\frac{12}{16} = \frac{21}{28}$

3. $n = 12$ $n = 5$ $n = 9$
4. $n = 25$ $n = 25$ $n = 7$
5. $\frac{7}{20}$; 0.35; 12%; 0.12
6. 60%; $1\frac{27}{50}$; 1.54
7. $\frac{9}{50}$; 0.18; 70%
8. $12\frac{1}{2}$%; 0.125; $\frac{1}{25}$; 0.04
9. $2\frac{1}{4}$; 2.25; 15%; 0.15
10. 420%; $4\frac{1}{5}$; $\frac{9}{25}$; 0.36
11. $80; $880
12. $1,200; $1,416
13. $6\frac{1}{2}$%
14. $92.05; $1,592.05

Page 60

	a	b	c	d
15.	$3\frac{3}{8}$	$\frac{7}{20}$	$13\frac{5}{12}$	
16.	1156885	1604	19.0608	35r91
17.	284.446	8.56143	335066	249.376
18.	$3\frac{1}{6}$	1658.449	54.6	10747844
19.	14 c.	.00106 km	11 ft.	
20.	9.5 dm	182 sec.	4260 g	
21.	146 oz.	1.19 L	$9\frac{2}{3}$ ft.	
22.	$3\frac{3}{4}$ gal.	1.056 g	0.42 m	
23.	2,300 g	$8\frac{1}{2}$ lb.	20.5 L	
24.	168 in.	29 L	$2\frac{1}{2}$ pt.	
25.	4.42 m	279 sec.	0.029 g	
26.	36 oz.	4600 mL	$9\frac{1}{4}$ ft.	

Page 61

27. $515.11
28. $7.20
29. 3 hr. 35 min.
30. $1.79
31. Peter's; 0.226 kg or 226 g
32. 20%
33. $5\frac{5}{6}$
34. 2,870 mi.

Grade 8 Answers

Page 62
35. 5.5% **36.** 10 lbs. 5 oz. **37.** $2\frac{1}{4}$ c.
38. 1,683 mi. **39.** $14.13 **40.** 0.087 kL or 87 L
41. 237 **42.** 2 gal. 1 qt.

Chapter 6

Pretest, page 63
1. $200 **2.** 10%; 36° **3.** 54° **4.** Colin
5. 4 **6.** 30 **7.** 8 **8.** 9; 30 **9.** 0–12 or 12; 8

Pretest, page 64
10. 12;

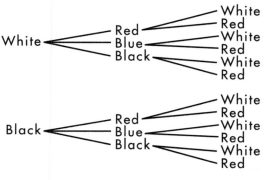

11. 3 **12.** 4 **13.** 9 **14.** 8 **15.** 24 **16.** 11–15
17. $\frac{1}{3}$ **18.** $\frac{1}{2}$ **19.** $\frac{1}{8}$ **20.** $\frac{5}{8}$

Lesson 6.1, page 65
1. 28 **2.** teddy bears **3.** 1 **4.** 3
5. Sam and Marco **6.** Lisa and Kiki **7.** 4 **8.** 2

Lesson 6.2, page 66
1. math test **2.** the 7th **3.** 25 points
4. the 5th **5.** 1 season **6.** 0.220; 0.320
7. 0.245 **8.** 0.040 points

Lesson 6.3, page 67
1. 15 **2.** 9 mi. **3.** 1 mi. **4.** 45 mi. **5.** 2:20
6. 40% **7.** 85% **8.** 4 hrs.

Lesson 6.4, page 68
1. 25%; 90° **2.** 33.3%; 120° **3.** 12.5%; 45°
4. 16.66%; 60° **5.** 12.5%; 45° **6.** 33.3%; $20
7. 25%; $15

Lesson 6.4, page 69
1. $1,500 **2.** 40%; 144° **3.** 20%; $\frac{1}{5}$ **4.** $\frac{1}{15}$; 24°
5. 20%; $1\frac{1}{2}$ **6.** 1 hour; $\frac{2}{15}$ **7.** 10%; 45 min.

Lesson 6.5, page 70
1. age and height
2. positive
3. 30
4. People stop growing after a certain age.
5. price of entrée and number ordered
6. negative
7. Some expensive entrées are still popular.
8. Possible answer: People will pay a lot for certain house specialties.

Lesson 6.6, page 71

	a	b
1.	9	80
	76, 78, 80, 80, 84, 86, 88, 90, 94	84
		18
		84
2.	8	78
	67, 75, 77, 78, 78, 81, 82, 84	78
		17
		77.75
3.	7	none
	99, 107, 111, 115, 119, 124, 127	115
		28
		114.6
4.	7	$21
	$13, $15, $18, $21, $21, $22, $25	$21
		$12
		$19.29

Lesson 6.7, page 72
1. $\frac{7}{61}$ **2.** $\frac{23}{61}$ **3.** $\frac{19}{61}$ **4.** $\frac{12}{61}$ **5.** 61 **6.** 4 **7.** 2
8. 5 **9.** 6 **10.** 8 **11.** 3 **12.** 80–89 **13.** 50–99

Lesson 6.8, page 73
1. 6 books; 18 **2.** 26; 8 **3.** 0, 18
4. 80; 34 points **5.** 16; 81.2

Lesson 6.9, page 74
1. 5 in.
2. 57 in.
3. 51 and 54 in.
4. 66 in.
5. 13 in.
6. 4 in.

Lesson 6.10, page 75

1. 8;

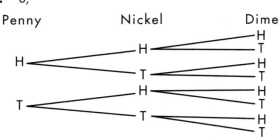

Penny	Nickel	Dime

2. 18;

Sneakers	Pants	Sweatshirts

3. 6;

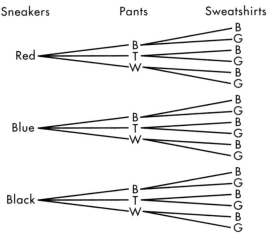

Lesson 6.11, page 76

1. B
2. skiing
3. playing video games
4. hiking
5. no

Lesson 6.12, page 77

1. $\frac{1}{2}$ 2. $\frac{3}{10}$ 3. $\frac{1}{5}$ 4. $\frac{7}{10}$ 5. $\frac{1}{3}$ 6. $\frac{1}{6}$ 7. $\frac{1}{6}$
8. $\frac{5}{12}$ 9. $\frac{1}{3}$

Lesson 6.12, page 78

1. $\frac{1}{6}$ 2. $\frac{1}{2}$ 3. $\frac{1}{5}$ 4. $\frac{2}{5}$ 5. $\frac{1}{4}$ 6. $\frac{1}{3}$ 7. $\frac{0}{12}$ or 0

Posttest, page 79

1. time spent studying and test scores
2. positive
3. Possible answer: Students studied earlier.
4. 1 semester
5. 2.0
6. Spring 2004
7. 1.2 points
8. 12 months or 1 year
9. August; 80°
10. between October and November

Posttest, page 80

11. 8; 66 in.
12. 67 in.; 67.125 in.
13. 13 in.
14. 16 yr.; 18
15. 11 yr.
16. upper extreme
17. a 3-by-4 matrix
18. sports
19. theater and volunteer work
20. paid work

Chapter 7

Pretest, page 81

1. $\overleftrightarrow{EF}$
2. ∠2, ∠3, ∠6, ∠7
3. ∠1, ∠4, ∠5, ∠8
4. ∠1/∠4, ∠2/∠3, ∠5/∠8, ∠6/∠7
5. ∠1/∠8, ∠2/∠7
6. ∠3/∠6, ∠4/∠5
7. $\sqrt{289}$; 17
8. $\sqrt{120}$; 11
9. $\sqrt{319}$; 17.9
10. right, scalene ; acute, equilateral ; isosceles, obtuse
11. $\frac{6}{5}$; $\frac{12}{10} = \frac{6}{5}$, $\frac{18}{15} = \frac{6}{5}$; yes

Pretest, page 82

12. (−4, − 1); (−1, −1); (−1, −5)
13. (0, 4); (3, 4); (3, 0)
14. translation
15. 20; 20; 24; 18
16. 60; 25
17. 40; 18

Grade 8 Answers

Lesson 7.1, page 83

1. line segment PQ; P(or Q) ——————— Q(or P)

2. line ST; S(or T) ←——————→ T(or S)

3. point P; P or ● P

	a	**b**	**c**
4.	$\overleftrightarrow{UV}$, $\overleftrightarrow{VU}$	$\overline{LM}$, $\overline{ML}$	Z $\overleftrightarrow{}$
5.	$\overline{IJ}$, $\overline{JI}$	K	LM, ML

Lesson 7.2, page 84

1a. $\overrightarrow{LM}$

1b. ∠MNO, ∠ONM, ∠N

1c. ∠DEF, ∠FED, ∠E

2a. ∠HIJ, ∠JIH, ∠I

2b. $\overrightarrow{BA}$

2c. ∠PQR, ∠RQP, ∠Q

3. angle BCD;

4. ray RS;

5. angle Q;

(Letters and angle may vary, but vertex must be Q.)

Lesson 7.3, page 85

	a	**b**
1.	120°, obtuse	75°, acute
2.	90°, right	50°, acute
3.	100°, obtuse	90°, right

Lesson 7.4, page 86

1. ∠FBE/∠EBD, ∠GIH/∠HIJ

2. ∠ABC/∠CBE, ∠CBD/∠DBF, ∠CBE/∠EBF,
∠EBF/∠FBA, ∠FBA/∠ABC, ∠LIK/∠LIH,
∠LIK/∠KIJ, ∠LIG/∠GIJ, ∠LIH/∠HIJ, ∠JIK/∠LIK

3. ∠ABC/∠FBE, ∠CBE/∠FBA, ∠KIL/∠HIJ,
∠LIH/∠KIJ

4. H (Answers may vary.)

Lesson 7.5, page 87

1. ∠1/∠2, ∠3/∠4, ∠5/∠6, ∠7/∠8
∠1/∠4, ∠2/∠3, ∠5/∠8, ∠6/∠7

2. ∠4 and ∠6   3. ∠1/∠7

4. ∠1/∠2, ∠2/∠4, ∠6/∠8, ∠8/∠7
∠7/∠5, ∠3/∠1, ∠5/∠6, ∠3/∠4

5. ∠3/∠6, ∠4/∠5   6. ∠1/∠8, ∠2/∠7

7. ∠1/∠4, ∠2/∠3; ∠5/∠8, ∠6/∠7

Lesson 7.6, page 88

1. triangle B   **2.** triangle A   **3.** triangle C

	a	**b**	**c**
4.	right	obtuse	obtuse
5.	acute	right	acute

Lesson 7.7, page 89

	a	**b**	**c**
1.	isosceles	scalene	isosceles
2.	equilateral	scalene	scalene
3.	isosceles	equilateral	scalene

Lesson 7.8, page 90

1. $\frac{24}{36} = \frac{2}{3}$; $\frac{28}{42} = \frac{2}{3}$; $\frac{36}{54} = \frac{2}{3}$; similar

2. $\frac{18}{12} = \frac{3}{2}$; $\frac{12}{8} = \frac{3}{2}$; $\frac{12}{10} = \frac{6}{5}$; not similar

3. $\frac{30}{40} = \frac{3}{4}$; $\frac{27}{36} = \frac{3}{4}$; $\frac{24}{32} = \frac{3}{4}$; similar

Lesson 7.8, page 91

	a	**b**
1.	21 ft.	10 m
2.	24 m	25 in.
3.	15 cm	10 ft.

Lesson 7.9, page 92

	a	**b**	**c**
1.	4	8	5
2.	10	1	3
3.	6	9	2
4.	9	10	9
5.	4	5	4
6.	5	6	6
7.	8	9	8
8.	6	7	7

Lesson 7.9, page 93

There are no answers for this page.

Lesson 7.10, page 94

1. 2 $\overline{97}$; 9.85   **2.** 2 $\overline{74}$; 8.6   **3.** 2 $\overline{45}$; 6.71

4. 2 $\overline{85}$; 9.22   **5.** 2 $\overline{61}$; 7.81   **6.** 2 $\overline{34}$; 5.83

7. 2 $\overline{85}$; 9.22   **8.** 2 $\overline{100}$; 10   **9.** 2 $\overline{53}$; 7.28

10. 2 $\overline{89}$; 9.43

Lesson 7.10, page 95

1. 2 $\overline{256}$; 16   **2.** 2 $\overline{100}$; 10   **3.** 2 $\overline{39}$; 6.24

4. 2 $\overline{120}$; 11   **5.** 2 $\overline{624}$; 25   **6.** 2 $\overline{81}$; 9

7. 2 $\overline{81}$; 9   **8.** 2 $\overline{5929}$; 77   **9.** 2 $\overline{3025}$; 55

10. 2 $\overline{288}$; 17

Lesson 7.10, page 96

1. 21   **2.** 9   **3.** 8.66   **4.** 65   **5.** 15.3

Grade 8 Answers

Lesson 7.11, page 97

	a	b	c
1.	60	20	52
2.	30	24	51
3.	35	12	16

Lesson 7.11, page 98
1. 25; 60 2. 35; 30; 28 3. 31.8; 45

Lesson 7.12, page 99
There are no answers for this page.

Lesson 7.12, page 100
1. $(-4, 1)$; $(-1, 1)$; $(-1, 4)$; $(-2, 4)$
2. $(-4, -1)$; $(-1, -1)$; $(-1, -4)$; $(-2, -4)$
3. reflection
4. $(-5, 1)$; $(-1, 1)$; $(-1, 4)$
5. $(-2, -2)$; $(2, -2)$; $(2, 1)$
6. translation
7. $(-4, 3)$; $(0, 3)$; $(-2, 1)$; $(-6, 1)$
8.

9. dilation

Posttest, page 101
1. obtuse, scalene; right, isosceles; acute, equilateral
2. $\frac{18}{27} = \frac{2}{3}$; $\frac{16}{24} = \frac{2}{3}$; $\frac{10}{16} = \frac{5}{8}$; no

	a	b
3.	60; 20; 52	30

4. $(2, 3)$; $(5, 3)$; $(4, 1)$; $(1, 1)$
5. $(-1, 2)$; $(-1, 5)$; $(1, 4)$; $(1, 1)$
6. rotation

Posttest, page 102
7. $\overleftrightarrow{MN}$ and $\overleftrightarrow{OP}$
8. $\overleftrightarrow{QR}$
9. $\angle 1, \angle 4, \angle 5, \angle 8$
10. $\angle 2, \angle 3, \angle 6, \angle 7$
11. $\angle 1/\angle 4, \angle 2/\angle 3, \angle 5/\angle 8, \angle 6/\angle 7$
12. $\angle 1/\angle 8, \angle 2/\angle 7$
13. $\angle 3/\angle 6, \angle 4/\angle 5$
14. $2\overline{149}$; 12.2
15. $2\overline{203}$; 14.2
16. 30; 20
17. 12

Chapter 8

Pretest, page 103

	a	b	c	d
1.	54; 36	115.2; 46	24.5; 25	
2.	192; 56	14; 44	11; 44	
3.		18	56.52	254.34
4.	5.5		34.54	94.99
5.		8.4	26.38	55.39
6.	432	565.2	395.64	

Pretest, page 104

	a	b	c
7.	588	445.1	489.84
8.	602.88	400	560

9. 561 10. 50.24 11. 0.025

Lesson 8.1, page 105

	a	b	c
1.	10.5	10	90
2.	26	42	42
3.	$25\frac{1}{3}$	104	154

Lesson 8.2, page 106

	a	b	c
1.	54	84	56.25
2.	15	6	135
3.	165	12.5	11

Lesson 8.3, page 107

	a	b	c
1.	210	14	199.5
2.	270	162	272
3.	348	230	312.5

Lesson 8.4, page 108

	a	b	c
1.		4	12.56
2.	9		56.52
3.	4.6		28.89
4.		11	34.54
5.		24.4	76.62
6.	2.5		15.7
7.		34	106.76
8.		7	21.98
9.	6.5		40.82
10.	1.9		11.93

Grade 8 Answers

Lesson 8.5, page 109

	a	b	c
1.		8	50.24
2.	6		113.04
3.		3	7.07
4.		22	379.94
5.	0.4		0.50
6.		180	25,434
7.		10	78.5
8.	4.5		63.59
9.	4.1		52.78
10.	5.5		94.99

Lesson 8.6, page 110

	a	b	c
1.	624	450	651
2.	306	157.5	137.5
3.	65.55	100	6.12

Lesson 8.7, page 111

1. 66; 270 **2.** 21.98; 38.47 **3.** 210 **4.** 70
5. 28

Lesson 8.8, page 112

	a	b	c
1.	862	144	1,720
2.	90	1,710	1,270
3.	334	324	188

Lesson 8.9, page 113

	a	b	c
1.	2,340	3,600	968
2.	300	324	1,728
3.	1,056	648	375

Lesson 8.10, page 114

1. 396; 331 **2.** 0.97 **3.** 270; 247.5
4. 5.25; 0.68 **5.** 240

Lesson 8.11, page 115

	a	b	c
1.	628	401.92	314
2.	452.16	320.28	408.2
3.	351.68	381.51	979.68

Lesson 8.12, page 116

	a	b	c
1.	942	502.4	1,607.68
2.	678.24	549.5	1.13
3.	552.64	14.13	1,256

Lesson 8.13, page 117

1. 395.64; 508.68 **2.** 6,430.72; 2,009.6
3. B; 116.18 **4.** 602.88 **5.** 1,334.5

Lesson 8.14, page 118

	a	b	c
1.	219.8	301.44	1,205.76
2.	395.64	3,077.2	417.62
3.	1,130.4	602.88	371.46

Lesson 8.15, page 119

	a	b	c
1.	200.96	376.8	39.25
2.	769.3	50.24	314
3.	94.2	9,231.6	47.1

Lesson 8.16, page 120

	a	b	c
1.	240	540	217
2.	459	260	1254
3.	235.45	198.75	644

Lesson 8.17, page 121

	a	b	c
1.	256	825	168.75
2.	546.88	1296	400
3.	122.5	0.72	11,200

Lesson 8.18, page 122

1. 0.384 **2.** 30.62 **3.** 14.13 **4.** 1,130.4
5. 3333333.33

Posttest, page 123

	a	b	c	d
1.	12; 48	19.25; 18	270; 90	
2.		5	15.7	19.63
3.	4.5		28.26	63.59
4.		3	9.42	7.07
5.	1,582.56	314	300	
6.	489.84	420	423.12	

Posttest, page 124

	a	b	c
7.	432	3,920	188.4
8.	1440	409.77	784

9. 1,017.36; 2,373.84 **10.** 642

Chapter 9

Pretest, page 125

1. $n - 7 = 13$
2. $8n - 5 = 27$
3. $n \times 6 = 42$
4. $n \times 1 = n$
5. $a(b + c) = (a \times b) + (a \times c)$
6. $a + b = b + a$

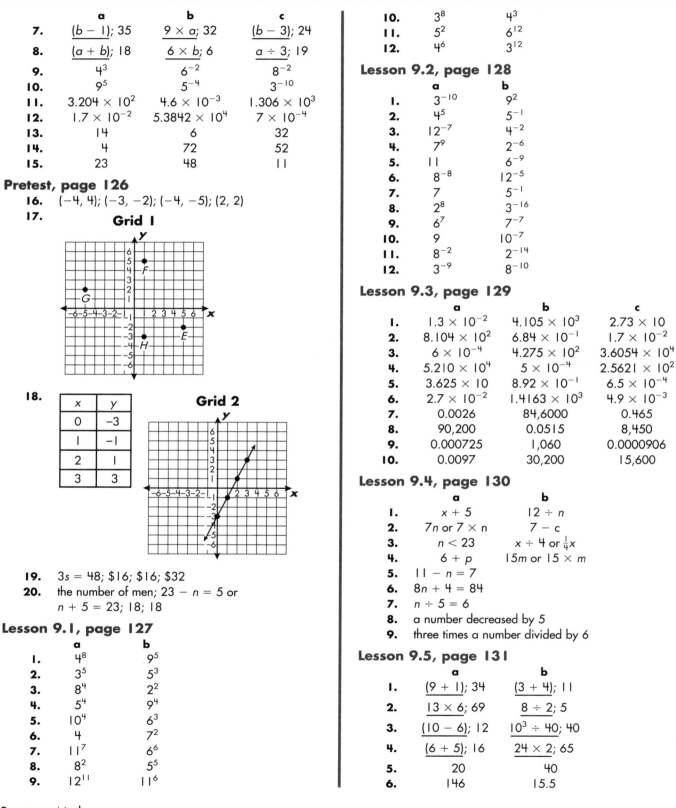

	a	b	c
7.	$(b-1)$; 35	$9 \times a$; 32	$(b-3)$; 24
8.	$(a+b)$; 18	$6 \times b$; 6	$a \div 3$; 19
9.	4^3	6^{-2}	8^{-2}
10.	9^5	5^{-4}	3^{-10}
11.	3.204×10^2	4.6×10^{-3}	1.306×10^3
12.	1.7×10^{-2}	5.3842×10^4	7×10^{-4}
13.	14	6	32
14.	4	72	52
15.	23	48	11

Pretest, page 126

16. $(-4, 4)$; $(-3, -2)$; $(-4, -5)$; $(2, 2)$

17.

Grid 1

18.

x	y
0	−3
1	−1
2	1
3	3

Grid 2

19. $3s = 48$; $16; $16; $32
20. the number of men; $23 - n = 5$ or $n + 5 = 23$; 18; 18

Lesson 9.1, page 127

	a	b
1.	4^8	9^5
2.	3^5	5^3
3.	8^4	2^2
4.	5^4	9^4
5.	10^4	6^3
6.	4	7^2
7.	11^7	6^6
8.	8^2	5^5
9.	12^{11}	11^6
10.	3^8	4^3
11.	5^2	6^{12}
12.	4^6	3^{12}

Lesson 9.2, page 128

	a	b
1.	3^{-10}	9^2
2.	4^5	5^{-1}
3.	12^{-7}	4^{-2}
4.	7^9	2^{-6}
5.	11	6^{-9}
6.	8^{-8}	12^{-5}
7.	7	5^{-1}
8.	2^8	3^{-16}
9.	6^7	7^{-7}
10.	9	10^{-7}
11.	8^{-2}	2^{-14}
12.	3^{-9}	8^{-10}

Lesson 9.3, page 129

	a	b	c
1.	1.3×10^{-2}	4.105×10^3	2.73×10
2.	8.104×10^2	6.84×10^{-1}	1.7×10^{-2}
3.	6×10^{-4}	4.275×10^2	3.6054×10^4
4.	5.210×10^4	5×10^{-4}	2.5621×10^2
5.	3.625×10	8.92×10^{-1}	6.5×10^{-4}
6.	2.7×10^{-2}	1.4163×10^3	4.9×10^{-3}
7.	0.0026	84,6000	0.465
8.	90,200	0.0515	8,450
9.	0.000725	1,060	0.0000906
10.	0.0097	30,200	15,600

Lesson 9.4, page 130

	a	b
1.	$x + 5$	$12 \div n$
2.	$7n$ or $7 \times n$	$7 - c$
3.	$n < 23$	$x \div 4$ or $\frac{1}{4}x$
4.	$6 + p$	$15m$ or $15 \times m$
5.	$11 - n = 7$	
6.	$8n + 4 = 84$	
7.	$n \div 5 = 6$	
8.	a number decreased by 5	
9.	three times a number divided by 6	

Lesson 9.5, page 131

	a	b
1.	$(9 + 1)$; 34	$(3 + 4)$; 11
2.	13×6; 69	$8 \div 2$; 5
3.	$(10 - 6)$; 12	$10^3 \div 40$; 40
4.	$(6 + 5)$; 16	24×2; 65
5.	20	40
6.	146	15.5

7.	34	125
8.	31	10
9.	38	5
10.	53	1
11.	56	18
12.	26	935

Lesson 9.6, page 132

	a	**b**
1.	$n + 17$	n
2.	$x + (y + 2)$	1
3.	$p \times m \times n$	$s + r$
4.	0	p
5.	35	120
6.	41	12
7.	0	1
8.	80	3
9.	11	36
10.	270	45

Lesson 9.7, page 133

Answers may vary.

1a. $(22 \times 100) + (22 \times 2) = 2{,}244$
1b. $(40 \times 25) - (1 \times 25) = 975$
2a. $(146 \times 30) + (146 \times 3) = 4{,}818$
2b. $(30 \times 16) - (2 \times 16) = 448$
3a. $(30 \times 35) + (6 \times 35) = 1{,}260$
3b. $(50 \times 106) + (1 \times 106) = 5{,}406$
4a. $(20 \times 256) - (1 \times 256) = 4{,}864$
4b. $(40 \times 17) + (5 \times 17) = 765$
5a. $(57 \times 40) - (57 \times 2) = 2{,}166$
5b. $(48 \times 40) + (48 \times 5) = 2{,}160$
6a. $5m + 5n$ **6b.** $f \times (12 + 15)$

	a	**b**
7.	$p \times (16 + 9)$	$(12 \times 4) + (12 \times e)$
8.	$(16 \times 9) - (16 \times r)$	$17 \times (b - c)$
9.	$11 \times (2 + n)$	$15p - 15q$
10.	$(14 \times 17) - (14 \times p)$	$12(n + m)$
11.	$p\,(r + s)$	$14(t - v)$
12.	$s(t + v)$	$(9 \times f) - (9 \times e)$

Lesson 9.8, page 134

	a	**b**	**c**
1.	13	12	37
2.	15	14	55
3.	22	48	35
4.	21	18	24
5.	28	33	28
6.	23	9	14
7.	12	32	8
8.	39	24	16
9.	8	55	22
10.	7	15	7

11.	5	14	56
12.	4	41	6

Lesson 9.9, page 135

	a	**b**	**c**
1.	7	64	6
2.	28	11	6
3.	8	2	5
4.	80	5	15
5.	77	200	90
6.	4	12	13
7.	42	11	15
8.	24	12	63
9.	13	54	3
10.	72	12	72

Lesson 9.10, page 136

1. the number of Jaden's cards; $n - 35 = 52$; 87
2. the number of tickets; $\$6.95n = \$55.60$; $8
3. the width of the room; $1.5n = 18$; 12
4. the Grizzlies' score; $n + 11 = 92$; 81

Lesson 9.11, page 137

	a	**b**	**c**
1.	7	15	36
2.	3	5	120
3.	48	10	11
4.	81	13	72
5.	8	120	272
6.	14	45	20
7.	60	8	42
8.	18	56	11
9.	65	96	21

Lesson 9.11, page 138

1. $1.5n = 90$; 60; 30
2. $2n - \frac{3}{4} = 5\frac{1}{4}$; 3 miles; $2\frac{1}{4}$ miles
3. $2n + 12 = 98$; $43; $55

Lesson 9.12, page 139

1-5.

Grid 1

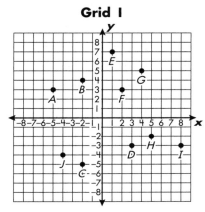

Grade 8 Answers

6. (−5, −3); (2, −2)   7. (5, −4); (−4, 4)
8. (4, 5); (1, 2)   9. (−6, 2); (6, 2)
10. (1, −4); (−3, −5)

Lesson 9.12, page 140

1. (−3, 3); (2, −2)   2. (6, 2); (2, 5)
3. (−6, 1); (−6, −3)   4. (−3, −4); (6, −3)
5. (−6, 6); (3, −6)

6–10.

Grid 2

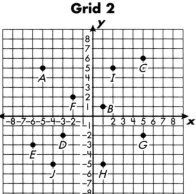

11. parallelogram 12. triangle 13. square

11–13.

Grid 3

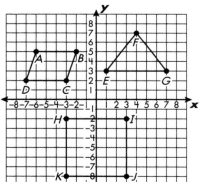

Lesson 9.13, page 141

1.

a	b	c
y	y	y
	−2	−7
	0	−5
6	4	−2
9	8	0
11	14	3
14	18	8

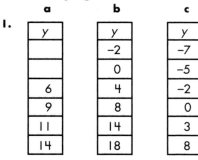

2.

y	y	y
6	−2	−6
1	1	−4
−2	1	−2
−3	2	0
6	3	1

3.

y	y	y
−7	−2	0
−4	−1	1
2	1	2
8	2	4
17	3	5

Lesson 9.13, page 142

1. Values chosen for x may vary but should create a whole number value for y.

x	y	x	y	x	y
2	−6	−6	0	−9	−1
4	−5	−3	1	−4	0
6	−4	6	4	1	1
8	−3	9	5	6	2
10	−2	12	6	11	3

2. Values chosen for x may vary but should create a whole number value for y.

x	y	x	y	x	y
−1	−12	−2	2	−6	3
0	−3	0	0	0	2
1	6	2	2	6	1
2	15	4	8	12	0
3	24	6	18	18	−1

	a	b	c	d
3.	x − 1	−3x	$\frac{x}{2} + 1$	x^2

Grade 8 Answers

Lesson 9.14, page 143

1a.

x	y
0	−3
2	−1
4	1
6	3

1b.

x	y
−2	−3
−1	−1
0	1
1	3

2a.

x	y
−2	−3
0	−2
2	−1
4	0

2b.

x	y
−4	−2
−1	−1
2	0
5	1

Lesson 9.14, page 144

1a.

1b.

2a.

2b.

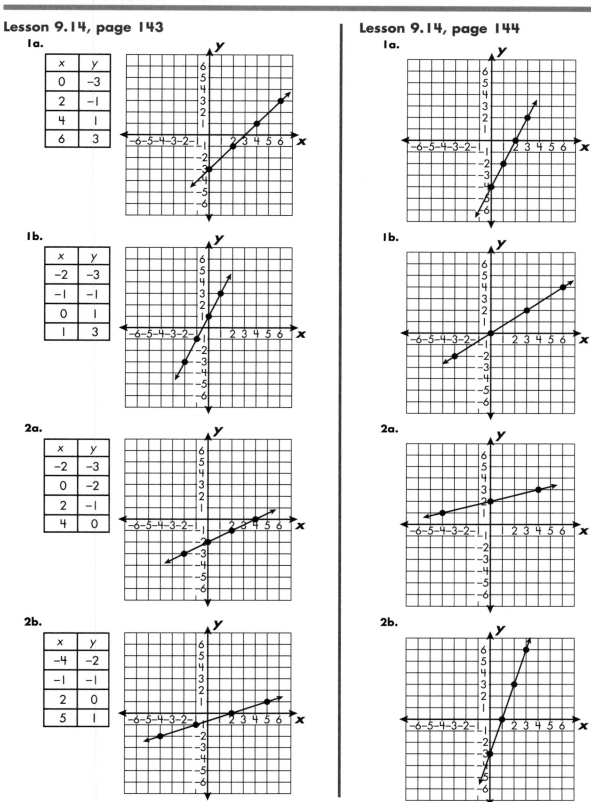

Grade 8 Answers

3a.

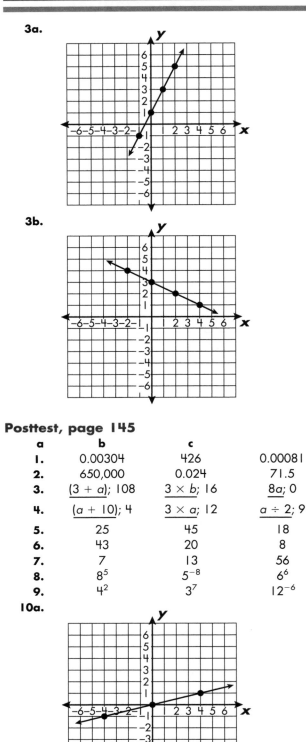

3b.

Posttest, page 145

	a	b	c
1.	0.00304	426	0.00081
2.	650,000	0.024	71.5
3.	$(3 + a)$; 108	$3 \times b$; 16	$8a$; 0
4.	$(a + 10)$; 4	$3 \times a$; 12	$a \div 2$; 9
5.	25	45	18
6.	43	20	8
7.	7	13	56
8.	8^5	5^{-8}	6^6
9.	4^2	3^7	12^{-6}

10a.

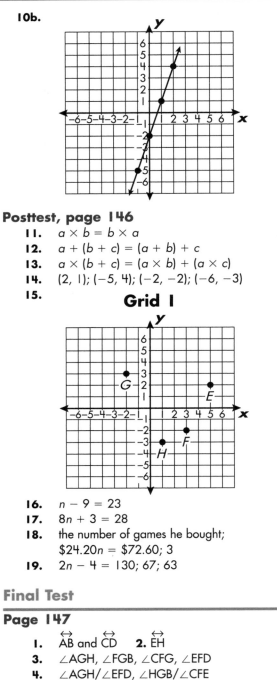

10b.

Posttest, page 146

11. $a \times b = b \times a$

12. $a + (b + c) = (a + b) + c$

13. $a \times (b + c) = (a \times b) + (a \times c)$

14. $(2, 1)$; $(-5, 4)$; $(-2, -2)$; $(-6, -3)$

15.

Grid 1

16. $n - 9 = 23$

17. $8n + 3 = 28$

18. the number of games he bought; $\$24.20n = \$72.60$; 3

19. $2n - 4 = 130$; 67; 63

Final Test

Page 147

1. $\overleftrightarrow{AB}$ and $\overleftrightarrow{CD}$ **2.** $\overleftrightarrow{EH}$

3. $\angle AGH$, $\angle FGB$, $\angle CFG$, $\angle EFD$

4. $\angle AGH / \angle EFD$, $\angle HGB / \angle CFE$

5. $\angle AGF / \angle GFD$, $\angle CFG / \angle FGB$

6a. acute; equilateral   **6b.** right; scalene

6c. obtuse; isosceles

Grade 8 Answers

	a	b	c
7.	0.3	9	0.75
8.	200	1,200	8
9.	1,500	0.85	15
10.	50	10	0.0054
11.	304	0.002	4.2
12.	102	2	30,000

Page 148

	a	b	c	d
13.	270; 90	2.16; 6.6	96; 56	
14.	4.5		28.26	63.59
15.		10	31.4	78.5
16.	0.7		4.4	1.54
17.	20	33.44		
18.	200	280		
19.	81.6	75		

20. 6 **21.** 1,200; 1,290 **22.** 3
23. 82.43; 1,082.43 **24.** 18.09; 1,218.09

Page 149

	a	b	c
25.	29; 31.5; 30	24; 18; 25	
26.	1.036×10^2	0.42	8.2×10^{-2}
27.	586	1.93×10^4	0.076
28.	3.604×10^3	0.005	6.3×10^{-3}
29.	3^7	2^{-8}	5^3
30.	4^{14}	8^{-1}	10^{-10}
31.	6^{-6}	11^{10}	7^{-1}
32.	7	7	16
33.	105	18	13
34.	4	60	18
35.	8	9	105
36.	10	13	55

37. $\frac{n}{2} - 7 = 3$ **38.** $n + 13 = 24$

Page 150

	a	b	c	d
39.	2297472	$36\frac{1}{4}$	206.2051	$23\frac{11}{60}$
40.	$3\frac{5}{9}$	22.088	95047	18.3329
41.	32.266	12.6	$26\frac{5}{24}$	$4\frac{5}{28}$
42.	$\boxed{\frac{14}{16} = \frac{21}{24}}$		$\boxed{\frac{15}{18} = \frac{25}{30}}$	$\boxed{\frac{18}{21} = \frac{42}{49}}$
43.		$\boxed{\frac{8}{6} = \frac{20}{15}}$		
44.	$n = 5$	$n = 14$	$n = 8$	
45.	$n = 25$	$n = 2$	$n = 24$	

Page 151

46. 5 **47.** 15 **48.** 22 **49.** 27 **50.** 28 **51.** 28
52. 1; 10 **53.** 23; 90 **54.** 25; 89.36
55. 6; 28.8° **56.** 30; $\frac{2}{5}$; 144°

Page 152

57a.

x	y
−2	2
0	3
2	4
4	5

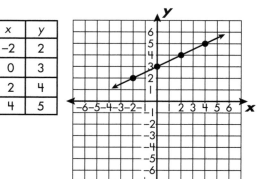

57b.

x	y
0	−4
1	0
2	4
3	8

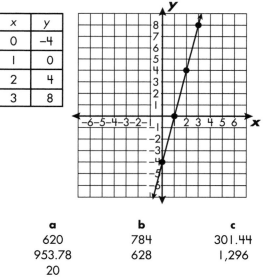

	a	b	c
58.	620	784	301.44
59.	953.78	628	1,296
60.	20		
61.	15		

Notes